Latinx Curriculum Theorizing

Race and Education in the Twenty-First Century

Series Editors

Kenneth J. Fasching-Varner, Louisiana State University; Roland Mitchell, Louisiana State University; and Lori Latrice Martin, Louisiana State University

This series asks authors and editors to consider the role of race and education, addressing questions such as "How do communities and educators alike take on issues of race in meaningful and authentic ways?" and "How can education work to disrupt, resolve, and otherwise transform current racial realities?" The series pays close attention to the intersections of difference, recognizing that isolated conversations about race eclipse the dynamic nature of identity development that play out for race as it intersects with gender, sexuality, socioeconomic class, and ability. It welcomes perspectives from across the entire spectrum of education from Pre-K through advanced graduate studies, and it invites work from a variety of disciplines, including counseling, psychology, higher education, curriculum theory, curriculum and instruction, and special education.

Titles in the Series

Intersectional Care for Black Boys in an Alternative School: They Really Care about Us, by Julia C. Ransom
Culture, Community, and Educational Success: Reimagining the Invisible Knapsack, edited by Toby S. Jenkins, Stephanie Troutman, and Crystal Polite Glover
Whiteness at the Table: Antiracism, Racism, and Identity in Education, edited by Shannon K. McManimon, Zachary A. Casey, and Christina Berchini
The Classroom as Privileged Space: Psychoanalytic Paradigms for Social Justice in Pedagogy, by Tapo Chimbganda
Curriculum and Students in Classrooms: Everyday Urban Education in an Era of Standardization, by Walter S. Gershon
Race, Population Studies, and America's Public Schools: A Critical Demography Perspective, edited by Hayward Derrick Horton, Lori Latrice Martin, and Kenneth Vasching-Varner
The Lived Experiences of African American Women Mentors: What It Means to Guide as Community Pedagogues, by Wyletta Gamble-Lomax
Race, Gender and Curriculum Theorizing: Working in Womanish Ways, edited by Denise Taliaferro Baszile, Kirsten T. Edwards, and Nichole A. Guillory
African Immigrants' Experiences in American Schools: Complicating the Race Discourse, by Shirley-Mthethwa Sommers and Immaculee Harushimana
Centering Women of Color in Academic Counterspaces: A Critical Race Analysis of Teaching, Learning, and Classroom Dynamics, by Annemarie Vaccaro and Melissa Camba-Kelsay
Asian/Americans, Education, and Crime: The Model Minority as Victim and Perpetrator, edited by Daisy Ball and Nicholas Daniel Hartlep
Race and Pedagogy: Creating Collaborative Spaces for Teacher Transformations, by Susan R. Adams and Jamie Buffington-Adams

The Journey Unraveled: African American Students' Career and College Readiness, edited by Jennifer R. Curry and M. Ann Shillingford

Big Box Schools: Race, Education, and the Danger of the Wal-Martization of Public Schools in America, by Lori Latrice Martin

Latinx Curriculum Theorizing, edited by Theodorea Regina Berry, Crystal A. Kalinec-Craig, Mariela A. Rodríguez

Latinx Curriculum Theorizing

Theodorea Regina Berry
Crystal A. Kalinec-Craig
Mariela A. Rodríguez

LEXINGTON BOOKS
Lanham • Boulder • New York • London

Published by Lexington Books
An imprint of The Rowman & Littlefield Publishing Group, Inc.
4501 Forbes Boulevard, Suite 200, Lanham, Maryland 20706
www.rowman.com

6 Tinworth Street, London SE11 5AL, United Kingdom

Copyright © 2019 by The Rowman & Littlefield Publishing Group, Inc.

All rights reserved. No part of this book may be reproduced in any form or by any electronic or mechanical means, including information storage and retrieval systems, without written permission from the publisher, except by a reviewer who may quote passages in a review.

British Library Cataloguing in Publication Information Available

Library of Congress Cataloging-in-Publication Data

Names: Berry, Theodorea Regina, 1963- editor. | Kalinec-Craig, Crystal A., 1979- editor. | Rodríguez, Mariela A., 1970- editor.
Title: Latinx curriculum theorizing / [edited by] Theodorea Regina Berry, Crystal A. Kalinec-Craig, and Mariela A. Rodríguez.
Other titles: Latino curriculum theorizing
Description: Lanham, Maryland : Lexington Books, [2019] | Series: Race and education in the twenty-first century | Includes bibliographical references and index.
Identifiers: LCCN 2018043739 (print) | LCCN 2018055769 (ebook) | ISBN 9781498573818 (Electronic) | ISBN 9781498573801 (cloth) ISBN 9781498573825 (pbk) Subjects: LCSH: Hispanic Americans—Education. | Education—Curricula.
Classification: LCC LC2669 (ebook) | LCC LC2669 .L395 2019 (print) | DDC 371.829/68073—dc23
LC record available at https://lccn.loc.gov/2018043739

Dedicated to my siblings—
Richard, Jr. (deceased), Kevin, Kimberlee, and Andre.
—*Theodorea Regina Berry*

Dedicated to those who embrace the brilliance of
Latinx children, families, and communities, I stand in solidarity.
—*Crystal A. Kalinec-Craig*

I dedicate this work to Latinx English Learners.
Estamos unidos en la lucha.
—*Mariela A. Rodríguez*

Contents

Prologue   xi
   Theodorea Regina Berry

Acknowledgments   xv

Introduction   xix

Part I: Latinx Curriculum and Content/Subject Matter   1

1. Insurrection and the Decolonial Imaginary at Academia Cuauhtli: The Liberating Potential of Third-Space Pedagogies in a Third Space   3
Angela Valenzuela

2. "To Serve the People": Transformational Praxis of the Chicago Young Lords   13
Ann Aviles, Richard Benson, and Erica Davila

3. Mathematics for Borderland Identities   33
Cristina Valencia Mazzanti and Martha Allexsaht-Snider

Part II: Latinx Curriculum in Schools: Addressing Goals, Objectives, and Purposes   49

4. Southern Latinxs: Toward a Curricular Epistemology of Dissent and Possibility   51
Juan F. Carrillo and Lucia I. Mock Muñoz de Luna

5. "Illegality" and the Curriculum: Making New Civics with Undocumented Activists   65
Jesús A. Tirado

6. Radical Literacy: Building Curriculum on Mexican American Youths' Lived Experiences   77
Stacy Saathoff

Part III: Latinx Currere, Latinx Curriculum as Autobiographical   97

7. Conocimientos Míos: Engaging Possibilities for School Curriculum   99
Alba Isabel Lamar and Lynette DeAun Guzmán

8 "Un Puño de Tierra": Curriculum and Pedagogy
   Theorizing along the U.S./Mexico Border   117
   Ganiva Reyes

9 *Currere* from the Borderlands: An Exercise in Possibilities
   for Latinx Transgender Visibility   135
   Mario Itzel Suárez

Epilogue   151
   Theodorea Regina Berry and Mariela A. Rodríguez

Index   153

About the Editors and Contributors   155

Prologue

Theodorea Regina Berry

Scholarship in curriculum studies in the United States often begins with understanding the history of U.S. education. Much of what we know begins with colonial education modeled after early British education. Students were, typically, White males of land-owning families. Wealth families could hire a tutor or governess to educate children of these families. Curriculum focused on students' need to gain knowledge in Latin, mathematics, philosophy, geography, French, and German. The perceived goal was to prepare children of these families to go to college, in the United States or Great Britain, so that they would be prepared to inherit the wealth entitled to them.

As the United States gained its independence and grew, statesmen like Thomas Jefferson promoted the value of education as a tool for building democracy. As such, schooling and curriculum became more formalized. Schoolhouses became more commonplace, and the knowledge deemed most worth knowing involved both intellectual and practical pursuits. Still in mostly male environments, students began to learn penmanship and arithmetic in addition to other subjects already present.

Curriculum continued to focus on a Eurocentric viewpoint when the Committee of Ten moved to make secondary education align with collegiate requirements. In the meanwhile, scholars like John Dewey and Maria Montessori were influencing how students should think and learn in the early years. Curriculum became more standardized in the height of the post–Civil War and industrial revolution and in the midst of the demand for working-class and poor children to be educated and the presence of more women in teaching. This standardization later promoted the work of such scholars as Franklin Bobbitt and Ralph Tyler.

I taught this information to numerous Masters-level graduate students in curriculum courses for years. As John Goodlad would say, I was teaching the way I was taught. However, somewhere along the way, I began inserting the scholarship of Black curriculum scholars into the standard curriculum canon of my classroom. Typically, I began this insertion with the significant scholarship of Dr. William H. Watkins published in the *Harvard Educational Review* entitled "Black Curriculum Orientations: A Preliminary Note" (1989). In this work, Watkins eloquently articulates the stages of evolution of Black curriculum development and skillfully aligns this development with social and political issues connected with each stage. I use these stages as a format for discussing the scholars and scholarship of both Black and White scholars, including discussions on Drs. Anna Julia Cooper, Carter G. Woodson, Alain LeRoy Locke, and William Edward Burghardt DuBois with discussions on John Dewey, Maria Montessori, George Counts, and Ralph Tyler. I often discussed with my students the ways in which the scholarship of all of these scholars occurred concurrently without being in conversation with one another. I often asked my students, "What could these scholars have learned from one another?" Most of the time, students were quite receptive to engaging in learning outside of the traditional canon. However, there have been two instances where students challenged the necessity of such information.

In the first instance, I taught a doctoral-level course on curriculum theory using a well-respected comprehensive text that included curriculum understandings from a variety of perspectives. In Understanding Curriculum, we discuss curriculum from reconceptualist positionalities covering curriculum as racialized, gendered, political, theological, and aesthetic. All except two of the students enrolled in this course objected to the way in which I centered race in connection with the other ways curriculum functions (Berry, 2018).

In the second instance, students challenged the limited presence of Chicanx/Latinx voices in the curriculum canon. In a Masters-level curriculum course I taught, the long-standing curriculum text typically used for his type of course included only one chapter that addressed curriculum in the context of the Mexican-American experience. In the *Curriculum Studies Reader*, Flinders and Thornton include the scholarship of Angela Valenzuela. But at a Hispanic-Serving Institution where many of the Masters-level graduate students self-identified as Latinx and/or taught in schools where the majority of the students self-identified as Latinx, this was a glaring insufficiency. Also noted was the singular chapter on Black curriculum orientations. However, when this particular class took place, Carl Grant, Keffrelyn D. Brown, and Anthony L. Brown had just released *Black Intellectual Thought in Education: The Missing Traditions of Anna Julia Cooper, Carter G. Woodson, and Alain LeRoy Locke* (2016), and I made this a recommended text for the course.

The students were absolutely right. Their challenge encouraged me to begin a search for curriculum theory scholarship with Chicanx/Latinx orientations. I needed the scholarship to be accessible for both novice and veteran teachers. I needed scholarship to address racial, social, and political connections to what knowledge is deemed most worth knowing. I needed the voices of this scholarship to come from within the community as people who get to decide what knowledge is most worth knowing. I needed historical and contemporary scholarship reflecting Chicanx/Latinx experiences as knowledge. Angela Valenzuela's work provides such significant empirical community voice. But my search failed to identify anything else like it. So, I found myself teaching these classes centering my students' voices and experiences as knowledge and leaning on other scholarship as a framework for the articulation of such voices. But I found this approach to be woefully insufficient. The other scholarship was not developed with these voices in mind. It did not speak to the historical, social, and political experiences connected to curriculum for the Chicanx/Latinx community.

My concerns were confirmed with the release of the text written by Wayne Au, Anthony L. Brown, and Dolores Calderon entitled *Reclaiming the Multicultural Roots of U.S. Curriculum* (2016). In the chapter on Mexican-American education and curriculum, the authors clearly depict the diversity and challenges of the Mexican-American experience with curriculum in New Mexico and Texas. While I was excited to include this text as required reading for the curriculum theory course, only one chapter addressed the Chicanx/Latinx experience and only for Mexican-Americans. While it was much more than I had before the release of this book, I still felt more was needed. Students who had the opportunity to engage with this text were delighted to have information they didn't have before this class. Much to my own surprise, many of the Latinx students in my class had no idea of the history of curriculum within their community.

The limitations of the Chicanx/Latinx voice for/in curriculum is not a new phenomenon. Franklin Bobbitt's report on San Antonio (TX) schools provides some insights on the ways curriculum for the Latinx community was understood and the ways Latinx students were viewed. Additionally, Enrique Aleman's educational documentary, Stolen Education, depicts an empirical narrative that highlights the deliberate absence of the Latinx voice in curriculum.

When I discussed this dilemma with my colleague, Mariela A. Rodríguez, she confirmed what I already knew; if the information isn't available, I should write it. She was right. But I felt like matter out of place on this issue. As a Black curriculum scholar, I firmly believe in making present what is absent. I have taken up the charge to position curriculum as racialized, gendered, political, social, theological, and aesthetic. For me, curriculum is centered on Herbert Spencer's two very important questions: What knowledge is most worth knowing and who determines what knowledge is most worth knowing? As a Black curriculum scholar who teaches and researches in curriculum theory, I was poised to explore and examine these issues toward the benefit of my students.

However, I paused because it was not my story to tell. I do not possess the voice to, authentically, engage in this work. I do not share the historical, social, and political identity with those who are centrally connected to this work. But the work was needed—and I committed to the work.

In doing so, I placed two conditions. First, the work would be an edited volume. This would allow for contributing scholars with experience on this subject matter within the field. Second, the contributing scholars would come from within the Chicanx/Latinx community. Other scholars could serve as coauthors, but this decision is rooted in one key idea: representation matters.

My Masters-level graduate students enrolled in my curriculum theory classes solidified the significance of representation. They voiced the importance of being able to see themselves in the work for/by/about curriculum. They wanted to know how to think about and engage in curriculum for/by/about Chicanx/Latinx K–12 students. They wanted to do so in ways that avoid deficit perspective replete with missed-understandings.

This book is a gift to those students.

Acknowledgments

THEODOREA REGINA BERRY

First, in all things I give thanks to the Divine Trinity. Thanks to my family for their love and support. I sincerely appreciate the love and support of my parish family at Holy Redeemer Catholic Church in San Antonio, Texas. Special thanks to my coeditors, Drs. Crystal A. Kalinec-Craig and Mariela A. Rodríguez for their willingness to work with me on this very important project. Your collegiality and compassionate professionalism should serve as an example to academic scholars everywhere. As a woman of color working in privileged space, I fully acknowledge that my success story is not my own. Thanks to Drs. DeBrenna L. Agbenyiga, Denise Taliaferro Baszile, Kinitra Brooks, Corrie Davis, Sherick Hughes, James C. Jupp, Sonja Lanehart, Marvin Lynn, Paul Schutz, and David Stovall for always supporting me. Curriculum studies scholars are a small yet significant group of academics who vastly influence the field of education. Thanks to Drs. William Ayers, Ming Fang He, Petra Munro Hendry, Janet Miller, William Pinar, and William Schubert for your significant contributions to the field and to Drs. Todd Alan Price, Walter Gershon, Nichole Guillory, Robert Helfenbein, and M. Francyne Huckaby for your continued contributions to the field.

I want to express my gratitude to the contributing authors of this volume. Your work places an important focus on the questions connected to knowledge and experience within the Chicanx/Latinx diaspora. Thank you for your willingness to share.

Thanks to the students who inspired the need for this work. I firmly believe that teaching and learning is a spiral event for both professor and student. We engage in experiences and knowledge sharing simultaneously and concurrently. Curriculum does not belong solely in the domain of Eurocentric identity and space. Exploring Black curriculum orientations had been central to much of my work. However, working with graduate students at The University of Texas at San Antonio made present the glaring absences of Latinx curriculum theories and orientations. Thank you for providing this opportunity and the inspiration for this work.

CRYSTAL A. KALINEC-CRAIG

I am grateful to those who inspire my work with Latinx communities. The theoretical work of Funds of Knowledge by Luis Moll, Cathy Amanti, Deborah Neff, Norma Gonzalez, Marta Civil, Carlos Vélez-Ibáñez, and James Greenberg fundamentally shaped an entire generation of scholars like myself who look for ways to highlight the resources of Latinx homes and communities. The research groups of CEMELA (Center for the Mathematics Education of Latinos/as) and Teachers Empowered to Advance Change in Mathematics (TEACH Math) show how institutional research collaborations can move the needle in how we can teach mathematics and how we can prepare mathematics teachers using a Funds of Knowledge approach. My work with the Tucson GEAR UP grant and Elizabeth Arnot Hopffer at the University of Arizona inspired me to reimagine the way I saw mathematics curriculum and instruction. The Tucson High School teachers in the Mexican American Studies program exemplifies how teachers can seek change through solidarity and continued activism. My collaborations with the Guadalupe Cultural Arts Center and with Orlando Graves Bolaños at The DoSeum ground my teaching, research, and scholarship in the communities that I cherish and continue to serve. To my extended family in TODOS, I look forward to taking on more challenges as mathematics teacher educators in highlighting the resources of Latinx children, families, and communities.

MARIELA A. RODRÍGUEZ

Individuals/Groups who contribute to my success as a scholar and make it possible for me to engage in this work include my familia—my paternal side, Rodríguez, and my maternal side, Morales. They all taught me the value of hard work and commitment to a cause. My family members were my first teachers, in both Spanish and English. My parents graduated from high school and instilled in me the benefits that a great education would bring. They always encouraged me to reach further than what I thought was possible. Their unconditional love and support throughout my years of schooling helped me to achieve my dream of becoming a bilingual educator.

I'm grateful to the mentors and role models whom I've worked with across the years. In particular I'd like to acknowledge Dr. María Luisa González, who served as my dissertation chairperson at New Mexico State University. Malú, as she is affectionately known, has been more than my "academic mother." We share a special bond that has extended 15 years after I earned my degree. She is thoughtful, considerate, and loving. I am truly blessed to have her in my corner.

It was Malú who introduced me to a wonderful organization—the University Council for Educational Administration (UCEA). UCEA is a consortium of almost 100 universities with programs dedicated to high-quality school leader preparation. School leaders directly affect student achievement. Thus, the tremendous work that this organization does to support school leader preparation through research and programming is vital. Malú served as UCEA President in 2000–2001, and now I am excitedly serving as UCEA President (2017–2018). I think it's the ultimate way to give back to an organization that has done so much for me since my graduate-student days through the present.

Introduction

Portelli (1987, p. 354) states that curriculum can be described in three ways: "(1) as a referent to a substantive phenomenon, curriculum, (2) as a name of a system of schooling, and (3) as a title of a field of study." In this way, curriculum can be defined as experiences, a plan or course of study, or content. The following sections will unpack each of these in more detail.

Curriculum as experiences aligns with much of the scholarship by such scholars as John Dewey ([1938]1997) and Maria Montessori (2013). Dewey ([1938]1997, p. 25) notes that there is an "organic connection between education and personal experience." In doing so, the teacher/instructor must be mindful of the learner's past, what they know and bring into the classroom, with what is to be learned. This would create an "education of, by and for the experience" (p. 29). According to Dewey ([1938]1997, p. 33) experience, in the context of education, has two criteria: (1) continuity, or experiential continuum and, (2) interaction. "This principle is involved ... in every attempt to discriminate between experiences that are worthwhile educationally and those that are not" and that people rather than systems or procedures determine what is worthwhile. Montessori (2013, p. 25) was more specific, indicating that the child would make such a determination. She notes "the school must permit the *free, natural manifestations of the child.*" Interaction acknowledges that experiences occur both internally and externally, actions that influence the objective conditions of experience. Curriculum as experience encompasses worthwhile interactions from which we engage in learning.

As a concept in schools, curriculum is more closely defined as a plan for instruction. Ralph Tyler (1949) and Franklin Bobbitt ascribed to a praxis that purported this definition. However, while Tyler (1949) conceded objectives as a matter of choice, Bobbitt (2013, p. 13) articulated that curriculum-making in two ways: "(1) ... the entire range of experiences, both undirected and directed, concerned in unfolding the abilities of the individual; or (2) ... series of consciously directed training experiences that the schools use for completing and perfecting unfoldment." Bobbitt's work was directly influential in the curriculum of schools in San Antonio, Texas. Specifically, in 1914, Bobbitt was hired to develop and complete a survey report of San Antonio Public Schools and, subsequently, develop a plan for its schools. Upon completion of the report in May 1915, 21,930 students were enrolled in San Antonio Public schools. Mexican and Mexican American students were 38.5 percent of the schools' population of students ages 7 to 16.

Curriculum as content addresses what should be taught, specifically relating to subject matter. Bobbitt's survey report is a clear example of the ways in which subject matter aligned to student population and demographics. Regarding subject matter and specifically grammar, Bobbitt (1915, p. 128) notes that different racial groups of students, notably "children of the Mexican schools" and "Negro schools" will possess "different kinds of errors and needs of different kinds." However, Bobbitt's report clearly articulates the differences in subject matter available to girls versus boys, and varying by area of study: vocational education, education for citizenship, and education for leisure occupations.

However, the conceptual genesis of this volume rests on Pinar's (2012) definition of curriculum, the first way described in this proposal. In his seminal work *What Is Curriculum Theory*, Pinar describes curriculum as autobiographical. Centered on this definition is the notion of currere, the Latin infinitive meaning to run the course. Curriculum, as an autobiographical text, inhabits the social, political, racial, gendered, aesthetic, and historical ways of constructing knowledge and runs the course in 4 steps: regressive, progressive, analytical, and sythetical.

For more than 150 years, curriculum from all three perspectives has been centered on White/European/Male/Heteronormative viewpoints. Few women, regardless of race, are noted as key curriculum scholars. *Understanding Curriculum*, a seminal work by Pinar et al. (2000) on curriculum theory/curriculum studies, includes an entire section on gendered curriculum; however, this section does not have work that rests solely on the scholarship of women as curriculum scholars. Recently, a text focusing on three Black curriculum scholars was published (Grant, Brown, and Brown, 2016). While this text provides significant, in-depth work on Black intellectual thought within the context of education and curriculum studies regrading three scholars whose work is foundational to Black curriculum scholarship, much more can be said about many more Black curriculum scholars.

A cursory examination of course syllabi and Black curriculum scholarship also revealed that little to no curriculum scholarship for/from Latinx perspectives exists in curriculum studies/curriculum theory courses and led to these questions: (1) What is the significance of the presence and absence of Latinx curriculum theorizing? (2) In what ways is Latinx curriculum theorizing connected to (a) curriculum, as a general; concept, (b) schools' purposes, goals, and objectives; and (c) curriculum as autobiographical?

The first question is embedded in curriculum . . . as historical, racialized, gendered, political, social, and aesthetic. The Latinx collective is a group of peoples in different geographical spaces whose work and/or identities addresses the independent origins (historical) and indigenous histories (racialized, historical) that were individually influenced (social) by Spanish imperial conquests (political). As such, various aspects of the lived experiences in these spaces are an amalgamation of indigenous and imperial notions (Moreno, 1999). Not excluded as an aspect of these experiences is curriculum. Not unlike the Black curriculum experience inside and outside of the United States, the Latinx collective curriculum experience embodies the values, beliefs, customs, and traditions of a people that incorporate the knowledge determined necessary to know with what Grant, Brown, and Brown (2016) would describe as knowledge connected to "the problems a people will face."

Language is a component that is critically tied to the learning experiences of Latinx students in U.S. public schools (Gándara & Contreras, 2009). As such, curricular aspects regarding learning English as a second language must be addressed as Latinx students who are English Learners (ELs) speak languages at home other than English, primarily Spanish. In particular a critical review of restrictive language policies (Gándara & Hopkins, 2010) and their impact on curriculum for Latinx ELs must be addressed.

While some Latinx scholars address curriculum studies/curriculum theory, the most significant work that illustrates the nexus of knowledge (curriculum) as racialized, political, social, and historical for/by/about Latinx students is Angela Valenzuela's (1999) *Subtractive Schooling*. This work addresses the ways in which tensions exist between curriculum as goals and objectives and curriculum as lived experiences for Mexican American students. This text has also helped give a name to the implicit and explicit marginalization of Mexican American students in American schools that historically value European American perspectives and ways of learning and teaching.

There is no text that specifically focuses on Latinx collective curriculum theorizing. This volume is unique in two ways. First, it is divided based on the three ways curriculum is described according to Portelli (1987). No single work addresses curriculum from multiple perspectives specifically for/by/about Latinx students.

Second, recognizing, acknowledging, accepting, and respecting Latinx as collective, this volume will also address curriculum from voices representative of the varying geographical, historical, and political spaces identified as Latinx including (but not limited to) Mexico, Puerto Rico, Dominican Republic, and Panama. Additionally, this work invites the perspectives and scholarship of non-Latinx whose praxis benefits members of the Latinx collective who are students and/or teachers. Such work takes a critical examination of the researcher/scholar identity within the Latinx community (Darder & Torres, 2013).

EDITORS' POSITIONALITIES

This work is deeply rooted in the identities and practices of the editors. As a Black, American-born woman with Bahamian, Bajan, Cherokee, and Irish roots, Theodorea Regina Berry is a critical race curriculum studies scholar whose work is situated at the interdisciplinary nexus of African American studies, curriculum studies, women and gender studies, and qualitative research methodologies. Raised in a middle-class, multicultural northeastern city, Berry interacted with people with varying racial, ethnic, and social backgrounds. Starting her life as a classically trained vocalist, Berry viewed the world in musical ways; for her, the world possessed universal understandings within multicultural contexts. But as she began to pursue her professional academic life, she came to understand that what is known and understood isn't often universal. It was during her Masters-level graduate degree program that she came to understand the significance of curriculum studies and its reconceptualist notions for what is valued as knowledge and who gets to decide what is valuable to know, regardless of context. Such understandings have fueled her pursuit of equitable representations of knowledge from a variety of cultural contexts.

Crystal A. Kalinec-Craig openly acknowledges that she is a white mathematics teacher educator who teaches in a large, public, Hispanic Serving Institution. As a native of the Texas coast, she was raised in a middle-class suburban home in Houston. After graduating from my teacher preparation program, she worked in various parts of the southern and southwest United States as a middle and high school mathematics teacher. It was not until she taught middle school for an American military base in Germany and a high school in Tucson, Arizona, did she realize that mathematics was not a culture-free, universal language. While studying mathematics teacher education, she began to question her assumptions about what elementary mathematics was and how children learned mathematics—it was much more complex and sophisticated than what she had assumed as a teacher. Kalinec-Craig's experience in Tucson was transformational to her journey as a teacher educator. She acknowledges how English is a privileged language and how her future teachers need to learn ways that value the linguistic resources of each child, especially those children who are emerging bilinguals. Her experience in Tucson also helped her to see how teachers and communities can mobilize to demand change that protects and supports Latinx communities.

Now in San Antonio as a mathematics teacher educator, Kalinec-Craig continues in the spirit of what she learned in the United States and overseas. She places her students in schools that more closely reflect the cultural and linguistic diversity of the Latinx communities that we serve. Based on what she learned in Tucson, her math methods course is designed to support future teachers as they learn to incorporate children's funds of knowledge in their mathematics instruction. She not only wants her future teachers to learn how to teach mathematics, but also to not take for granted what they know or assume to know about teaching mathematics—they need to look for ways to honor what their students know and in the context of the communities that they serve.

Mariela A. Rodríguez works as a faculty member in a department of educational leadership at a Hispanic Serving Institution; this is a role that she takes very seriously. Rodríguez is committed to supporting graduate students who seek careers as school and district leaders. She believes that it's so important to help them understand how to best support culturally and linguistically diverse students and their families. Thus, she takes the time to select books and other readings that will help these aspiring leaders gain knowledge about students' "funds of knowledge" and the linguistic and cultural strengths that they bring to the school. These strengths should not be devalued if they do not appear to fit the "norm", like speaking Spanish as a native language and living the immigrant experience.

Rodríguez has these "positions" based on her own experiences as a bilingual learner. She still recalls during her kindergarten year having to stay one-hour after the other students had gone home so that a teacher could help her work on her English; her first language spoken at home was Spanish. Thus, her dream to become a bilingual teacher was deeply rooted in the positive experiences that she had with that teacher after school hours. Rodríguez remembers the teacher was kind and never belittled students for not mastering the English language.

So, when it comes to Latinx curriculum theorizing, Rodríguez bases this work on her own experiences as a bilingual learner and teacher. Often times she sought specific strategies that would help her best meet the academic and social needs of her students. The chapters presented in this volume offer thoughtful recommendations for educators across the educational spectrum. As an educational leadership scholar, it's critical for Rodríguez to be able to share the latest research with aspiring school leaders who can then apply it and share it with the teachers in their buildings.

THE KNOWLEDGE WITHIN

This volume is organized in three sections. The first section, entitled "Latinx Curriculum and Content/Subject Matter," includes work that addresses the ways in which people of the Latinx diaspora are included in content subject matter to include mis/representations and absences. This section is led with the work from Angela Valenzuela on a curriculum delivered at Austin's Academia Cuauhtli. In this work, Valenzuela explores the decolonial imaginary and third space pedagogies that live in a curriculum of insurrection.

Ann Aviles, Richard Benson, and Erica Davila employ a document analysis to emphasize the curricular and pedagogical contributions and political education employed by the Chicago Young Lords Organization (ChYLO) occurring from 1966 to 1975. Aviles and her colleagues chronicle the activism of ChYLO aimed at addressing deficiencies in the educational institutions in Chicago and the service of this group designed to "alleviate the injustice and exploitation of Puerto Ricans" (Flores-Rodriguez, 2011–2012, p. 109).

This section concludes with the scholarship of Cristina Valencia Mazzanti and Martha Allexsaht-Snider as they analyze the mathematics learning of Latinx children in the context of a general education kindergarten classroom, a dual language immersion kindergarten classroom, and in a series of workshops for Latinx families. The analyses focus on funds of knowledge and the windows and mirrors framework (Gutierrez, 2002). Through the analysis of the three different contexts (the two kindergartens and the workshops), Mazzanti and Allexsaht-Snider reflect on how curriculum is constructed and what forms of knowing come to be perceived as valuable when bilingual children, families, and educators engage in mathematics learning together.

The second section, "Latinx Curriculum in Schools: Addressing Goals, Objectives, and Purposes," includes work that addresses the ways in which schools, school leadership, and school systems develop and implement goals, objectives, and purposes of schooling with, for and/or against the Latinx educational community. In the first chapter of this section, Juan F. Carrillo and Lucia Mock center this work on concepts of visible and invisible narratives to examine the role of the University of North Carolina's Latin@/x Education Research Hub (LERH) in contesting curricular silence and hegemonic notions of place while also producing critical discourses, courses, and research germane to Latinx history, intellectual thought, culture, and community. Carrillo and Mock draw from collaborative testimonios (Espino, Vega, Rendón, Romero, & Muñiz, 2012) that explore how LERH resists a vision of subtractive schooling (Valenzuela, 1999) while also pointing to the prospects of agency and a counterassimilationist future.

In "'Illegality' and the Curriculum: Making New Civics with Undocumented Activists," Jesús A. Tirado examines the experiences of undocumented activists at the nexus of their identities and their involvement in the creation of a new civic education. This work centers on the significance of curriculum, illegality, and precarity.

Stacy Saathoff's "Radical Literacy: Building Curriculum on Mexican American Youth's Lived Experiences," explores a curriculum design that is rooted in the lived experiences of Mexican American youth. Through the content areas of language arts and social studies in a middle or high school setting students read one of three novels, journal about specific themes, meet in dialogue groups, and develop an autobiographical creative project. The theoretical foundation of the chapter uses the Critical Race Theory tenet of voice, along with intersectionality, to highlight students' lived experiences in the curriculum.

The final section of this volume, "Latinx Currere, Latinx Curriculum as Autobiographical," includes work that addresses the historical and cultural roots and contributions of curriculum from the Latinx diaspora and will also examine and explore currere as Latinx. In the first of four chapters of this final section, Alba Isabel Lamar and Lynette DeAun Guzmán use Latinx Critical Race Theory to describe the ways in which school curriculum can function as "a culturally specific artifact designed to maintain a White supremacist script" (Ladson-Billings, 1998, p. 421). The focus of this chapter will speak to the invaluable sociohistorical perspectives offered by Chicanx and Latinx communities, stemming from the Latinx diaspora. The authors draw on *testimonio* as a methodological approach to produce counternarratives that speak back to deficit framings and highlight curricula that decenter Whiteness to address the contributions from Latinx educators while envisioning school with *Conocimientos Míos*.

Ganiva Reyes discusses what happens when an environment of authentic care (Noddings, 2013) enables a teacher and her students to embrace their border identities and Mexicanness to create a sense of belonging. Using portraiture methodology (Lawrence-Lightfoot & Davis, 1997), this chapter presents a portrait of one classroom in an alternative school in RGV, in which regional music invoked stories about family and community. Engaged pedagogy (Berry, 2010; hooks, 1994), Chicana feminist theory (Moraga & Anzaldua, 1983), and ethics of care (Noddings, 2013) are used to understand how a science teacher and her students of Mexican-origin (including teen mothers) engaged in mutual interactions of vulnerability and storytelling through music. This chapter analyzes how caring pedagogical interactions allowed Latinx students to use their own border identities, experiences, and memories to coconstruct curriculum in the classroom.

In the final chapter of this section and the text entitled, "Currere from the Borderlands: An Exercise in Possibilities for Latinx Transgender Visibility," Mario Itzel Suárez presents an autobiographical narrative of a Latinx transgender man and former teacher (pronouns: he/him/his) from the border town of Eagle Pass, Texas. The narrative goes through the four moments of Pinar's (2012) *currere*: the regressive, the progressive, the analytical, and the synthetical moments. The author weaves in Anzaldua's (2007) *Borderlands/La Frontera* with *currere*, as he writes about his recollection of the first lesson learned as a child. The author, in the regressive moment, provides a narrative of learning the difference between males and females in a Mexican household. In the progressive moment, he walks through potential medical and therapy options for transitioning. In the analytical moment, the author considers his past and present "lives" in order to arrive at the synthetical moment, where he realizes that like Anzaldua, he is an embodiment of the *hieros gamos* (p. 41), a being that contains both female and male characteristics. In the synthetical moment, he starts to realize that his visibility, though dangerous, has possibilities to change people's minds toward a more empathetic one, so long as his does not betray him. Thus, that synthetical moment is relived every time he "outs" himself to different people as a way of educating others about his experience as a transgender man of color and the implications that has for other transgender, gender nonconforming, and gender nonbinary people of color who are in the land of the *atravesados* (p. 25).

REFERENCES

Anzaldúa, G. 2007. *Borderlands/La frontera: The new mestiza* (3rd ed). San Francisco, CA: Aunt Lute Books.

Berry, T. R. 2010. Engaged pedagogy and critical race feminism. *The Journal of Educational Foundations*, 24(3/4), 19–26.

Bobbitt, J. F. 1915. The San Antonio public school system: A survey. San Antonio, TX: The San Antonio School Board.

———. 2013. Scientific method in curriculum-making. In David J. Flinders and Stephen J. Thornton (eds.), *The Curriculum Studies Reader* (4th ed., pp. 11–18). New York: Routledge.

Darder, A., & Torres, R. D. 2013. *Latinos and education: A critical reader* (2nd ed.). New York: Routledge.

Dewey, J. (1938) 1997. *Experience and education.* New York: Touchstone.

Espino, M., Vega, I., Rendón, L., Ranero, J., & Muñiz, M. 2012. The process of reflexión in bridging testimonies across lived experience. *Equity & Excellence in Education*, 45(no. 3), 444–449. https://doi.org/10.1080/10665684.2012.698188

Flores-Rodriguez, A. G. 2011–2012. On National Turf: The Rise of the Young Lords Organization and Its Struggle for the Nation in Chicago. Op., *Citnum.* 20, 105–141.

Gándara, P., & Contreras, F. 2009. *The Latino education crisis: The consequences of failed social policies.* Cambridge, MA: Harvard University Press.

Gándara, P., & Hopkins, M. 2010. *Forbidden language: English learners and restrictive language policies.* New York: Teachers College Press.

Grant, C., Brown, K. L., & Brown, A. L. 2016. *Black intellectual thought in education: The missing traditions of Anna Julia Cooper, Carter G. Woodson, and Alain LeRoy Locke.* New York: Routledge.

Gutierrez, R. 2002. Enabling the practice of mathematics teachers in context: Toward a new equity research agenda. *Mathematical Thinking and Learning*, 4(2–3), 145–187.

hooks, b. (1994). *Teaching to transgress: Education as the practice of freedom.* New York: Routledge.

Ladson-Billings, G. 1998. Just what is critical race theory and what's it doing in a nice field like education? *International Journal of Qualitative Studies in Education*, 11(1), 7–24.

Lawrence-Lightfoot, S., & Davis, Jessica Hoffman. 1997. *The Art and Science of Portraiture.* Jossey-Bass.

Moraga, C., & Anzaldua, G. (Eds.). 1983. *This bridge called my back: Writings by radical women of color* (2nd ed.). Latham, NY: Kitchen Table/Women of Color Press.

Moreno, J. F. (Ed.). 1999. *The elusive quest for equality: 150 years of Chicano/Chicana education*. Cambridge, MA: Harvard Educational Review.
Montessori, M. (2013). A critical consideration of the new pedagogy in its relation to modern science. In David J. Flinders and Stephen J. Thornton (eds.), *The Curriculum Studies Reader* (4th ed., pp. 19–31). New York: Routledge.
Noddings, N. 2013. *Caring: A relational approach to ethics and moral education*. Berkeley: University of California Press.
Pinar, W. F. 2012. *What Is curriculum theory?* (2nd ed.). New York: Routledge.
Pinar, W. F., Reynolds, W. M., Slattery, P., & Taubman, P. M. 2000. *Understanding curriculum: An introduction to the study of historical and contemporary curriculum discourses*. New York: Peter Lang.
Portelli, J. P. 1987. On defining curriculum. *Journal of Curriculum and Supervision*, 2(4), 354–367.
Tyler, R. W. 1949. *Basic principles of curriculum and instruction*. Chicago: The University of Chicago Press.
Valenzuela, A. 1999. *Subtractive schooling: US Mexican youth and the politics of caring*. Albany: State University of New York Press.

Part I

Latinx Curriculum and Content/Subject Matter

ONE

Insurrection and the Decolonial Imaginary at Academia Cuauhtli

The Liberating Potential of Third-Space Pedagogies in a Third Space

Angela Valenzuela

On the morning of October 15, 2016, the majority of the children attending Academia Cuauhtli, a Saturday school, for fourth- and fifth-graders, in Austin, Texas, burst into a cacophony of demands for fairness, reflecting an enhanced sense of critical awareness espoused by the program's curriculum and pedagogy. This was a response to the culturally relevant instruction of Maestro (a respectful appellation for "teacher," in Spanish) Martínez, a seasoned bilingual education teacher, armed with a coconstructed, civil rights history curriculum, and a motivating text about a young, celebrated person in Texas history. He had taught a lesson on social justice with a text written by Carmen Tafolla and Sharyll Teneyuca (2008), titled, *That's Not Fair! / No Es Justo! Emma Tenayuca's Struggle for Justice/La Lucha de Emma Tenayuca Por la Justicia*.

The classroom experience was a peak moment where a social justice narrative translated into action with half of the class declaring *"huelga"* (or "strike"), much to the amusement and surprise of their teachers and others present like myself. By "coconstruction," I mean that Academia Cuauhtli's curriculum is a project that is grounded in community, but through the partnership with teachers and curriculum writings in the Austin Independent School District (AISD), it is a professional community that reflects the values, strengths, and opportunities of our community. Drawing from Perez's (1999) concept of the decolonial imaginary, I characterize herein this special moment as an "insurrection" because it illuminates the transformational potential of a community-anchored initiative that intentionally seeks to liberate teachers, children, and classrooms from the strictures of subtractive curriculum, schooling, and ways of "doing education" (Valenzuela, 1999).

Because Academia Cuauhtli exists as part of a three-way partnership that is physically located in a community cultural arts center provides a nuanced account of Bhabha's (1994) concept of the third space in order to fully account for the student insurrection (also see Gutiérrez, 2008; Gutiérrez, Baquedano-López, & Tejeda, 1999). I begin with theoretically exploring both the decolonial imaginary and the third space, and then provide a sense of the context by delving into a two-part narrative consisting of two parts: First I focus on Maestro Martínez's teaching about the life of Emma Tenayuca which provides insights into his pedagogy; and the second hones in on the insurrection itself as an instantiation of the decolonial imaginary. I end with concluding thoughts that complicate Bhabha's notion of the third space by according importance to the physical space *as a third space* where third space pedagogies simultaneously occur.

THE DECOLONIAL IMAGINARY AND THE THIRD SPACE

Ample research shows that Ethnic Studies or multicultural education as part of a larger educational curriculum provides substantive representation to students typically represented unequally (Sleeter, 2011). Stated differently, through an Ethnic Studies curriculum, historically underprivileged students develop a deeper sense of self in relation to family, community, and society. It does so by providing a mirror from which these populations can *see* themselves mirrored in the curriculum. In the case of Academia Cuauhtli, a Saturday program, children experience a culturally relevant curriculum in their mother tongue, underscoring the value of their community-based identities. Curriculum and instruction at Academia Cuauhtli therefore challenge the dominant narrative to which youth are regularly exposed. What is construed as "normal" in the context of official, and otherwise largely unchallenged, discourses of schooling gets disrupted (Apple, 2014), freeing the self to "a view of self" as liberated, representing the transformative potential that lays at the heart of the decolonial imaginary (Pérez, 1999). As diametrically opposed to the more common experience of fragmentation and alienation from the schooling process (Valenzuela, 1999; Valenzuela, 2016), Academia Cuauhtli offers a space of freedom to choose, experience, and see oneself as the embodiment of wholeness and grace.

Students can *see* themselves mirrored in the curriculum. Moreover, in places like Academia Cuauhtli, where children are able to experience culturally relevant curriculum in their mother tongue, their community-based identities get valued as central to the learning process, implicitly challenging the dominant narrative to which they are regularly exposed. That which gets construed as "normal" in the context of official discourses of schooling that otherwise largely go unchallenged (Apple, 2014) gets disrupted, creating space for a decolonial imaginary (Pérez, 1999). According to Pérez (1999), the decolonial imaginary is

> a rupturing space, the alternative to that which is between the colonial and postcolonial, that interstitial space where differential politics and social dilemmas are negotiated. (p. 6)

Pérez's decolonial imaginary builds on Bhabha's (1994) notion of culture as perpetually inflected with power relations between subordinate and dominant groups (also see Fay & Haydon, 2017). In the case of Academia Cuauhtli, the dominant group are the teachers and the adults while the subordinate group are the children. Also the boys generally speak more than the girls, many of whom seem shy, even at Academia Cuauhtli where we work hard to build cohesion, friendship, and solidarity. While it is a low-stakes environment where all children and parents are treated respectfully, it is equally true that these are communities that have been the target of Immigration and Customs Enforcement (ICE) raids long before Donald Trump became president.

For both Bhabha (1994) and Pérez (1999), spaces are not only imagined, but they also concretely exist, implying the limits of a binary that constructs space in either material or conceptual terms—that is, "space as material" or "space as a concept," existing in people's imaginations. In this vein, Pérez (1999) offers, "These interstitial gaps interrupt the linear model of time, and it is in such locations that oppositional, subaltern histories can be found" (p. 5).

If one relaxes this binary and allows for what Bhabha (1994) terms the "third space" where real and imagined spaces intersect, on the one hand, and accepts, on the other, the intellectual, moral, and pedagogical commitment to the decolonization of minoritized children's minds, bodies, and spirts (e.g., Saavedra & Nymark, 2008; Solyom & Brayboy, 2011), then the potential for a decolonial imaginary can become manifest, as in a classroom insurrection. It is at this point that the third space distinguishes itself from the decolonial imaginary in at least two ways.

First, this piece builds the argument that third space pedagogies themselves are differentially liberating depending on where they occur—in this case, a local, community arts institution. Second, while a decolonial imaginary always implies the third space, the reverse is not necessarily true. That is, while third spaces are invariably caught up with "elaborating strategies of selfhood" (Bhabha, 1994, p. 1), the production of radical subjectivities attuned to a memory, history, and critique of colonization is not automatic. I turn now to a textured description of the third space that

Academia Cuauhtli enjoys both because of its pedagogy and its situatedness at the ESB-MACC.

BACKGROUND CONTEXT: ELABORATING AN ECOSYSTEM OF POSSIBILITY

Established in 2014, Academia Cuauhtli (Nahuatl for "Eagle Academy") is a formal-legal partnership between a local community-based organization named Nuestro Grupo, of which I am a cofounder, the Austin Independent School District (AISD), and the City of Austin's Emma S. Barrientos Mexican American Culture Center (ESB-MACC). We serve predominantly first-generation, mostly Mexican, immigrant children from five East Austin, Title I schools and their families. While the scale of the Saturday academy is small, serving an average of 34 fourth- and fifth-grade students from five East Austin public elementary, Title I schools, Nuestro Grupo is having broader impacts. That is, Nuestro Grupo has prepared close to 100 teachers with a standards-aligned, coconstructed, research-based curriculum (prepared at Cuauhtli) that is also available districtwide for grades 3–7 and 11, filling a critical knowledge gap in the curriculum of Austin's increasingly diverse public schools.

Neither Nuestro Grupo nor Academia Cuauhtli is located either in the schools or the nearby University of Texas at Austin, but rather on the grounds of the ESB-MACC, generally regarded as Austin's premier Mexican American cultural arts institution. As a partner, the ESB-MACC provides free space and significant access to staff and opportunities with art exhibits, bilingual theater, films, musical performances, cultural celebrations, and access to numerous other arts-focused opportunities. Particularly through its after-school program that provides instruction to youth who participate in Academia Cuauhtli, it provides a sense of belonging in a world of exclusion where children and families can imagine not only new worlds of possibility, but also a sense of ownership of a public-serving institution that was itself born out of years of community struggle (Gutiérrez, 2008).

Drawing from Bhabha (1994), Academia Cuauhtli utilizes "third space" pedagogies by centering Mexican American and Tejano/a (meaning "Texas Mexican") culture and identity. This stands in stark contrast to its general absence in AISD schools. The very act of including a culturally relevant children's book into an educational space is arguably a kind of rupturing unto itself in the way Pérez (1999) suggests. The spiritual and intellectual desert created by a subtractive, K–12 curriculum that systematically deprives children of opportunities to see themselves represented in books, stories, and histories—much less in their own languages—creates potential for such texts—and our coconstructed curriculum, generally—to engender ways of thinking and knowing that resonate with students' values and experiences (Mo & Shen, 2003; Seto, 2003; Valenzuela, 1999).

Our Academia Cuauhtli volunteers include mostly undergraduate and graduate students from the University of Texas at Austin who work a school year that runs from September through May. Some volunteers only attend Nuestro Grupo's Wednesday night planning meetings, while others participate on Saturdays only, and a third group, myself included, meet at both times to the extent that travel schedules and family obligations permit.

Space does not permit an expansive elaboration on the myriad discussions and planning that took place in order to establish Academia Cuauhtli, but suffice it to say that Nuestro Grupo envisioned a cultural revitalization project offering lessons exclusively in Spanish. We also planned a critical, culturally rich focus on Tejano history, immigration/migration, danza Mexica (Aztec dance), indigenous heritage, and the cultural arts (Valenzuela, Zamora, & Rubio, 2015). In our regular Wednesday evening meetings in preparation for each Saturday class, we have conscientiously described ourselves as a "Chicana feminist space" to which the current account attests.

We desire for our curriculum and pedagogy to raise women and girls' silenced voices and histories to empower them, as well as our communities. These commentaries of dignity, self-empowerment, and self-actualization take the place of *flor y cantos* (indigenous flower and song incantations) at the beginning of each meeting. The lead discussants offer personal and inspirational thoughts that help build mutual trust and our sense of caring for one another (Valenzuela, 1999). In the Nuestro Grupo meeting immediately following the insurrection, Maestro Martínez shared, "We want girls to become the counter stories for those who consider them as less valuable, which is a common practice in our culture." These and other kinds of commentaries tend to get expressed in our *flor y cantos*.

Despite the opening account that focuses on a bilingual male teacher, most of our teachers are women. By design, our expert and novice bilingually certified teachers are experienced in Latino community activities like book fairs, educational conferences, and protests at School Board meetings, and at least 10 have participated in coconstructing the standards-aligned, research-based curriculum used in Academia Cuauhtli. The approximately fifty dual language teachers that have participated in our professional development workshops are also using our curriculum districtwide.

Nuestro Grupo has contributed to the establishment of an ecosystem of mutual support—through our informal partnership with teachers, school staff, parents, and children associated with the Austin Area Association for Bilingual Education (AAABE) teachers—for AISD bilingually certified teachers, school staff, parents, and children. This means that

Nuestro Grupo members regularly attend and participate in AAABE socials, events, and conferences, as well as wider networks within the district. In addition to annual funding support, AAABE provides Academia Cuauhtli with a rotating set of at least 10, preselected teachers annually who collaborate with our curriculum writers in developing the curriculum road map during the summer months. These teachers also attend professional development sessions and Academia Cuauhtli's annual retreats. Their responsibility is to teach on their assigned Saturdays from 9 a.m.–12 p.m. Since these teachers emanate from throughout AISD schools, Academia Cuauhtli additionally promotes camaraderie among them, as well as a sense of solidarity in advancing the education of Latina/o children.

Our annual graduation ceremonies are always large with between two and three hundred in attendance. Many parents and other family members work on Saturdays and are unable to accompany them to our classes or to pick them up afterward. Consequently, we have arranged for the district to provide a school bus to pick up and return children in the morning at specific locations. Families face many challenges associated with poverty, gentrification, and for some, undocumented status. This latter challenge has been of particular significance of late, given the emotional toll that deportations and threats of deportation have taken on our children, families, and schools. Building trust with families has been slow and painstaking. By our third year of operation, however, relations with Academia Cuauhtli parents, teachers, ESB-MACC staff, and Nuestro Grupo volunteers had definitely coalesced, allowing for a playful sense of freedom that I theorize further in my concluding comments.

TEACHING EMMA TENAYUCA

Tafolla and Teneyuca's (2008) children's book on Emma Tenayuca is the story of a small girl's growing up and coming into consciousness of poverty and inequality during the mid-1920s in San Antonio, Texas. Maestro Martínez taught from the book on that eventful October morning at Academia Cuauhtli. Since we encourage siblings to attend, the Raul Salinas room (our regular classroom space) was particularly packed that morning. As is customary, Nuestro Grupo volunteers and some parents were also present. Formerly a teacher from Mexico, Maestro Martínez is a gentle teacher who speaks in a clear, measured tone, while raising questions that help children to read and think deeply as he reads along to them aloud. I could tell that the students were attentive to his reading of the story. A girl recorded parts of his lesson with a phone as her mother sat by her, listening quietly, as well. She was one of only a few parents present for this instruction as the remainder were in another room participating in a *plática*, or conversation, with members of Nuestro Grupo assigned to assist them with the kinds of knowledge that they need in order for them to successfully navigate the public school system.

Prior to reading the text to the children, Maestro Martínez provided them with an overview of the book. He explained that Emma Tenayuca, born on December 21, 1916, was a major civil rights leader in Texas history and that authorities jailed her several times for her beliefs and leadership. He added that she was a young person who loved to read and advocated for the poor of San Antonio and that the book was about her coming into self-awareness by the age of 21. Emma Tenayuca was able to organize the largest strike in the city's history, involving pecan shellers, mostly women and some children facing unfair working conditions — long hours, low pay, and respiratory illnesses related to the task of shelling the pecans.

He walked the children through her life, page by page. He described how Emma Tenayuca saw, as a matter of course, hungry children, destitute families with little to nothing to live on, at least one friend within her proximity who was not able to read because she had to accompany her family on the migrant stream, and mothers and small children, hungry and poorly clad, weathering the unforgiving winter. "*No es justo!* That's not fair!" she told her grandfather one day. At this point, Maestro Martínez paused and asked, "What is fairness? What are some examples?" In Spanish, one child commented, "Like when some have more to eat than others." "Yes, that's a good example," Maestro Martínez responded. Another commented, "Like when your dad does a lot of work for someone and the boss refuses to pay him." The pained voice of this particular student intimated firsthand experience with this occasional exploitative practice toward immigrants. "Yes," Maestro Martínez responded in Spanish, "It's unfair that a boss doesn't pay his workers and this is what Emma also witnessed."

Maestro Martínez asked students for other examples of unfairness from their lives. He was clear that he was trying to elicit from them a response. Instead, they mostly sat quietly in their seats, several exhibiting nervousness with their lips pursed and tightly drawn facial expressions. "What is very important to us here at Academia Cuauhtli is your voice," he said in Spanish. "We want all of you to talk and share your views. Your voice is very important," he insisted. To this, there was continued silence. After a long quiet pause, he continued reading.

He reads about Emma's relationship with her grandfather and how he encouraged her to always do her part to correct injustices. "So you see, it is not enough to see an injustice, you also have to do something about it!" Maestro Martínez exclaimed in Spanish, sounding insistent. In time, and after the employers cut the wages of the pecan shellers, Emma Tenayuca organized a two-month strike that at its height involved more than 8,000 out of 12,000 total workers — ultimately forcing the owners to raise workers' salaries. This earned her the respect of so many people in San Antonio, as well as nationwide, he concluded. He repeated how Emma was not only a talker, but also a doer. Focusing his comments on the girls in the classroom, Maestro Martínez exclaimed in Spanish,

> Emma Tenayuca was a young girl. And it's especially important for you as young girls to speak, especially when you are experiencing or witnessing unfairness, just like Emma did. We in Academia Cuauhtli, really cherish your voices. Like Emma Tenayuca, you also have a voice. And you must speak up when there is an injustice! It's not enough to observe it. You must also do something about it.

With the assistance of his partnering teacher that day together with Nuestro Grupo volunteers and a few parents, the students then took an outdoor activity break while Maestro Martínez remained inside, with plans of rewarding the children with a bite-sized candy.

Insurrection and the Decolonial Imaginary

As the children made their way back into the classroom, they observed Maestro Martínez holding a large bag of Reese's chocolates in his hands and placing them on the children's seats. However, because by this point in time, Maestro Martínez had succeeded in placing the chocolates on only half of their seats, the other half felt put off. Those that had chocolates at their seats readily consumed them. The other half looked around, looking despondent, albeit playfully so. Although Maestro Martínez was literally in the middle of his task, he nevertheless played along, saying, "Well, what are you supposed to do when you see an injustice?" he asked them in Spanish.

At this point, the decolonial imaginary unfolded. The classroom was immediately transformed into a world where girls and boys now gave clear and personal expression to their concern over fairness. The small girl that had earlier been recording Maestro Martínez with her mother's phone, together with her older sister, sprinted into action. They immediately made their way to the front of the classroom, grabbing the large, "Academia Cuauhtli" poster board sign at the front of the classroom, and began yelling "*Huelga! Huelga!*" at the top of their voices, fist pumping in the air, demanding fairness.

The class as a whole reveled in what to an outsider might have looked like chaos, a loss of control. With broad smiles and triumphal gestures, the sisters led an equally impassioned chorus of protesters "at the picket line." This revealed that the students had learned Maestro Martínez' lesson well, with their action invoking a distant, yet palpable spirit of civil rights protest by transporting everyone present, if for a moment, into a space where children, especially girls, have voice, power, and a moral obligation to rectify injustice. They would have made Emma Tenayuca proud.

Although anticlimactic, a beaming Maestro Martínez gave the animated protesters their chocolates as the students and parents, sharing smiles and excitement, collected their items in the final remaining minutes of the class to catch the school bus awaiting them outside. Turning to me, Maestro Martínez and I exchanged knowing smiles. He told me in English and Spanish, "Los niños se pusieron en huelga! ("The children went on strike!") I didn't tell them to do that." While the specific action they took wasn't dictated by Maestro Martínez, it is clear that his quick thinking became a teachable moment with respect to Emma Tenayuca's ethic of fairness that engendered an extemporaneous expression of protest, reflecting a sense of self-awareness across time.

CONCLUSION

To say that the decolonial imaginary always implies the third space though the reverse is not necessarily so is helpful for understanding why matters played out as they did so powerfully in Maestro Martínez's classroom. What is not fully captured in this account, however, is how Academia Cuauhtli itself—as a physical space that resides outside of the formal institutional spaces of the public school and university system—is a liberating setting for all involved. For starters, the ESB-MACC is a local, community arts institution that *belongs* to Austin's Mexican American community. This means not only that things might happen there that might not ordinarily happen in regular schools where ways of knowing and being are predictably interreferential, with values, mores, and discourses getting reproduced. Conversely, clues to the magic of Academia Cuauhtli and Maestro Martínez's skillful teaching, generally, are captured in his own pedagogy that demonstrates openness to student expression, and most particularly, when he refers directly to what "we at Academia Cuauhtli want."

His use of the collective pronoun, "we," speaks not only to the power of ownership of a coconstructed curriculum, but also to the collective spirit of grassroots, community-based education where a sense of ownership over a local, community arts institution is also cultivated. Moreover, for a community that is under the gaze of a judgmental and demeaning high-stakes testing K–12 environment, as well as a hostile, anti-immigrant political context, the collective pronoun conveys both a shared history of oppression and a palpable sense of solidarity. The larger implication is that third space pedagogies are themselves not intrinsically free.

In short, what this narrative best captures is the liberating potential of third-space pedagogies when taught in actual third-space contexts that are explicitly values based in culturally resonant ways. In such spaces and places, the decolonial imaginary becomes a lived, concrete experience of the here and now where the very act of standing up to injustice is triumphant, lightening the burden of lived experience, if only for a moment.

REFERENCES

Apple, M. W. *Official knowledge: Democratic education in a conservative age*. New York: Routledge, 2014.

Bhabha, H. 1994. *The location of culture*. New York: Routledge.

Fay, S., & Haydon, L. 2017. *The location of culture*. New York: Macat Library.

Gutiérrez, K. D. 2008. Developing a sociocritical literacy in the third space. *Reading Research Quarterly, 43*(2), 148–164.

Gutiérrez, K. D., Baquedano-López, P., & Tejeda, C. 1999. Rethinking diversity: Hybridity and hybrid language practices in the third space. *Mind, Culture, and Activity*, 6(4), 286–303.

Mo, W., & Shen, W. 2003. Accuracy is not enough: The role of cultural values in the authenticity of picture books. In Dana L. Fox & Kathy G. Short (eds.), *Stories matter: The complexity of cultural authenticity in children's literature* (pp. 198–212). Urbana, IL: National Council of Teachers of English.

Pérez, E. 1999. *The decolonial imaginary: Writing Chicanas into history*. Bloomington: Indiana University Press.

Saavedra, C. M., & Nymark, E. D. 2008. Borderland-mestizaje. In Norman K. Denzin, Yvonna S. Lincoln, & Linda Tuhiwai Smith (eds.), *Handbook of critical and indigenous methodologies* (p. 255). Thousand Oaks, CA: Sage Publications.

Seto, T. 2003. Multiculturalism is not Halloween. In Dana L. Fox & Kathy G Short (eds.), *Stories matter: The complexity of cultural authenticity in children's literature* (pp. 93–97). Urbana, IL: National Council of Teachers of English.

Sleeter, C. E. 2011. The academic and social value of ethnic studies: A research review. National Education Association Research Department. Retrieved on February 19, 2016, http://www.nea.org/assets/docs/NBI-2010-3-value-of-ethnic-studies.pdf

Solyom, J. A., & Jones Brayboy, B. M. 2011. Memento Mori: Policing the minds and bodies of indigenous Latinas/os in Arizona. *California Western International Law Journal, 42*, 473.

Tafolla, C., & Teneyuca, S. 2008. *That's not fair!/No es justo! Emma Tenayuca's struggle for justice/La lucha de Emma Tenayuca por la justicia*. San Antonio, TX: Wings Press.

Valenzuela, A. 1999. *Subtractive schooling: U.S.-Mexican youth and the politics of caring*. New York: State University of New York Press.

——— (ed.). 2016. *Growing critically conscious teachers: A social justice curriculum for educators of Latino/a youth*. New York: Teachers College Press.

Valenzuela, A., Zamora, E., & Rubio, B. 2015. Academia cuauhtli and the eagle: Danza Mexica and the epistemology of the circle. *Voices in Urban Education, 41*, 46–56.

TWO

"To Serve the People"

Transformational Praxis of the Chicago Young Lords

Ann Aviles, Richard Benson, and Erica Davila

Chicago, a city established in 1833 by a Black Haitian trader, Jean Baptist DuSable, developed from its inception to become a center of commerce and political advancement for national prominence. By the mid-1800s, Chicago emerged to become a grandiose commercial site due to its location as a regional marketplace that attracted interests on a global scale. Labor needs of steel manufacturing giants made Chicago more than the city of 'big shoulders' that housed industry. Industry needs increased the incentives to attract people in need of work and in many cases, sociopolitical refuge. Global migration waves to Chicago produced multi-ethnic enclaves and diverse communities throughout the city at the beginning of 1900s.[1] This influx of immigrant populations that gravitated to Chicago at the dawn of the twentieth century became the bedrock for what the metropolis would be built upon. Postwar America ushered in the creation of cosmopolitan urban sites and the microcosm of Chicago attracted numerous ethnic populations of Irish, Italian, Polish, Puerto Rican, Jewish, Mexican, Greek, Lithuanian, and African American descent. Far from the attempts of becoming a "melting pot," Chicago came to epitomize a municipality of diverse cultures, neighborhood organizations, and unapologetic "glocal"[2] representations of nationalist pride—all found in the city by the lake.[3]

However, with the dreams and multi-cultural/ethnic representations that have made Chicago an international city also come the drama of political struggle that can never be divorced from critical historical narratives. For Chicago, the world has maintained a lens of fixation on the city made infamous for political corruption, Al Capone–style "gangsterism," and big city machine politics. However, as Chicago folklore serves a significance for a global consensus, the city cannot be truly understood without the equal pairings of counternarratives that explicate the tales of citywide multiethnic and racial migration waves, political struggles, community mobilizations, youth protests, and union organizing that has historically provided theater and militant aspirations for a national scene. At the core of political occurrences in Chicago is the thrust of independent politics that are rooted in a legacy of radical movements that have cultivated an eclectic array of activists.[4]

Antimachine activism in the city of Chicago is closely linked to shifts in national modes of organizational challenge to the totalitarian mayoral regimes that marginalized people of color in various urban centers nation-wide. However, Chicago was subjected to the fate of a unique political beast in the form of Richard J. Daley who held office for 20 years, and went unopposed in several mayoral elections. In *Black Power in Chicago*, scholars Doug Gills and Abdul Alkalimat provide a striking reflection of Daley's reign:

> He was a formidable opponent who could scream four-letter words on national television . . . and force prominent civil rights leaders to give him the Black Power handshake. In fact, when he did these things, working class ethnics loved him even more. As a point man for the Irish, Daley administered their disproportionate control of power and jobs despite their declining numbers and percentage of the population.[5]

Far from isolation, Daley's dominance reflected the political stranglehold that Irish Catholics exercised on Chicago's city government. Essentially, Chicago was a city far beyond the mere concepts of partisan government. By the mid-1960s, Chicago was best described by scholars of Chicago's "Communiversity," as a confederation of several immigrant nations. To which prompted the additional query, "Is the city of Chicago an ethnocracy or a theocracy? Perhaps it is both—an ethnotheocracy."[6] To those outside the scope of Chicago style politics, this merely translated as an assertion to marginalization, inequitable distribution of resources, cronyism, nepotism, and abuses of power that ensured the maintenance of poor people of color who will only inherit an increase of generational poverty in Chicago.

Taking notice of urban blight in Chicago, Dr. Martin Luther King Jr. and his momentum garnered from the Civil Rights Movement decided to take his advocacy interests North to Chicago and battle the Daley machine in 1965. King and the Southern Christian Leadership Conference's (SCLC) move to advance the Chicago Freedom Movement put the city on center stage as the nation paid special attention to housing inequalities and racial discrimination in the nation's most segregated city. King's sojourn North, though turbulent in Chicago, did yield success as more people took to the streets to protest in the open-housing marches. As a result, the presence of the SCLC in Chicago and the Student Non-Violent Coordinating Committee (SNCC) Black Power Project spurred Chicago youth of multiracial and ethnic backgrounds to challenge the Daley machine.[7]

As the nation continued to experience the restlessness of high school and college youth, more protest demonstrations erupted to protest the Vietnam War and support Third World Liberation anti-imperialist struggles. In community spaces of Chicago, more youth lashed out to challenge police violence and institutional racism. Black and Puerto Rican communities experienced more than their fair share of brutality, and "in June 1966 police shot and killed a young Puerto Rican named Cruz Arcelis, setting off the Division Street Riots in Humboldt Park, west of Uptown."[8] With an increase of national and local pressure, in a speech delivered to a Chicago audience on July 28, 1966, Stokely Carmichael openly referred to mayor Daley as a racist and chief custodian of Black exploitation in the city.[9] Daley continued to deepen racial strife in Chicago during the 1968 urban rebellions that arose from the assassination of Dr. King. As Black and Puerto Rican youth took to the streets in response to a festering tide of racial tension, Daley informed the Chicago police to "shoot to kill . . . shoot to maim looters" and further exacerbated tensions in the racially and economically torn city.[10] Only months later, as Chicago hosted the 1968 Democratic Convention, Daley again, issued additional orders of violent confrontation to Chicago police, who in turn attacked antiwar activists protesting at the convention.[11]

However, even more nonexistent to this narrative of unheralded community activists is the work and legacy of the Chicago Young Lords Organization (referred to as ChYLO throughout this chapter) who challenged the systemic and damning institutional traditions that Chicago became wrought for. As contemporaries of the aforementioned organizations, ChYLO emerges during a vital moment in the historical trajectory of Chicago's troublesome 1960s developments. Though complex sociopolitical phenomenon cultivates the emergence of ChYLO, it is critical to demand a clear analysis of ChYLO in the context of historical events that define the organization within both Chicago and national perspectives. Thus, this chapter will address three significant questions related to the legacy of ChYLO:

1. What is the role of community-based political education for the purposes of youth organizing/education?
2. What forms of counter-hegemonic curriculum and pedagogical tools did ChYLO utilize to achieve the aims and objectives of community mobilization?

3. How does ChYLO's community-political education inform curriculum development, specifically for Latinx and other marginalized groups?

IDEOLOGY AND ACTIVISM

We approach this work from the stance of critical scholar activists. Collectively, we inform and interpret this work from our roots as educators, community activists, and native Chicagoans resisting oppressive structures. Curriculum consists of more than static documents, instead as "[C]ritical theorists [we] analyze curriculum as an institutional set of arrangements that includes policies, contexts, identities, and pedagogy as well as explicit curriculum documents."[12] Within this theoretical framework we analyze the work of the Chicago Young Lords Organization (ChYLO) as a curricular project. Placing the practices of these youth activists at the center of our educational justice work shifts curricular narratives. Further, this work calls on others to consider this shift and dig into the knowledge constructed by the organic intellectual[13] work of ChYLO. Community educational formations were developed by ChYLO to address deficiencies identified within educational institutions, and to aid urban youth in combating the postindustrial, sociopolitical, and economic challenges of Chicago communities. The aims of ChYLO were to

> alleviate the injustice and exploitation of Puerto Ricans in the United States and on the island. The [Ch]YLO brand of militancy, however, did not stem from intellectual circles. It was developed and constantly redefined on the ground. . . . From a turf gang, the Young Lords became the Young Lords Organization (YLO), a voice for militant Puerto Rican nationalism, opposition to urban renewal, solidarity with the black freedom struggle, and support for revolutionary movements around the world. . . . The [Ch] YLO sought self-determination and greater control over space, but, and importantly, the re-establishment of self-pride, dignity, and a sense of solidarity among Puerto Ricans in Chicago.[14]

A document analysis of ChYLO materials, including archived interviews housed at DePaul University and Grand State Valley, was reviewed and follow-up interviews with key leaders of ChYLO were conducted to provide an historical account of the curricular development and pedagogy developed and employed by ChYLO in their efforts to: educate Latinx populations in Chicago regarding their history; understand impacts of colonialism and imperialism; and equip youth with ideological and transformative tools to change their individual, material, and community conditions. This work will rely on qualitative analysis of the stated organization's alternative pedagogical resources with significant attention provided to the various curricular examples provided by the ChYLO organization. In this chapter we aim to analyze, nuance, and discuss the actions taken by ChYLO as a form of curricular development and praxis.

BRIEF HISTORY OF CHYLO

The Chicago Young Lords (ChYLO)[15] began as a street gang, reflective of the repressive racial dynamics of Chicago described in the chapter opening. Orlando Davila established the Young Lords as a gang in approximately 1961.[16] The development of the gang was a form of protection for Puerto Rican youth in Chicago from Irish, Italian, and other white gangs. One of the early members of the gang, Jose "Cha-Cha" Jimenez spent time in and out of jail due to his gang and drug involvement, which eventually led to his development of consciousness and understanding of larger systems of oppression. Cha-Cha recognized the prevalence of problems among poor people, in particular Puerto Ricans. Cha-Cha was instrumental in reorganizing the Young Lords street gang into a "political organization fighting for self-determination of Latinos and other oppressed peoples."[17] In September 1968, ChYLO was reorganized by Cha-Cha into a "human rights movement for self-determination for Puerto Rico and other nations, and for neighborhood controlled development and empowerment."[18] In January 1969, ChYLO began to set up a formal organizational structure patterned after the Black Panther Party's ministerial configuration.[19] For the purposes of this chapter, we focus on three ministerial positions: General Secretary/Chairman of ChYLO, Jose "Cha-Cha" Jimenez; Minister of Information, Omar Lopez; and Minister of Education, Luis "Tony" Baez. These positions focused on the development of critical ideological concepts related to issues of welfare, health, childcare, police brutality, urban renewal, and Puerto Rico's status as a colony of the United States.[20] The leadership of ChYLO recognized the community concerns/dynamics impacting Latinxs in Chicago; the identification of these issues and the subsequent manner in which they were addressed are reflective of the pedagogical ideologies and subsequent practices of the organization.

While a specific plan was not formulated initially, ChYLO Chairman Cha-Cha Jimenez did develop a 12-point plan, while serving a year in Cook County jail; he was "fighting repressive conditions because then, like today the goal was to develop an organizing tool to help build structure for our [Latinx] protracted struggle and for barrio (neighborhood) empowerment."[21] The 12-point plan is as follows:

1. We want independence and self-determination for the People of Aztlan and Puerto Rico.
2. We want an end to all imperialist wars—economic and military.

3. We want an end to the mercenary nature of the U.S. military system and an end to oppression of Latinos and other poor and oppressed people by threats of imprisonment or by economically depriving them of their basic needs then forcing them to volunteer or allowing them to be drafted into unjust, imperialist wars.
4. We want equality for the sexes.
5. We want an end to the inner-city removal of Latinos and other poor and oppressed people. We want Latinos and all poor and oppressed people to control the housing to be built in their respective communities so that they can be sure it is fit for human beings and economically reasonable. We also want all existing housing brought up to comply with the codes.
6. We want a guaranteed income and full employment for Latinos and all poor and oppressed people.
7. We want bi-lingual education for Latinos. An education that teaches Latinos and all poor and oppressed people the true history of their past and exposes the true nature of this decadent society.
8. We want an end to the robbing of Latinos and all poor and oppressed people by GREEDY YANQUI BUSINESSMEN in the Latino community.
9. We want an end to the enormous drug problem caused by this decadent society. We want the drug pushers, the rich perpetrators of this society, arrested and tried by their victims. We want all those now in jail for crimes related to drugs discharged to community-controlled rehabilitation centers and provided with good and efficient medical care. We want research begun immediately so that the use of methadone on heroin addicts can be discontinued.
10. We want the same good and efficient health care that is given to the rich to be given to Latinos and other poor and oppressed people.
11. We want an end to the brutalization and cold-blooded murder of Latinos and all poor and oppressed people by Yanqui police in this country. We want police in Latino communities to be Latinos and under the control of the Latino community.
12. We want all Latinos released from federal, state, county and city jails, because they have not had fair trials, not have been tried by a jury of their peers as defined by the U.S. Constitution. They have been tried by Yanqui courts and jurors who have no basic understanding of Latinos nor of the conditions to which Latinos are subjected.

Cha-Cha Jimenez, General Secretary
Young Lords Organization
Cook County Jail
December 31, 1972

ChYLOs experiences with various issues as members of the Chicago Latinx community informed the stance they took on addressing the concerns outlined in their 12-point program. While we are not able to address all the points outlined by their plan in this chapter, we highlight it here to illustrate the comprehensive nature of the curricula (organizing tool) they developed and employed at various points in time, responding to the repressive conditions in Chicago, specifically among the Puerto Rican, and Latinx community.

RESISTANCE, INTELLECTUALISM, AND PRAXIS

In this section, we will discuss themes that arose from document analysis and interviews conducted with the three key leaders in the ChYLO organization. Themes consist of: organizational transformation, organic intellectualism, and practice. These themes emerged in our discussions with ChYLO leadership in which each emphasized the challenges of organizing Latinx youth who had negative experiences with education and other governmental institutions (specifically the Daley machine) that at best marginalized them and more often than not harassed and/or threatened their very existence.

ORGANIZATIONAL TRANSFORMATION

There is no negating the reality that ChYLO began as a street/turf gang. It rose out of a need to protect Latinx youth from white youth harassment and violence. "The Puerto Ricans—who by now had grown in number—began to organize themselves in self-defense."[22] Gang fights between rival gangs had become routine. In addition, members had begun doing drugs—"sniff glue, some marijuana, shoot heroin and become more active in crime . . . burglarize homes, strip cars, snatch purses, and stick up people."[23] These dynamics are highlighted not to disparage members of ChYLO, but instead to describe the complex dynamics of youth activities developed in response to sociopolitical conditions such as disinvestment, displacement, and poor treatment of the Puerto Rican community at this time, and to elucidate the challenges of transforming ChYLO from a gang to a human rights/political organization. This is not to justify the ways in which youth responded, but instead is meant to humanize and bring to the forefront the many issues negatively impacting youth in Chicago's communities. One of the main leaders, Cha-Cha was (self-admittedly) involved in many of these activities and as a result spent time in and out of jail. Ironically, it was Cha-Cha's frequent trips to prison that made him "trusted" by the gang members, leading to his development as president of ChYLO. Conversely, it was Cha-Cha's time in prison that exposed him to alternatives of violence and drugs in addressing community, social, and personal ills faced.

> Although confused for many years as to who the oppressor was, Cha-Cha used his time in jail to think. He left jail with a vague conception of an oppressor—a conception he sharpened as he experienced abuse. He saw that his problems were not unique but common among the poor, especially among Latinos. He reorganized the dissolving street gang—then on the verge of falling into drugs—and turned it into a political organization fighting for the self-determination of Latinos and other poor and oppressed peoples.[24]

According to the ChYLOs Minister of Education, Dr. Tony Baez, getting members to engage readings was not an easy task, "[we] had to find a way of taking people that were very undisciplined and getting them to stay put to read. . . . I created modules that were not too long—short enough so people could read the thing—couldn't expect people to read whole books, some of us had to read the whole book and then summarize it; so we had classes to do that."[25] Tony recognized that although ChYLO members were not engaged in formal educational processes (e.g. classroom learning), they were in fact, "educating themselves and the community around them."[26] Omar Lopez and Cha-Cha Jimenez recruited Tony to organize an educational movement, given that Tony had a more formal educational background.[27]

The Minister of Information, Omar Lopez, also expressed the difficulty of engaging youth in education, especially given that their experiences with school focused on Eurocentric curriculum, absent of learning and knowledge that would provide the tools needed to navigate dynamics of poverty, police brutality, and displacement. According to Lopez,[28] "it was a real challenge in politicizing [ChYLO] members especially around housing and police brutality. . . . In May 1969 members [were] still very reluctant to become political. . . . [I] believe what changed them was the killing of Manuel Ramos"[29]—this event pushed members to become political. It is critical to note the resistance youth demonstrated as it parallels current resistance Latinx youth exhibit when they are disengaged and/or reluctant to complete school readings, assignments, or other schooling requirements. It was the murder of a ChYLO member that created a connection, urgency, and motivation to engage readings and a shift in ideology from gang activity to political organizing for many ChYLO youth.

The killing of a comrade, Manuel Ramos, also sparked ChYLO's organizing and action. This tragic event led to a large rally and march in which members of ChYLO called on many community members within and across Chicago to protest police brutality. When marching, the group came across rival gang territory, and the leadership soon realized that ChYLO cadres had not obtained permission to march through this neighborhood. As a result, an impromptu meeting/dialogue occurred between ChYLO leadership and the BlackStone Rangers.[30] One of the ministers had to quickly explain the purpose of the march in order to avoid conflict with this rival gang. His ability to explain the situation and make a compelling argument resulted in no violence/conflict and the rival gang even joined the march.[31] This situation reflects the transformation ChYLO underwent as they negotiated their roles/identity from street gang to political organization. Rather than using brute force/violence, the leadership utilized their understanding of police brutality not only in the Latinx community but also in Black communities across Chicago. This allowed for the identification of a "common enemy," and the leadership of the gang was able to relate based on their lived experiences with police harassment and the brutality that accompanied it. ChYLO leadership though not formally trained as educators were able to make connections between what was happening in their communities, developing youth ideologies around issues such as police brutality, simultaneously making connections to larger systems/structures within the City of Chicago, nationally, and globally—a sincere reflection of translating their organizing skills and knowledge of community issues to work toward transforming conditions of injustice.

ORGANIC INTELLECTUALS

We are utilizing the term "organic intellectuals" as coined by Antonio Gramsci who stated; "organic intellectuals are distinguished less by their profession, which may be any job characteristic of their class, than by their function in directing the ideas and aspirations of the class to which they organically belong."[32] The grounded approach of ChYLO is critical in our own work, heeding caution in recognizing our positionality as university faculty; however, we also understand the complex nature of our identities--which for all of us, is first and foremost folks of color from Chicago. As we analyzed primary source documents and interview data, we embraced our perspectives as critical educators seeking hope within the brilliance of young folks of color comprising ChYLO who fought for Chicago and for oppressed people on a global scale. As Gramsci argued, "It is through this assumption of conscious responsibility, aided by absorption of ideas and personnel from the more advanced bourgeois intellectual strata, that the proletariat can escape from defensive corporatism and economism and advance towards hegemony."[33]

> We were not um . . . our knowledge was not academic. And ya know that was one of the things we always said, it doesn't mean that if don't go to school or you're not in college that you are not smart, or that you cannot analyze a situation where you get involved. We always emphasized that fact, we always hammered that into the cadres so that they

would understand that they were smart. And in fact, the leadership, and I'm talking specifically about Cha-Cha, he was pretty intelligent. So, to be able to organize what used to be a gang into this type of human rights organization, it takes a lot of maneuvering, ya know, a lot of maneuvering, so he's pretty skillful on things like that.[34]

It wasn't difficult for the Latinx youth to understand what Cha-Cha was saying about urban renewal, racism, police brutality, etc. After all, they lived it. "At first Cha-Cha turned his apartment into an office and organized classes. . . . The Young Lords held meetings in Lincoln Park on the problems of housing and urban renewal."[35] Further, Cha-Cha notes,

> The first Young Lords actually had political education classes in the living room . . . listening to records from Fidel, Che, Malcolm X . . . then we would go to the street corner and we would be talking about the *Red Book*,[36] and still drinking wine and smoking weed on the corner, that was our office. So, we really have to understand how we organized the group, so that means you have people from the street, little gang bangers and everything else talking about *On Contradiction* [Tse-Tung, 1968] and theory and practice and that practice is more important than theory . . . that theory comes from practice. And this is how the Young Lords in Chicago were developing.[37]

As Cha-Cha reflects back to his time organizing with ChYLO during the 1960s, it is critical to take note of the movements happening during this same moment in education, and more specifically curriculum studies. At this time radical scholars were conceptualizing social justice educational frameworks. As academics today, we clearly see movements on the ground, such as Black Lives Matter, impacting the work of academia and vice versa. Our exploration identifies how the movements ChYLO mobilized on the ground in Chicago informed the work of scholars who were part of these moments in curriculum studies that helped define concepts such as hidden curriculum[38] and ethnic studies[39] among many other concepts that made a significant shift in the field of education. As Cha-Cha stated, "We had very few Latino students here at the time, there were no Latino Studies in Illinois, maybe on the east coast but we didn't have any here."[40] The absence of Latinx students and studies was (and is) not just an issue at the post-secondary level as expressed by Cha-Cha, the absence of Latinx curriculum K–12 is even more evident. Furthermore, ChYLO serves to inform the scholarship of curriculum studies, recognizing their processes of teaching and learning. The pedagogical practices of ChYLO should be included in the field of curriculum studies (K–16) and the larger discussion of Latinx people; naming and claiming their histories, struggles, and victories within the United States.

ChYLOs 12-point plan highlighted above provides a critical piece of curriculum. First, in order to craft this plan, Cha-Cha and the members of ChYLO deeply analyzed the needs of their community. They did the work that academics might describe as deep qualitative research, talking to people on the ground and sifting through any documents they could get their hands on, be it news media or government policies. Another example of the youth's organic intellectualism is reflected in sending youth out to talk to "professionals" and "professionals in training"; one of ChYLOs 17-year-old members was sent to Northwestern University in Evanston, Illinois, to speak to medical students about the importance of preventive community medicine.[41] Engaging in these types of activities exposed this particular group of medical students to the critical need of community medicine. These efforts also served as a recruitment mechanism in which interested medical students would then become volunteers in the community clinic run by ChYLO out of the basement of the People's Church.[42]

If we consider the process ChYLO undertook to do this work, one can start to see the power of their intellect. Furthermore, it was not simply asking the powers that be for the needs of their local communities, they went deeper examining how their struggle was connected to a wider global project of control and power. For example, ChYLO was very vocal regarding their stance on the inhumane consequences of military practices. As Flores-Rodriguez states, "Cha-Cha and his fellow Chicago Lords understood forced removal [gentrification] in the city as an extension of the colonial program on the island."[43] As ChYLO shifted from turf gang to political organization, they began reading radical texts, such as Karl Marx and Mao Tse-Tung, framing their struggle within the global political context of power, poverty, and capital. Not distinct to the movement in curricular studies during the same historical moment. As noted during a conversation with Dr. Tony Baez, "We were not intellectuals trying to produce papers, [our] goal was deeper understanding—development of intellect, to share with community.... [The ChYLO] Newspaper was the organizing tool—[it] let the community know what was going on locally and globally."[44] Further the newspaper was bilingual, reflecting an appropriate pedagogical approach to meeting community needs via culturally responsive practices.

As critical scholars, we must (re)create and question the discourse around intellect and knowledge production. The work of ChYLO ruptures the anti-intellectualism woven in the current structure of our nation. The implications of this work clearly demonstrate the need to value the efforts of the organic intellectuals who (re)assembled as ChYLO. Their work is grounded in grassroots intellectual practice that took consistent reflection, and exemplifies education rooted in liberation and emancipation. Specifically framing the work of ChYLO as that of critical pedagogues embeds them within a larger conversation that rethinks teaching and curriculum. While ChYLO resisted the injustices of their communities in the 1960s and 1970s, critical academics were asking significant questions about the purpose of education and naming teaching as a political act; we contend, these practices in and outside of the academy were not exclusive, instead they were reciprocal, informing one another's work. We must recognize the intellectual work of ChYLO, and document how these youth became "teachers" in their community—sharing curriculum on the street corner or in the People's Church they occupied while feeding breakfast to some of the very youngest impacted by unjust social policies and practices. While ChYLO assembled in Chicago (1960s), there were many antiwar movements, decolonization movements, and efforts to hold institutions and the government accountable for institutional racism, sexism, and other forms of discrimination. ChYLO's work emerged during this historical moment, creating spaces where they learned together about the ways their people were being oppressed, not simply noting that there was a need to serve the people, but that this need was engineered to keep folks poor in order to keep others rich. ChYLO wanted folks in Chicago to understand how they were part of this larger project focused on profit over people and to arm the community with information in resisting oppressive practices and policies. Describing their "syllabus," Cha-Cha states,

> We read books like Frantz Fanon, *The Wretched of the Earth* ... we read Military Writings of Mao Tse-Tung and one of the important writings was the part on "Encirclement and Suppression" campaigns which was very important, I have used this to keep the Young Lords alive after all these years, basically what it said was that the enemy is constantly trying to circle the wagon to try and destroy us so we have to be able to know when to retreat not in a cowardly way, but an active retreat in order to re-educate your members, we call it raising the level of consciousness.[45]

This glimpse inside the intellectual work of ChYLO provides critical insight on how they actively produced and translated knowledge to empower their community. Delving into their story of teaching and learning, we see the powerful contributions they offer to the Latinx body of curriculum. Learning about Latinx people in most school settings means many absences and misrepresentations; when Latinx narratives are included in school curricula many of these master narratives are steeped in deficiency and tokenism. Instead of placing Latinx histories and lived experiences in a damage-centered context,[46] ChYLO provides a counter narrative that lifts the power of Latinx people.

ON PRACTICE

The last prevailing theme we will discuss that emerged from reviewing the archival data and conducting follow-up interviews with key members was the notion of "practice." ChYLO members were about action and change, focusing less on the development of position papers and/or theoretical discussions of oppression and liberation. Dr. Tony Baez, the Minister of Education, noted that prior to joining ChYLO, he was involved in political organizing and action in Puerto Rico. He expressed his admiration for the tactics the Chicago youth engaged:

> People in Chicago were more 'aggressive' and daring to do more things . . . [they were] willing to engage in action, daring to get arrested, daring to go to the streets, have demonstrations. I found myself engaging in these actions—marched/demonstrated in NYC at the UN. I would have never done that in Puerto Rico. [Engage in] marches on Division St. I was surrounded by people resisting and fighting back against injustices such as the death of Fred Hampton. All of that talk/discourse was affecting me personally. Now if I had certain skills in education, I had to put those skills to work; I had to work with others to identify literature being read by folks in the movement to better understand what was going on everywhere. I started to read more economics, Marx, Mao, etc. It was important not because of who they were, but because they gave me additional tools to understand contradictions about what was going on.[47]

As noted above, ChYLO had a very practical approach to their work that was inspired by philosophers such as Mao Tse-Tung:

> [W]e [ChYLO leadership] used to quote Mao on all those things, ya know your ideas don't come from the sky, they don't fall from sky; Ideas come from practice, so the whole approach is ok, you do and then you learn from that doing, then you analyze it and find out what went wrong and then you do again. So, we're saying knowledge comes out of practice, and not where you just sit down and read books and put 'em together and ya know come out with a position paper.[48]

Practice as described by Mao focuses on learning through one's actions:

> If man wants to succeed in his work, that is, to achieve the anticipated results, he must bring his ideas into correspondence with the laws of the objective external world; if they do not correspond, he will fail in his practice. After he fails, he draws his lessons, corrects his ideas to make them correspond to the laws of the external world, and can thus turn failure into success.[49]

Mao further states, "The struggle of the proletariat and the revolutionary people to change the world comprises the fulfillment of the following tasks: to change the objective world and, at the same time, their own subjective world—to change their cognitive ability and change the relations between the subjective and objective world."[50] Drawing from this framing, ChYLO made this an integral part of their community educational efforts, in particular as a tool for youth engagement, analysis, and action. ChYLO's minister of information went on to explain,

> Everything that developed from the Young Lords was very organic. It wasn't ok here's our strategic plan, let's go step-by-step, no. It was very

> organic, it was developing—as we were taking actions it was developing ... the two basic issues were police brutality and housing—and those were really affecting the youth and those were affecting the families of the youth in the community. So that when you begin to decipher that, when you begin to talk to the people, to the younger members about why—how come your family or your friend's family is being pushed out? How come? Then they had to start saying, yea, how come? Who did it? How did it happen? So, it would develop like that. So, you go from again Mao, says you go from the simple to the complex—you don't go from the complex to the simple, ya know. Yea and so I think that was what we always would tell 'em—you know how to analyze a problem, you know what's going on, and you're feeling it. Just analyze it; and then to back that up ... So I think the 12-point program was basic also in educating not just the members, but I think also in educating the community. When it comes out of practice, then it makes sense to the regular people. If you do it in a vacuum and if people don't see themselves being touched by whatever you're talking about, they stay home. So that was, in terms of hammering that uh, basically, how you learn. How is knowledge acquired and that was Mao, ya know what we used.[51]

This description of ChYLOs approach to education connects the themes of transformation, organic intellectualism and practice. Individuals contribute to the creation of knowledge by engaging in practices that are rooted in community needs and struggles. As exemplified by Omar's description of practice, youth were able to understand and make connections to larger sociopolitical issues of imperialism, racism, and police brutality because they were living it, they then took action to enact change. Curriculum must be connected to people's experiences and identities. The failure of many institutions that espouse education is the focus on rote memorization and abstract learning that has little to no connection to their everyday lives. This is not to say that there are not educators and/or educational institutions that engage in culturally sustaining pedagogies[52] as those described by ChYLO; however, these educators and institutions are too often the exception and not the rule.

Further describing the ways in which practice was integral to youth learning, transformation and subsequent action, Omar shares:

> Because you know we had the church on Armitage so people always ended up at the church after 5–6p, after whatever they were doing. And that's when that kind of education would happen. Open discussions and if Tony was around he would probably lead some of those discussions; just about every Young Lord had a Red Book, so if we want to talk about "on practice" they could get that from the Red Book. Tony developed a module more like on the history of PR; of course, it was a leftist view of PR history, and that was one that we wanted everyone to learn. And everybody was pretty versed on the history of PR, I was really impressed. So that's how it used to happen, it was not,

like everything that was going in those years, even in education, it was the open classroom and the student is the one that evaluates the teacher. So, it was that kind of thing, so we couldn't probably say ok sit down, read that, now give me a report. No, it was all very open—they didn't even feel it and they were learning. [53]

Engaging in this practical type of learning also allowed for better organizing and support from community youth. ChYLOs roots in the community facilitated strong community support. "For example, when [ChYLO] put out a call for marches [we] could get mass numbers of people. We were able to get ~1,500 people in less than 24 hours; this often consisted of youth—[we] referred to them as 'rally' [Chi] Lords."[54] This approach proved helpful when ChYLO members put their education into practice: taking over the Church on Armitage Ave., known as the "People's Church" (located in a predominantly Puerto Rican community); taking over a meeting involving urban renewal; engaging in a five-day take-over of the McCormick Theological Seminary; and engaging in a rally/march to bring awareness to the police brutality occurring in their community. ChYLO engaged in what contemporary educators would refer to as praxis—focusing on a reciprocal relationship between education/theory and action.

CONTRIBUTIONS TO LATINX CURRICULUM/THEORIZING

The historical and political contexts throughout the city of Chicago pushed youth of color to mobilize against structural and institutional inequities that pervaded the fiber of Chicago municipalities. The gross absence of grand narratives exists that explicate the marginalized counter-narratives of community-youth led organizations whose political work and organizing helped to define Chicago during an era of national turbulence. Groups such as the Illinois Chapter of the Black Panther Party, the Young Patriots, and the Conservative Vice Lords have been sparsely mentioned to fully absent from Chicago history that addresses community uplift, race/ethnic consciousness and pride, mobilization efforts for community control, and alternative forms of community, youth, and adult education services.

Highlighting, analyzing, and replicating the educational efforts of Latinx youth organizations such as ChYLO are needed to inform educational practices that better meet the needs of Latinx youth and to create coalitions/connections across various groups—locally, nationally, and globally. This begs many questions, such as: why are the pedagogical narratives of groups such as ChYLO missing from standard/required curriculum? Why aren't colleges of education and other programs such as community health, public policy, medicine, and nursing using the practices of ChYLO in their curriculum as examples of culturally relevant/sustaining pedagogies? How can educators learn from and utilize the work of organic intellectuals such as ChYLO to better engage and teach the required subjects of math, English, government, history, etc., in a more radical and transformative matter?

ChYLO demonstrated the organic, comprehensive, and relevant curriculum/pedagogy being generated and shared by mostly Puerto Rican youth in post War Chicago. Protests, sit-ins, and takeovers coordinated by ChYLO resulted in direct service outcomes, such as the creation of a law office, and The People's Church. The model and approach taken by ChYLO warrants documentation and dissemination given their relevance in this current sociopolitical historical moment. As Watkins states,

> I have always accepted that Black education, and all, public education, was a product of historically, politically, and socially constructed ideas. I have observed Black education as a "political" act. I have viewed this act as influenced by hegemonic social relationships, labor market economics, class stratification and racial division. . . . I acknowledge that schools, curriculum, culture, and social ideas are all contested terrain. . . . As such, democracy does confront power. Common people do have ideas, engage in action, and indeed, mightily influence social processes.[55]

The ongoing push for privatization, rote memorization/test skills being emphasized in schools, and racial disparities perpetuated by and within schools, are a testament to the need for community members, especially youth, to be intimately involved in curriculum development—specifically, counter-hegemonic curriculum that facilitates and nurtures critical thinking, structural analysis of systems, and community-led/driven solutions for the liberation of all people.

Tactics and pedagogical approaches taken by ChYLO have implications for the field of urban education, youth development, and curriculum studies. The average age of ChYLO members ranged from 17 to 21, exemplifying that youth have been, and continue to be, agents of change and transformation. We must center youth as curriculum creators, honoring their abilities, knowledge, and innovation. Educators must create spaces that facilitate "problem-posing"[56] approaches to curriculum. ChYLOs Minister of Education, Dr. Tony Baez shared, "Involvement in movements was really about humanizing the way things are done in schools/education. . . . Lesson I've learned is that when you become a part of the movement in your youth, when you are 'in' it and part of it you grow with it."[57] The model implemented by ChYLO was the impetus for ongoing development and growth of youth who were otherwise marginalized or discounted. ChYLO played an integral role in the development of justice-based, youth driven curriculum and direct action in community and political spaces.

Considering that many Latinx youth continue to be shut out by schools (e.g., anti-immigration rhetoric/policies) and endure curricula that are irrelevant, dehumanizing, and disempowering, we must continue to learn from and advocate for liberatory education—within and outside of school space(s). ChYLO efforts remind us that schooling and education are not synonymous. Counter-hegemonic curricula grounded in community realities and struggle are necessary components of public education. Focusing on nurturing the talents and genius of Latinx (and all youth of color) calls for an education that reflects the efforts of ChYLO. Documenting the educational efforts, challenges and progress of ChYLO contributes to the historical and curricular record by illuminating their intellect, innovation, persistence, and contribution to anti-imperialism, resistance through self-determination, community control, collaboration, and coalition building—locally, nationally and globally.

NOTES

1. Abdul Alkalimat and Doug Gills, *Harold Washington and the Crisis of Black Power in Chicago: Mass Protest* (Chicago: Twenty-First Century Book and Publications, 1989), 10; for additional information on the legacy of Black activism, organizing, and politics in Chicago see, *Civil Rights and Beyond: African American and Latino/a Activism in the United States* by Brian D. Behnken; *Running for Freedom: Civil Rights and Black Politics in America since 1941*; also, by Alkalimat see, "Chicago Black Power Politics and the Crisis of the Black Middle Class," in the *Black Scholar*, Vol 19., No. 2, March/April 1988.

2. "Glocal" in the context of this article is defined as a phenomenon reflecting both local and global considerations. The term is derived from the Japanese concept, *dochakuka*, which means global localization. For more information on the concept and its etymology, see "Glocalization as Globalization: Evolution of a Sociological Concept," *Bangladesh e-*Journal of Sociology, Vol. 1, No. 2, July, 2004.

3. Thomas Dyja, *The Third Coast: When Chicago Built the American Dream* (New York: Penguin Books, 2013), 282–286.

4. Alkalimat and Gills, *Black Power in Chicago*, 17; Drs. Anderson Thompson and Harold Pates, interview by Richard D. Benson II, September 7, 2010 (interview in author's possession).

5. Alkalimat and Gills, *Black Power in Chicago*, 18; also, see, *Who Runs Chicago?* by Michael Kilian, Connie Fletcher and F. Richard Ciccone.

6. The Communiversity, "Who Controls Black Destiny," *The Communiviews*, May 1970, 2, Ansel Wong Papers, Black Cultural Archives of London, Britain, Box 7; Established in 1969 as a response to the national call for a "Black University", the Communiversity became a think tank and counter-hegemonic space of critical learning of Black life in Chicago and the Pan-African world. The Communiversity addressed critical aims of teaching and learning for students, teachers, activists, Black Nationalists, Pan-Africanists, Marxists, and community organizers which sought educational and curricular refuge from Eurocentric supremacist methodologies in American schooling. Founding members included Dr. Robert Starks, Dr. Harold Pates, Dr. Anderson Thompson, Professor Robert Rhodes, Dr. Jacob Carruthers, Professor Yvonne Jones, Dr. Conrad Worrill, the Honorable Judge Bernetta Bush, Professor Leon Harris, and Ruwa Chiri. Founding members of the Communiversity participated locally and nationally in cultural, political and community conferences, and international Pan-Africanist activities from 1969 to the early 1980s. For more information on the Communiversity and the legacy of Black activism in Chicago see, "Part 2: Chicago and the

African Centered Movement" by Dr. Conrad Worrill in *The South Side Current*, June 2017 issue.

7. Amy Sonnie and James Tracy, *Hillbilly Nationalists, Urban Race Rebels, and Black Power: Community Organizing in Radical Times* (Brooklyn, NY: Melville House, 2011), 43; "SCLC Starts Movement to End Slums," *Southern Christian Leadership Conference Newsletter*, January–February 1966, 6. Black History Collection/James Bevel Collection, University of Illinois at Chicago Archives, Box 1, Folder 11; for more information on the legacy of the Black Freedom Struggle and the mayoral campaign of Harold Washington, see *Chicago Divided: The Making of a Black Mayor* by Paul Kleppner and also see "Harold," *The People's Mayor: An Authorized Biography of Mayor Harold Washington* by Dempsey Travis. For an analysis of Washington's campaign support that was steeped heavily in the Black church, see *The Black Church and the Harold Washington Story: The Man, The Message, The Movement*, edited by Henry J. Young.

8. Sonnie and Tracy, *Hillbilly Nationalists, Urban Race Rebels, and Black Power*, 47–48; Vincent Harding, "Black Students and the 'Impossible' Revolution," *Ebony Magazine*, August 1969, 141–148; for additional information on college and youth activism in higher education and high schools nation-wide, see *Black Revolution on Campus* by Marth Biondi and see *Fighting for Our Place in the Sun: Malcolm X and the Radicalization of the Black Student Movement 1960–1973* by Richard D. Benson II.

9. "Black Power Issue: Notes and Comment Published by: Student NonViolent Coordinating Committee," August Issue. Black History Collection/James Bevel Collection, University of Illinois at Chicago Archives, Box 1, Folder 11; further supporting the historical account is autobiography of Kwame Ture, *Ready for Revolution: The Life and Struggles of Kwame Ture (Stokely Carmichael)*, pp. 538–540.

10. Dave Potter and Bob Hunter, "Black Office Holders Rap Daley's Shoot, Kill Edict", *Chicago Daily Defender*, April 18, 1968, 3; Donald Mosby, "Black Cops, Lawyers 'Shocked' By Shoot to Kill Statement", *Chicago Daily Defender*, April 16, 1968, 3; Guest Editorial, *Milwaukee Star*, April 24, 1968.

11. Mike Royko, *Boss: Richard J. Daley of Chicago* (New York: Plume, 1988), 195.

12. Lyn Yates, "Curriculum and Critical Theory," in *International Encyclopedia of Education*, eds. Penelope Peterson, Eva Baker, and Barry McGaw, p. 494. Oxford: Academic Press, 2010.

13. Antonio Gramsci, *Selections from Prison Notebooks* (New York: International Publishers Company, 1971).

14. Angel G. Flores-Rodriguez, "On National Turf: The Rise of the Young Lords Organization and its Struggle for the Nation in Chicago," *Op. Cit.*, num. 20. 109

15. We delineate and name The Young Lords of Chicago as much of the documented historical writings focus on The Young Lords chapter in New York. This delineation is an effort to specifically document the work of the Chicago Young Lords. While based on similar ideologies, the dynamics and on-the-ground tactics of the Chicago and New York chapters differed, and this work seeks to highlight the work of ChYLO given said differences.

16. Jose Jimenez. "Que Vive El Pueblo: A biographical history of Jose Cha-Cha Jimenez, General Secretary of the Young Lords Organization." *Young Lords History: Documents and Resources*. https://ylohistory.wordpress.com/primary-documents/

17. Ibid., 3.

18. Young Lords Timeline, http://nationalyounglords.com/?page_id=13

19. Ibid.

20. Jimenez, *Que Vive*, 1.

21. Jose Cha-Cha Jimenez, personal email communication with Ann M. Aviles, January 18, 2018.

22. Jimenez, *Que Vive*, 8.

23. Ibid., 9.

24. Ibid., 1.

25. Dr. Tony Baez, interview by Ann M. Aviles, phone interview, February 23, 2017.

26. Ibid.

27. Baez studied at the University of Puerto Rico before coming to Chicago.

28. Omar Lopez, Interview by Ann M. Aviles. Phone interview. October 25, 2017.

29. Manuel Ramos was killed by an off-duty Chicago police officer, James Lamb, on May 3, 1969, during a party occurring at the home of Orlando Davila, a Young Lords cofounder. Lamb was never arrested for Ramos's murder. See M. R. Gonzales, *Ruffians and Revolutionaries: The Development of the Chicago Young Lords Organization,* 2015, Thesis and Dissertations Paper 807.

30. The Blackstone Rangers were a street gang formed in the late 1950s on Blackstone Street on the south side of Chicago, Illinois. The Blackstone Rangers were founded by two teenagers, Jeff Fort and Eugene Hairston, while they were at the Illinois School for Boys in St. Charles. In their earliest days the Rangers were mostly local neighborhood kids who banded together for protection against other rival gangs. Their intentions, however, began to expand as the gang turned to profitable criminal activity. By 1965, the Blackstone Rangers ballooned to 5,000 members. For more information see http://www.blackpast.org/aah/blackstone-rangers-black-p-stone-nation-el-rukns-c-1957–c-2000

31. Omar Lopez, interview by Ann M. Aviles, phone interview, October 25, 2017.

32. Gramsci, *Selections*, 131.

33. Ibid., 131–132.

34. Omar Lopez, interview by Ann M. Aviles & Erica R. Davila, in-person interview, November 17, 2017.

35. Jimenez, *Que Vive*, 17.

36. The 'little red book' that explained to the people of China the ideology of the Chinese Communist Party. Available at https://www.marxists.org/reference/archive/mao/works/red-book/.

37. Jose Jimenez, interview by Ann M. Aviles and Erica R. Davila, in-person interview, December 22, 2017.

38. Phillip W. Jackson, *Life in classrooms* (New York: Holt, Rinehart and Winston, Inc.), 1968.

39. Django Paris and Samy H. Alim, (eds.). *Culturally Sustaining Pedagogies: Teaching and Learning for Justice in a Changing World* (New York: Teachers College Press. 2017).

40. Jose Jimenez, interview by Ann M. Aviles & Erica R. Davila, in-person interview, December 22, 2017.

41. Omar Lopez, interview by Ann M. Aviles, phone interview, October 25, 2017.

42. The People's Church provided free breakfast, childcare, and health services to the Puerto Rican/Latinx community.

43. Flores-Rodriguez, *On National Turf,* 112.

44. Dr. Tony Baez, interview by Ann. M. Aviles, phone interview, February 23, 2017.

45. Jose Jimenez, interview with Ann M. Aviles and Erica R. Davila, in-person interview, December 22, 2017.

46. Eve Tuck, "Suspending Damage: A Letter to Communities," *Harvard Educational Review*, 79, no. 3 (2009), 413.

47. Dr. Tony Baez, interview by Ann M. Aviles, phone interview, February 23, 2017.

48. Omar Lopez, interview by Ann. M. Aviles and Erica R. Davila, in-person interview, November 17, 2017.

49. Mao Tse-Tung. *Four Essays on Philosophy* (Foreign Language Press. Peking. 1968), 7.

50. Ibid., 19–20.

51. Omar Lopez, interview by Ann M. Aviles and Erica R. Davila, in-person interview, November 17, 2017.

52. Paris and Alim, *Culturally Sustaining*, 2017.

53. Omar Lopez, interview by Ann M. Aviles and Erica R. Davila, in-person interview, November 17, 2017.

54. Omar Lopez, interview by Ann M. Aviles, phone interview, October 25, 2017.

55. William Watkins. *The White Architects of Black Education: Ideology and Power in America, 1865–1954* (New York: Teachers College Press, 2001), 179.
56. Paulo Freire, *Pedagogy of the Oppressed*. New York: Continuum, 2000.
57. Dr. Tony Baez, interview by Ann M. Aviles, phone interview, February 23, 2017.

REFERENCES

Alkalimat, A., & Gills, D. 1989. *Harold Washington and the crisis of black power in Chicago: Mass protest*. Chicago: Twenty-First Century Book and Publications.
The Communiversity. 1970. Who controls black destiny. *The Communiviews*, May, 2. Chicago, IL.
Dyja, T. L. *The third coast: When Chicago built the American dream*. New York: Penguin Books, 2013.
Flores-Rodriguez, A. G. 2011–2012. "On National Turf: The Rise of the Young Lords Organization and its Struggle for the Nation in Chicago," *Op. Cit.*, num. 20, 105–141.
Freire, P. *Pedagogy of the oppressed*. New York: Continuum, 2000.
Gonzales, M. R. 2015. *Ruffians and revolutionaries: The development of the Chicago Young Lords Organization*. MA thesis, University of Wisconsin Milwaukee.
Gramsci, A. 1971. *Selections from prison notebooks*. New York: International Publishers Company, Incorporated.
Guest Editorial. 1968, April 24. *Milwaukee Star*. Milwaukee, WI.
Jackson, P. W. *Life in classrooms*. New York: Holt, Rinehart and Winston, Inc., 1968.
Jimenez, J. 1972. Que vive el Pueblo: A biographical history of Jose Cha-Cha Jimenez, General Secretary of the Young Lords Organization. *Young Lords History: Documents and Resources*. https://ylohistory.wordpress.com/primary-documents/
Mosby, D. 1968, April 16. Black cops, lawyers "shocked" by shoot to kill statement. *Chicago Daily Defender*. Chicago, IL.
Paris, D., & Alim, H. S. (eds.). 2017. *Culturally sustaining pedagogies: Teaching and learning for justice in a changing world*. New York: Teachers College Press.
Potter, D., & Hunter, B. 1968, April 18. Black Office Holders Rap Daley's Shoot, Kill Edict. *Chicago Daily Defender*. Chicago, IL.
Royko, M. 1988. *Boss: Richard J. Daley of Chicago*. New York: Plume.
Sonnie, A., & Tracy, J. 2011. *Hillbilly nationalists, urban race rebels, and black power: Community organizing in radical times*. New York: Melville House.
Southern Christian Leadership Conference. 1966, January–February. SCLC Starts Movement to End Slums. *Southern Christian Leadership Conference Newsletter* (p. 6). Black History Collection/James Bevel Collection, University of Illinois at Chicago Archives, Box 1, Folder 11.
Tse-Tung, M. 1968. *Four essays on philosophy*. Peking: Foreign Language Press.
Tuck, E. 2009. Suspending damage: A letter to communities. *Harvard Educational Review*, 79(3), 409–428.
Watkins, W. 2001. *The white architects of black education: Ideology and power in America, 1865–1954*. New York: Teachers College Press.
Williams, P. B. 2015, April 2. Declaration. *Chicago Magazine*. Chicago, IL. http://www.chicagomag.com/Chicago-Magazine/April-2015/Phillip-Williams-Gladys-Nilsson/
Yates, L. 2010. Curriculum and critical theory. In Penelope Peterson, Eva Baker, & Barry McGaw (eds.), *International Encyclopedia of Education* (pp. 494–499). Oxford: Academic Press.
Young Lords Historical Timeline. National Young Lords, accessed January 1, 2018. http://nationalyounglords.com/?page_id=13

THREE
Mathematics for Borderland Identities

Cristina Valencia Mazzanti and Martha Allexsaht-Snider

Perhaps you have heard or think yourself that mathematics is a universal language that transposes borders and cultures, that universally communicates and is experienced by everyone as one. Perhaps, like us, you have experienced mathematics in different contexts, coming to know that mathematics is bound to the humans that practice it, their languages, and cultures. These stances represent two ways of looking at mathematics that are significantly different and consequently shape our understanding and teaching of mathematics in specific ways. In this chapter, we share some of the ways we have come to know mathematics through the second stance: mathematics as a human practice, as well as some of the frameworks and experiences that help us see it as such. We then reflect on how this has informed our understanding of how to teach and learn mathematics with Latinx[1] bilingual children.

In this chapter, we draw on a range of different perspectives to explore our interests in mathematics learning and our perspective of mathematics as a human endeavor. We first focus on Anzaldúa's notion of the *mestiza* and Collins's notion of the *outsider within*[2] as possible avenues for understanding the ways of being and identities of Latinx children in the United States. We draw on these to frame our exploration of mathematics learning in the context of a series of mathematics workshops for Latinx families as well as Cristina's (the first author) experiences in two kindergarten classrooms in public schools in Northeast Georgia.

We also make connections to Style's (1988) idea of curriculum as windows and mirrors to make visible the links between learning and the ideas developed through Anzaldúa and Collins regarding borderland identities. We seek to elucidate the many bridges we see between our research and our stances as well as the formal and informal learning spaces in which we conceptualized mathematics learning, particularly in regard to our experiences with language and the perspectives that stem from those experiences. We see these different contexts and frameworks as more generative ways to imagine the education of Latinx children, and that they better allow us to see the humane and contextual nature of mathematics and mathematics education.

BORDERLAND IDENTITIES: LEARNING FROM THE MESTIZA CONSCIOUSNESS AND THE OUTSIDER WITHIN

As we seek to explore the complexities of what it means to understand mathematics knowing and learning as a human endeavor, particularly for Latinx children in the United States, we find it is particularly helpful to consider some ways to understand what it means to be Latinx and the experiences that it brings as well as what it means to know and learn as a Latinx person. Consequently, we situate our thinking about knowledge, curriculum, and learning for Latinx children in the context of the work of two feminists of color, Anzaldúa and Collins. We draw on feminist perspectives and epistemologies because they allow us to uncover the relations between knowledge and identity as well as the power dynamics that envelope knowledge. Feminist perspectives help us see the contextual nature of knowledge and how it is impossible to see any standpoint as unquestionable (Delanty and Strydom, 2003). We examine the idea of the *outsider within* by Collins and the *mestiza* by Anzaldúa as we see in them possibilities for understanding the ways of being of Latinx children and how this may allow us to understand their experiences with knowledge and learning and imagine new possibilities for them.

In her book, *Borderlands/La Frontera: The New Mestiza*, Anzaldúa (2012) develops the concept of la mestiza in relation to Vasconcelos's idea of the cosmic race. She writes:

> Jose Vasconcelos, Mexican philosopher, envisaged *una raza mestiza, una mezcla de razas afines, una raza de color—la primera raza sintesis del globo*. He calls it a cosmic race, *la raza cósmica*, a fifth race embracing the four races of the world. Opposite to the theory of the pure Aryan, and to the policy of racial purity that white America practices, his theory is one of inclusivity.... This mixture of races, rather than resulting in an inferior being, provides hybrid progeny, a mutable, more malleable species with a rich gene pool. From this racial, ideological, cultural and biological cross-pollinization, an alien "consciousness is presently in the making—a new *mestiza* consciousness, *una conciencia de mujer*. It is a consciousness of the Borderlands." (Anzaldúa, 2012, p. 99)

This *raza mestiza* that Anzaldúa constructs in her book offers a way to see the world and the ways of being of borderland identities and particularly Latinx people that is more generative. This way of being of the *mestiza* goes beyond needing to belong to just one culture or assimilation, it accepts a complex way of being in which it is possible to belong to more than one culture and be in more than one world, to be in the borderlands. Anzaldúa's words are also transformative in the sense that they turn such identities into powerful ways of being. Similarly, Aigner-Varoz (2000) writes, "Gloria Anzaldúa constructs a mestiza consciousness as a dynamic "new mythos" capable of breaking down dualistic hegemonic paradigms. Anzaldúa targets paradigms representing culturally determined roles imposed on individuals and peoples from the outside" (p. 47). In Aigner-Varoz's argument and understanding of Anzaldúa's work there is a way of seeing the feminist's words as powerful metaphors with the ability to transform.

Anzaldúa's way of conceptualizing the mestiza is also powerful in that it acknowledges a way of being multicultural, immigrant, and Latinx, a way of being in the borderland that is empowering but not naïve. A resonating question is the question of the constant duality—or multiality—that comes with belonging to more than one world, culture, or language and the inherent contradiction that this way of being brings; "the *mestiza* faces the dilemma of the mixed breed: which collectively does the daughter of a darkskinned mother listen to?" (Anzaldúa, 2012, p. 100). However, this powerful way of being, this dilemma of the mestiza does not seem to carry the negative connotation that it has been assigned in other spaces; the way Anzaldúa draws on Vasconcelos's raza cósmica allows for a creative and productive way of naming such dilemma and is again a metaphor that has the power to transform and reframe the experiences of borderland identities, of Latinx people. Anzaldúa frames this position and way of being of the *mestiza* in the dilemma as also the possibility to know and to discover something new and form a different perspective; "In perceiving conflicting information and points of view, she [la mestiza] is subjected to a swamping of her psychological borders. She has discovered that she can't hold concepts or ideas in rigid boundaries" (p. 101).

In regard to the possibilities and ways of knowing Anzaldúa envisions through the mestiza, it is also very important to mention the relation between this way of being and language. The ways Anzaldúa uses language in the above quotes carry a strong message and imply a connection between these ways of being, this mestiza identity, and a being in the world that is multilingual. In Anzaldúa's work, belonging to more than one world inherently brings a multiplicity of languages. Her constructions of language allow us to see multiple ways to be in the world through multiple languages as well as multiple ways to understand language. At the same time her presentation of language opens possibilities for seeing knowledge, and learning, generated through the use of more than one language, not as deficient or incomplete but as a way of being that is complete. This is to say that unlike other frameworks in which proof of proficiency, of completeness, means being able to use just one language to express oneself, Anzaldúa embodies the notion that mixing languages reflects a full and complete way of being.[3]

In *Learning from the Outsider Within: The Sociological Significance of Black Feminist Thought*, Collins (1986) develops the concept of the outsider-within, which in many ways is sister to the notion of the *mestiza*. In her article, Collins vividly depicts the image of African-American women traveling, living, and intimately knowing the lives of white families without ever belonging or being a part of them, becoming outsiders-within. Years later in a reflection on her original article she writes, "I chose the term outsider within because it seemed to be an apt description of individuals like myself who found ourselves caught between groups of unequal power" (Collins, 1999, p. 85). In this, the parallels with Anzaldúa's notion of the *mestiza* are striking; for both there is the idea of an identity, of a way of being and knowing, that is shaped by the mixture of two worlds, of two cultures and a concern for a sense of belonging. However, there is also a sense of distance in how these two identities may come to belong to more than one world. Collins' introduction of the idea of power is worth noticing, as it allows us to think differently and more complexly about the dilemma of inhabiting more than one world. Collins herself redefines the concept of the insider-within in a later reflection, tying it to border spaces. She writes, "I now use the term *outsider-within* to describe the social locations or border spaces occupied by groups of unequal power" (1999, p. 86).

Two other very relevant ideas that Collins (1986) contributes in the context of the *outsider within* are the ideas of self-definition and self-valuation. In the author's own words, "Self-definition involves challenging the political knowledge-validation process that has resulted in externally defined, stereotypical images of Afro-American womanhood. In contrast, self-valuation stresses the content of Black women's self-definitions—namely, replacing externally-derived images with authentic Black female images" (Collins, 1986, p. s17). These ideas allow us to think about Latinx identities, ways of being, learning, and relation to knowledge from new perspectives.

Like Anzaldúa, Collins's construction of the outsider within comes from a deep knowledge and experience, is not naïve. In fact, Collins problematizes the insider within ways of being and position in two important ways. First, she argues "people who find themselves in outsider-within locations do not necessarily produce knowledge dedicated to fostering social justice" (Collins, 1999, p. 87). This idea reminds us of the heterogeneous nature of any group of people. It also speaks to the complexity of the links between our identity, the experiences that we have, and how we shape our positionalities. Second, Collins brings important awareness to the fact that, highlighting the positive features of the ways of being of the outsider within status does not deny the issues and the power imbalances inherently imbedded in that role and the fact that this status has been well established and understood as problematic. She writes,

> By stressing the potentially positive features of outsider-within status, I in no way want to deny the very real problem this social status has for large numbers of Black women. American sociology has long identified marginal status as problematic. However, my sense of the "problems" diverge from those espoused by traditional sociologists. For example, Robert Park states, "the marginal man . . . is one whom fate has condemned to live in two societies and in two, not merely different but antagonistic cultures (1950, p. 373)." From Park's perspective, marginality and difference themselves were problems. This perspective quite rationally led to the social policy solution of assimilation, one aimed at eliminating difference, or if that didn't work, pretending it was not important. In contrast, I argue that it is the meaning attached to difference that is the problem. (Collins, 1986, p. s15)

Collins's perspective is unlike that of Anzaldúa, who sees the mestiza as something that one is, inherently inhabiting more than one world because of one's own racial identity and cultural origin. Collins's concept of the outsider within inherently brings a process of becoming, of the outsider becoming the insider. When thinking about the two concepts together, the concepts of the *mestiza* and the *outsider within* allow us to think of borderland identities, of those of us who live in imaginary frontiers, and our relations to knowledge and learning, from new perspectives. We are better able to imagine the ways of being and understanding of borderland identities and the identities of Latinx people. We no longer are limited to that into which we are born, but we also enter into the process of constant becoming, which seems so inherent to any emigration and immigration story. Belonging is no longer rigidly defined by outside geographic or national constraints, is instead fluid, and comes from the lived experiences of people. At the same time, it also allows us to disconnect the ways of understanding the borderland identities of Latinx people from nationalist views of immigration.[4]

WHOSE MATHEMATICS?

Collins's and Anzaldúa's conceptualizations of the mestiza consciousness and the outsider within elucidate the bridges between knowing and identity, allowing us to understand how knowing can be seen as a way of being and how this might look for borderland identities. In this section we focus on the possibilities such conceptualizations and perspectives offer for the mathematics education of Latinx people. We will explore some examples of the spaces created by students, educators, and researchers to imagine new ways and possibilities for being, knowing, and learning in mathematics classrooms.

In the introduction we discussed how a contextual way of understanding mathematics, in which mathematics is known as a human endeavor bound by culture and language, allows us to question if we should all know and practice the same mathematics or different ones that respond to our cultural ways of being and linguistic practices.[5] The complexity of this question is magnified by other thinkers who have argued that to ensure equality and quality education for minoritized students, it is necessary that everyone has access to the same education in the same way. As we think about different directions and ways in which we address the educational needs of Latinx children and our experiences in schools in the United States, a feeling of confusion arises. We have come to wonder if what minoritized children are experiencing in the United States today is access to the same education that all citizens of the world should have or instead an education that corresponds to what dominant peers have historically received and are expected to receive.

This question is made even more problematic for us by the perspectives of other researchers and educators with similar commitments to ours regarding the education of Latinx people. Bustos Flores et al. (2014) have argued that "in spite of this tremendous complexity of today's educational world, educational systems and teachers continue to compel their students to trade in their precious cultural capital for a dominant one that is ostensibly more powerful in the marketplace (Cummins, 1996; Walsh, 1991; Nieto, 1994). Adopting a canonical language and culture has never ensured the participation of all" (p. 20). The final point made in this quote is one of particular significance to us as it offers possibilities to reimagine the educational practices and policies currently in place for minoritized students. We do not see receiving an education that corresponds to the dominant culture and language as synonymous with receiving an education that provides opportunities for deep and meaningful mathematics learning.

If we take this perspective as a starting point, then there are many possibilities to reconceptualize our current approaches to the mathematics education of children, particularly those who are minoritized. For us it means finding ways to imagine and create educational experiences that offer more opportunities for minoritized students and it starts with our work in the previous section, thinking about the ways of being of Latinx people and how we may find new ways to see them and understand their experiences and how these are ingrained in our identities and the intrinsic power dynamics of knowledge. We believe that doing so allows us to see differently and to make connections to others who share similar commitments and have thought of different possibilities for the learning of minoritized children.

Although there are many different ways to think about curriculum or define it, in the context of this chapter we understand curriculum as the collection of the learning experiences children have in a particular setting. In this instance we consider three different settings: a general education kindergarten classroom (Classroom 1), a DLI[6] education classroom (Classroom 2), and a series of family workshops (Familias Aprendiendo). Our reflection on these three different settings allows us to consider the possibilities for curriculum for Latinx children in formal and informal settings as well as the complementary roles that these settings may play in the education of Latinx children.

BEING OF MULTIPLE WORLDS: LATINX CHILDREN CROSSING BORDERS AND LEARNING MATHEMATICS

Latinx children come to kindergarten classrooms in the United States filled with knowledge and more often than not with knowledge and experiences in both Spanish and English.[7] Although their experiences in classrooms in the United States vary greatly, most of them include learning in English and learning mathematics. Their experiences also include an encounter with dominant culture in the United States, an educational system that reflects it, and the culture of the educational system itself.[8] In this section we focus on Cristina's experiences in two kindergarten classrooms and how they led us to think about the experience of formal schooling as a kind of border crossing with the potential to allow Latinx children to assume and explore their own identities in transformative new ways.

One way to understand the importance of the powerful ways of being of borderland identities for learning, as beings able to transcend borders and see from multiple perspectives, is highlighted by Style (1988) in *Curriculum as Window and Mirror*. Style uses the metaphor of curriculum needing to be like a window and a mirror to highlight the importance of multiple perspectives; she writes "If the student is understood as occupying a dwelling of self, education needs to enable the student to look through window frames in order to see the realities of others and into mirrors in order to see her/his own reality reflected. Knowledge of both types of framing is basic to a balanced education which is committed to affirming the essential dialectic between the self and the world" (p. 1). From this perspective, the idea of windows and mirrors seems highly relevant to the mathematics education of Latinx children as it provides a way of transposing the borders and being in a borderland space by acknowledging who we are through mirrors and opening possibilities and new ways of being through windows.

It also opens the possibility of Latinx children's bilingualism and biculturalism as an intrinsic advantage and skill for seeing from multiple perspectives. In fact, Style (1988) has argued that the idea of curriculum needing to function as windows and mirrors is also closely tied to the idea of multiple perspectives; "the need for curriculum to function both as window and as mirror, we need to acknowledge that this perspective is in line with the ancient liberal arts tradition which pursues multiple perspectives (in insisting on a variety of disciplinary paradigms)" (p. 3). Her arguments and examples about the need for curriculum to reflect multiple perspectives seem particularly appealing. Style writes, "This multiplicity, in turn, enables both students and teachers to be engaged in conversation about an evolving definition of the beautiful." (p. 1).

The way Style (1988) articulates the idea of windows and mirrors in this last quote makes it interesting to consider the possibilities of imagining the idea of a global society as a context for mathematics education and how it allows us to still conceptualize the individual borderland space as a way of being. The idea of the global community allows for the multiplicity that comes with belonging to our specific borderland spaces while also allowing an unequivocal and unified sense of belonging to a space that is one and is all encompassing, the global community. If we think about this in the context of mathematics education, then the possibilities for curriculum become even more complex as they have the possibility to reflect the multiple ways in which we are with others. Along with this perspective it is also interesting to consider how Dominguez (2016) connects the idea of windows and mirrors to idea of student noticing, noticing as a way of knowing one's own knowledge (mirror) and one's own learning (window). These perspectives make the argument for an education that encompasses multiple perspectives fundamental to any educational approach that truly seeks to support Latinx children through Anzaldúa's conceptualization of the *mestiza* consciousness.

Latinx researchers with deep commitments to an equitable mathematics education, particularly for Latinx people, have also found the window and mirror framework as a helpful way of conceptualizing the learning of Latinx children. In an article about Latino children working with word problems, Dominguez (2016) writes,

> I suggest using a windows-and-mirrors framework for encouraging students to be problem posers. Like a window, a problem should be an opportunity for students and teachers to look out for what makes sense to solve the problem. Simultaneously, like a mirror, a problem should be an opportunity for students and teachers to look into what students notice as relevant for solving a problem. Is the window too wide, too open or, on the contrary, too narrow; or is it just right? For the same matter, does the mirror allow students to recognize in the situation something that they know and that can be useful for solving a prob-

lem? Readjusting the window and/or the mirror—as it is recognized in word problems—signifies reformulating a problem. (p. 360)

As we focus on Cristina's experiences in the kindergarten classrooms, we find new depths to the ideas we have explored in this chapter. In her stance as a Latina who assumes the role of a volunteer teacher within the classroom, and who is a fluent speaker of English and Spanish, we found the possibility to understand children's experiences and perspectives as they engaged bilingually in mathematics learning. As Cristina has worked with Latinx children in the context of mathematics teaching and learning, questions have opened up about the connections between identity and language as well as what it means to belong.

When we think of the children's use of English and Spanish, we reflect on the way children often made conscientious choices about what language to use to position themselves and their knowledge in the context of the classroom. Their choice often served as an opening to notice complex and metacognitive thinking about languages and mathematics, where they were navigating multiple identities and knowledge. In the way a child would count first in Spanish and then in English, another would recognize a quantity in Spanish but need to count in English to know how to write the number, in the way a child would translate from one language to another to explain to a peer, or take pride in teaching their peer the numbers in a different language, we started seeing how children would thrive when they had opportunities to make sense of their learning from a borderland space that allowed for multiple languages. Through time it also became apparent that allowing for a borderland space for language allowed for a borderland space for knowledge and learning. Through Spanish, children could share stories about their families or popular Spanish-speaking TV shows and connect them to the mathematics that they were learning, opening the possibility to connect both their home and school worlds. This way of connecting their knowledge, of moving back and forth through languages, has opened many possibilities for learning, but more importantly it has opened doors for students to understand the value of their previous knowledge and experiences as they start developing their identity as students.

KNOWING THROUGH SELF-DEFINITION AND SELF-VALUING: LEARNING FROM FAMILY WORKSHOPS

We learned about the importance of creating spaces for self-definition and self-valuing for Latinx children and families in a series of family workshops focused on mathematics. The workshops were originally conceptualized as a space for Latinx families with parents whose dominant language was Spanish. They were a response to Cristina's experience with English-only policies in local schools and her outlook on the beliefs about language in those contexts, where speaking languages other than English is seen as a significant disadvantage particularly for people who do not belong to the dominant culture. Consequently, as we conceptualized the workshops for Latinx families, we focused on creating opportunities to reinforce Spanish and bilingualism as valuable learning resources.

The workshops take place once a year and are designed to last for a semester. They alternate between family sessions and sessions in which parents and children work separately; the workshops' main focus is mathematics but we also discuss other ideas concerning education and schooling, such as language and language acquisition. During family sessions, parents and children work together on creative projects related to mathematics. The family sessions offer possibilities for parents to see their children through new perspectives, especially when it comes to mathematics learning. During parent sessions, the children work in another room on mathematics activities set in stations while the parents engage in whole group conversations around the activities they engaged in during the family sessions, concerns parents have around their children's education, and their own experiences with learning and parenting. Parents would often direct the conversation in these sessions toward their own schooling, the schooling of their children, being an immigrant, and the power dynamics behind language. In many ways, parent sessions offered a peer group for the parents to validate their own perspectives of their children as mathematics learners, their language beliefs and practices, and their own value to their children's education.

It is through time and the conversations with parents that we have come to see the workshops as a space of self-definition and self-valuation for families; a space for and claimed by parents to see in a new light their role in the education of their children and their children's mathematics ability. In this regard, the workshops served as a complement and counterpoint to the experiences parents and children were having in school. The workshops helped us reflect on how school can be an experience in which children and parents do not have much control, where children are evaluated by teachers according to standards and assessments in which parents have little to no input and for which they often only see the resulting final grade. The nonevaluative nature of the workshops gave space for the parents to shift the focus of learning away from the pressures and concerns given by others and focus on what they were noticing about their children as learners. We see many parallels with this experience and the process of self-definition as understood by Collins (1986), which entails challenging the political processes of knowledge validation that are intrinsically external and carry stereotypical images in them.

Having a peer group in other parents who shared their cultural background and language as well as the shared experience of the workshops allowed for parents to reinforce this process of self-definition, to reinforce the new ways in which they were seeing their roles as parents and their children as able mathematics learners. In fact, we saw in the opportunities to build community the necessary movement from self-definition, to self-valuation. We reviewed earlier how Collins's (1986) conceptualization of self-valuation entails stressing the content of self-definition, replacing externally created images with authentic ones that come from others with a shared identity. The opportunities for intentional conversation in the parent sessions create a space in which parents share with each other their own narratives of learning, for themselves and for their children, providing narratives and images for each other to learn from and imitate, allowing the parents to assume their identities in new ways and transform themselves.

CONCLUSION

Gutierrez (2002) opens an important question when thinking about school mathematics; she helps us think critically about why students are required to adapt to school mathematics, instead of school adapting to them. This seems highly relevant in terms of the questions we have raised about embracing a dominant education as well as the connections we have traced between education and borderland identities. When talking about the ideas developed by Style (1988), Gutierrez (2012) explains how thinking about curriculum providing a window and mirror to students is an issue of equity. In her article Style writes,

> Of course, students' educational diet is not balanced if they see themselves in the mirror all the time. Likewise, democracy's school curriculum is unbalanced if a black student sits in school, year after year, forced to look through the window upon the (validated) experiences of white others while seldom, if ever, having the central mirror held up to the particularities of her or his own experience. Such racial imbalance is harmful as well to white students whose seeing of humanity's different realities is also profoundly obscured. (p. 5)

We are challenged to imagine what kind of windows and mirrors we want to construct within the mathematics curriculum for classrooms including Latinx and other multilingual and immigrant children.

As we consider the different possibilities for the education of Latinx children, of children who are racially, culturally, and linguistically diverse, this consciousness of the complex nature of equity seems highly relevant to us. Commitments towards a more equitable mathematics are well established,[9] however, understanding the close link between equity and inequity seems like a way for us to move forward in different and more generative directions. It also allows us to understand the importance of grounding our commitment to a more equitable education for

Latinx children in their perspectives and identities, and not only on what we may imagine is equitable or inequitable. This is fundamentally what allows us to see mathematics as human and contextual.

In reimagining the education of Latinx children, we think it is essential to rethink some of the fundamental ways we think about education. The most important perhaps is to stop thinking about education in terms of a possible future. Many approaches and decisions for mathematics instruction have been made based on specific goals for mathematics instruction and the context in which mathematics will be used (e.g., Krasa and Shunkwiler, 2009). However, our limitations for knowing the future have long been established, and we are more and more aware of the ways in which thinking about education in terms of an imagined future is problematic (Jones, 2012). This is significant when thinking about the education of children, which is often shaped by goals and designed to meet the needs they will have as future adults and users of mathematics. If we seek to move away from such ways of thinking about mathematics education, we need to be able to find new ways to think about it and imagine it, and conscientiously grounding ourselves in Latinx people's experiences and identities seems like a very relevant way of doing it.

At the end of *Reflections on the Outsider Within* Collins (1999) makes an important call for structural and institutional changes that are systematically more inclusive and limit the ways in which people remain outsiders within structures. In her words, "Organizations should aim to eliminate outsider-within locations, not by excluding the individual Black women who raise hard questions, but by including them in new ways. More importantly, for those African American women who have gained access to places denied their mothers, new ways of inclusion, outsider-within and otherwise, provide new opportunities for fostering social justice" (p. 88). Collins's call for systemic change proves to still be necessary in the context of this chapter. It also makes it seem relevant to revisit the understanding that Anzaldúa's mestiza identity brings, the idea that being an outsider is intrinsically part of who we are, and consequently that perhaps the systematic change that we need is to redefine the ways we see ourselves and each other when occupying border spaces, outsider spaces, and how doing so may be transformative.

POSITIONALITY STATEMENT

We came to be interested in mathematics and particularly in teaching and learning mathematics with Latinx children through different paths. For Cristina (the first author), her interest in mathematics stems from her own experiences as a student. She was taught mathematics multilingually in connection to philosophy and art, coming to see mathematics as a deep expression of the meaning of the human condition. She finds that she enjoys teaching mathematics to young children the most; as she appreciates the complexity of teaching multilingual children the deep connections that exist between mathematics and language, and particularly how knowing more than one language may give us more tools as mathematicians. For Cristina, her identity as an immigrant, a Latina,[10] and a multilingual person, and the identity of the students and families she teaches are intrinsically tied. Her choice to work with Latinx children comes from these nuanced connections to her own identity as well as the unintentional and situational realities of her current context.

Martha's (the second author) interest in mathematics and language grew as she worked in the 1980s and 1990s as an ESOL (English for Speakers of Other Languages) teacher and in mathematics professional development programs with teachers of immigrant and refugee children and their families. For Martha, new wonderings about ways to create mathematics curriculum to support bilingual Latinx children and parents have begun to emerge through recent collaborative work with Cristina. Martha's perspectives as a white teacher educator and a bilingual speaker of English and Spanish enrich the understandings we developed through her enduring commitment to learning with immigrant and multilingual people and Latinx communities.

NOTES

1. We used the term Latinx in this chapter because we believe it reflects an honest attempt to use language that is more reflective and inclusive of all people. We would also like to problematize it as we understand that no one term can represent the heterogeneous nature of any group of people and the intersectional identities of all individuals in one group. We think it is particularly important to acknowledge that it is our understanding that most Latinx people in this chapter would identify as Latino or Latina and Latinos as a group. Furthermore, we find problematic that many Latinx people (especially those who only speak Spanish) would not identify with the term Latinx or even recognize it, particularly when considering that the term is not actually representative of the Spanish language or currently exists in it. Unlike Latino/a/os/as, which exist in both Spanish and English, currently Latinx only reflects the English grammar and language.

2. We would like to acknowledge the complexity and perhaps problematic nature of drawing on the experiences of African-American women to understand the experiences of Latinx children in the United States. Although these are different ways of being and experiencing the world, we find that the ability to read and see ourselves in others is fundamental for understanding oneself and making sense of our experiences. As we draw on Collins's knowledge and experience to make sense of our own, of the experiences of Latinx, we seek to honor and respect her wisdom. Furthermore, we believe that our ability to learn from her is in the fundamental spirit of this chapter and of our research in which we embrace the opportunities to learn from others who are like us and unlike us, in a true celebration of diversity, while also acknowledging that knowledge is never neutral and intrinsically brings the power dynamics through which it is generated. In the next section, we will also draw on a white American (Style) and other Latinx people besides Anzaldúa, to make sense of the experiences of Latinx people. We do this in the same spirit as when we draw from Collins. We would also like to explicitly state that we are intentional in selecting whom we draw and

learn from, purposefully trying to frame Latinx people from perspectives that are generative and go beyond traditional white Western points of view, which historically have been detrimental to those of us that are other or outsiders.

3. Due to the many focuses of this chapter we have chosen not to expand on the important arguments and ideas translanguaging theory has contributed to redefining the way language and bilingualism are viewed for Latinx people. Translanguaging theory offers powerful ways of understanding the language practices of Anzaldúa and has made important contributions in understanding how simultaneously using more than one language (like mixing Spanish and English) is a valid and important language practice.

4. In this regard, we again want to highlight the heterogeneous nature of Latinx people. We believe that current narratives of Latinx people in the United States may tie Latinx identities to immigration, when we know that most Latinx people in the world are not immigrants. I, Cristina, would also like to acknowledge that for me my Latina identity is intrinsically tied to immigration.

5. This question has many layers and it does not disclose the many assumptions that it carries, for instance assumptions about what is and is not considered mathematics.

6. DLI stands for Dual Language Immersion program and is designed to support native speakers of English and Spanish in becoming bilingual and biliterate in both languages.

7. The idea of children coming to school with rich experiences that contribute to their learning reflects the understandings developed by González et al. (1995). The fact that these experiences are bilingual reflects the understandings from the 2015 report by the United States Census Bureau, according to which two-thirds of people who speak Spanish at home also speak English very well.

8. We see this, for instance, in the form of standards, standardized assessments, and simply by giving children the opportunity to participate in larger community (classroom/school) that reflects the structure of society.

9. This is evident in NCTM's (National Council of Teachers of Mathematics) commitment to access and equity that has become more visible through time. Their statement reads: "Creating, supporting, and sustaining a culture of access and equity require being responsive to students' backgrounds, experiences, cultural perspectives, traditions, and knowledge when designing and implementing a mathematics program and assessing its effectiveness. Acknowledging and addressing factors that contribute to differential outcomes among groups of students are critical to ensuring that all students routinely have opportunities to experience high-quality mathematics instruction, learn challenging mathematics content, and receive the support necessary to be successful. Addressing equity and access includes both ensuring that all students attain mathematics proficiency and increasing the numbers of students from all racial, ethnic, linguistic, gender, and socioeconomic groups who attain the highest levels of mathematics achievement."

10. I (Cristina) chose to use the term Latina instead of Latinx to define my own identity. I see this as something central to my identity, as I can be Latina in all languages through which I am in the world (Spanish, Italian, and English). The ability of this word to define and transpose linguistic borders feels essential to me when I take into account my intersectionalities, far beyond any other labels. This again reflects the complex and heterogeneous nature of Latinx people and their ways of being, and shows the problematic nature of the term Latinx, particularly when it is imposed on others.

REFERENCES

Aigner-Varoz, E. 2000. Metaphors of a Mestiza consciousness: Anzaldúa's borderlands/La Frontera. *MELUS,* 25(2), 47–62. https://doi:10.2307/468218

Anzaldúa, G. 2012. *Borderlands/La Frontera: The new Mestiza*. San Francisco: Aunt Lute Books.
Bustos Flores, B., Vasquez, O. A., & Riojas Clark, E. 2014. Generating transworld pedagogy: reimagining la clase mágica, n.p. UGA GIL-Find Catalog,EBSCOhost
Collins, P. 1986. Learning from the outsider within: The sociological significance of black feminist thought. *Social Problems, 33*(6), s14–s32. https://doi:10.2307/800672
———. 1999. Reflections on the outsider within. *Journal of Career Development, 26*(1), 85–88.
Delanty, G., & Strydom, P. (eds.). 2003. *Philosophies of social science: The classic and contemporary readings*. Maidenhead, England: Open University.
Dominguez, H. 2016. Mirrors and windows into student noticing. *Teaching Children Mathematics, 22*(6), 358–365. https://doi:10.5951/teacchilmath.22.6.0358
Gonzalez, N., Moll, L., Tenery, M. F., Rivera, A., Rendon, P., Gonzales, R., & Amanti, C. 1995. Funds of knowledge for teaching in Latino households. *Urban Education, 29*(4), 443–470. https://doi.org/10.1177/0042085995029004005
Gutierrez, R. 2002. Enabling the practice of mathematics teachers in context: Toward a new equity research agenda. *Mathematical Thinking and Learning, 4*(2–3), 145–187.
———. 2012. Embracing Nepantla: Rethinking "knowledge" and its use in mathematics teaching. *Journal of Research in Mathematics Education, 1*(1), 29–56. https://doi: 10.4471/redimat.2012.02
Jones, S. 2012. Trauma narratives and Nomos in teacher education. *TeachingEducation, 23*(2), 131–152.
Krasa, N., & Shunkwiler, S. 2009. *Number sense and number nonsense: Understanding the challenges of learning math*. Baltimore, MD: Paul H. Brookes.
National Council of Teachers of Mathematics. n.d. Access and equity in mathematics education. Position statement. Accessed January 28, 2018, from http://www.nctm.org/Standards-and-Positions/Position-Statements/Access-and-Equity-in-Mathematics-Education/
Style, E. 1988. Curriculum as window and mirror. In Margaret E. Crocco (ed.), *Listening for All Voices, Gender Balancing the School Curriculum* (pp. 6–12). Summit, NJ: Oak Knoll School Monograph. https://nationalseedproject.org/images/documents/Curriculum_As_Window_and_Mirror.pdf
U.S. Census Bureau. 2015, October 1. Data. Accessed January 11, 2018, https://census.gov/data/tables/2013/demo/2009-2013-lang-tables.html

Part II

Latinx Curriculum in Schools: Addressing Goals, Objectives, and Purposes

FOUR
Southern Latinxs

Toward a Curricular Epistemology of Dissent and Possibility

Juan F. Carrillo and Lucia I. Mock Muñoz de Luna

North Carolina has experienced tremendous growth in its Latinx population. Yet, the stories, curriculum, and *critical hope* (Duncan-Andrade 2009) of the Latinx population is still largely absent in the education scholarship. Drawing from Au, Brown, and Calderon's (2017) notion of visible and invisible narratives, we examine how the University of North Carolina's Latin@/x Education Research Hub (LERH) works to address silences in the topography of Latinx knowledge, hope, and community in North Carolina and in the New Latinx south. We situate our chapter in our collaborative testimonios (Espino et al. 2012) in an effort to document, analyze, and center our collaborative approaches to scholarship and social change.

LATIN@/X EDUCATION RESEARCH HUB

First, we provide some context germane to Latin@ Education Research Hub. LERH was founded in 2016 with the collective efforts of students, alumni, faculty, and many others. LERH is located at a tier one, Predominantly White Institution in the New Latinx South. This university has a small but growing Latinx student population and has struggled for years to address diversity issues on campus. Isolation, frustration, and the limited opportunities to find a critical space at UNC Chapel Hill, were some of the key issues that led to the development of LERH. The hub is made up of three core pillars: public pedagogy, critical Latin@/x education research, university-community/school partnerships. As this chapter will show, the space is also central to producing links between individuals that are looking to create a collaborative and critical scholarly community in the New Latinx South. LERH has a national level faculty and student affiliate program, a lecture series, and various ongoing university-community school projects. Additionally, the podcast Block Chronicles is a way by which the hub space is used to disseminate knowledge and dialogue with the community beyond the ivory tower.

THEORETICAL GROUNDING

The New Latinx South: The Case of North Carolina

Since 1990, North Carolina has become a new gateway state for Latinx immigrants. From 1990 to 2010, the state saw the fastest increase in immigrant population in the United States, with the number of Latinx residents increasing from 77,000 in 1990 (1.2% of the population), to over 913,640 in 2015—accounting for 9.1% of the state's population (Rong & Hilburn, 2017). This shift in demographics has had a dramatic impact on North Carolina's educational system; overall, one in five students in K–12 public schools is either foreign-born or a child of foreign-born parents and during the 2015–2016 school year, 16.5% of students identified as Latino/a American (Rong & Hilburn, 2017). Latinx students, although still underrepresented, are also increasing their presence in the higher education communities in North Carolina; in the UNC system they are the second-fastest growing group of nonwhite students, with a 9% enrollment increase in the fall of 2015 (University of North Carolina Enrollment Report, 2015). As Latinx students become a growing part of the public school and higher education community, they are writing a new chapter in the history of the state (Carrillo & Rodriguez, 2016).

However, North Carolina's relationship with its Latinx students and families has been fraught, as Latino/a communities have complicated the traditional black-white binary discourse around diversity that receiving communities are unaccustomed to (Cervantes-Soon & Turner, 2017). The responses to these nuances have been varied, at times characterized by high rates of segregation (Carrillo, 2016; McDaniel et al., 2017), resistance to change and outright hostility (Byrd, 2014; Cuadros, 2006; "Hate group protests in Troy," 2014), and a reliance on the oversimplified national narrative around immigrant populations (Murillo, 2002; Portes & Salas, 2015). In schools, these dynamics have played out in under-funded support programming for English Language Learner students (Shofer, 2017), problematic Dual-Language immersion programs that have commodified Latinx students' resources (Cervantes-Soon, 2014; Cervantes-Soon &

Turner, 2017), and subtractive schooling experiences (Green et al., 2017; Valenzuela, 1999; Villenas, 2002).

Not surprisingly, Latinx students in North Carolina schools are often framed through deficit frameworks. These limited narratives have led to a notable lack of critical literature on Latinx/Chican@ student identity and experiences in North Carolina (Carrillo, 2016), in addition to additive approaches that center students and their families as active agents in their scholarly communities. Despite this marked exclusion in educational scholarship, Latinx students are often at the center of critical discussion and activism on their college campuses in North Carolina, including their leadership in the community response to the HB2 bill targeting transgender citizens (De Guzman, 2016) and the community response to the decision to end the Deferred Action for Childhood Arrivals (DACA) program in late 2017 (Lennon, 2017).

Testimonios

We draw from important scholarship on testimonios to share our collective voice in efforts to challenge systemic erasure, demand a more nuanced take on our memories and histories and cultures, and reimagine the role space and power and identity construction in the New Latinx South. We are inspired and draw theoretical insight from testimonio work (Beverley 2000; Cervantes-Soon 2012; The Latina Feminist Group 2001) that centers that role of naming violence all while narrating avenues for agency and social justice. Testimonios have their roots in Latin America, often outlining the struggles of indigenous communities and exploring the polemic realities of government-related violence (Menchú & Burgos-Debray, 1984; Poniatowska, 1971; Smith, 2012). We also draw theoretical guidance from testimonio scholarship that offers analyses of working-class high school students in Ciudad Juarez, Chihuahua, Mexico and immigrant mothers (Cervantes-Soon, 2012; González, 2006). Our testimonios are rooted in this work, seeking to offer witness on how suffering and dislocation is a material, ontological, and epistemological attack, one we seek to remedy in community.

Visible and Invisible Narratives

We also draw from Au, Brown, and Calderon's (2016) notion of visible and invisible narratives to show how we resist our erasure, center our steps toward equity and justice, and document the role that LERH has had in putting forth a community that is situated at the intersections of theory, action, and critical work. Located in the southeastern United States, a place where the agency of Latinx communities and allies is rarely if ever documented, we share our narratives of dissent and possibility.

METHODS

Collaborative Testimonios

Soja (2010) contends that we are "embedded in the geographies around us in much the same as we are integral actors in the social contexts and always involved in one way or another in the making of our individual biographies and collective histories" (71). In part, we seek to make sense of space and geography while engaging our stories, methods, and praxis as dimensions of clarity, social justice, and change as it relates to our scholarly work and in terms of our commitment to Latinx communities. We met in the state of North Carolina during a graduate class at UNC Chapel Hill in the fall of 2017. It was space, geography, and our desire to make some changes at curriculum and philosophical/political levels that in part bounded our stories and cemented the methodological approach that we use in this chapter. Juan F. Carrillo is a university professor, and Lucia Mock Muñoz de Luna is a graduate student. During a class that addressed many issues of power and critical work as it relates to Latinx communities, we began to discuss what LERH means to us as a space of hope, community, and resistance at the Whitestream university. We also acknowledged how LERH served a unique role within our campus as certain tensions arose over the years related to race, critical work, and grassroots movements and action. The LERH physical space is located in the basement of the UNC School of Education, and that spatial reality also became a process by which to "get away" and regroup as we faced various challenges during the semester.

Drawing from a collaborative testimonio approach (Espino et al. 2012), we discuss the following three prompts:

1. What role does LERH have as a place of resistance?
2. How has LERH helped you in producing critical work?
3. What role does LERH have in producing a community and sense of belonging at a Predominantly White Institution (PWI)?

These prompts were the result of themes that came up over the course of four months. We discussed the role of LERH in class, at student-related events and meetings, coffee shops, and over email. Resistance, the importance of critical work, and the role of community were core areas of focus that consistently came up in our discussions. These themes are also the result of contextual, climate issues on campus where critical work and current leadership provided lots of tension around doing critical scholarship and engaging in humanizing trajectories. Moreover, the context of being in a Predominantly White Institution (PWI) located in the south led to various feelings of isolation and frustration over the limited opportunities to find spaces for doing critical work on Latinx issues in education. Hence, LERH became a gathering place, a place of creation, an inventive place, and a unified front for challenging hegemonic spaces that produced violent narratives.

OUR TESTIMONIOS

Below, we share our testimonios. We break this process up into three questions/prompts and we also respond to each other.

Prompt 1: What role does LERH have as a place of resistance?

Juan

My father used to always joke about power, always make fun of it, implying how absurd it is as a social construct. My mother was similar, she resisted being "controlled." I call my mother and she often is nowhere near where she says she is going to be when I go visit. She is always shifting, adjusting, trying to live her truest life. The hub space to me, in part, is part of that legacy, of working how we want to work in the name of some notion of humanization. I know the constraints, but I am mindful of how we can follow our values as it relates to changing things; a space to write about specific things we care about, and act in the community in ways that are true to our views of the world. Being in an elite university can be a surreal experience of detachment with many silences—so I use this hub space as a speaking point, a place that can help with addressing those gaps. I travel a lot for work-related activities, and when I get back to UNC, the hub space is where I feel at home. Like I can take the energy, disappointment, and hopes I have to move some projects forward. I can also feel the power of the people that have been there the day before or a few minutes prior. It is there, in the air. What is interesting too is the way this space of various individuals has led to the development of courses, mentorship, talks, and other actions that push back against assimilationist, deficit, and integrationist approaches to the Latinx community.

Lucia

When I think about resistance, my mind automatically goes to Star Wars, and the "The Resistance"—a group of radicals fighting against an authoritarian galactic empire. It helps add some levity for me. But then I remember walking out of the theater last month after watching the latest Star Wars movie and seeing the tears in my mom's eyes about Princess Leia; knowing this was her last movie (given Carrie Fisher's death last year). This moment has stuck with me because my mom has always reminded me of Princess Leia, especially lately as the older generation of rebels still fighting tirelessly against injustice, hatred, Darth Vader. Mi mama has always embodied resistance to me—her life reflects a battle against patriarchy and disregard for humanity; she and my father fled fascist Spain in the 1970s, and in doing so she was forced to leave behind her two oldest children (my half-siblings) and then spent the next thirty years fighting to free herself, and them, of the weight of this decision. She's still fighting. Her story, the story of our family, has defined my life in many ways, too many to talk about here. But somehow this critical part of my being has never felt like part of my academic, scholarly identity; there's never been space for it. Instead there's been this imposition of a difference between the cerebral and the spiritual, the lived and the learned. One of the great ironies to me in my experience as a graduate student so far has been that for all of our talk about "humanizing" those we research and write about (the very nature of research in my eyes is trying to extract stories), we rarely examine, or reveal, our own humanity. Rarely do we exact the same curiosity, critique, questioning of ourselves that we do of others; hold that same mirror up to ourselves that we so readily impose on others. Maybe we wouldn't like what we see.

The hub is this mirror. It's the place where The Resistance lives. Walking into that office in the basement for the first time last year—with the music blasting and the windows open, letting in the warm breeze—I felt myself step into a space that demanded my humanity, demanded my family, my mom, my experience as a white, queer, immigrant, Spanish-speaking woman come in with me. Not for observation, for representation, for diversity—but for my own well-being. And then in return it gave me compañeros—a group of people to walk with in this journey through academia; compañeros to talk to about the latest Arsenal game and about my doubts around doing my research with Syrian and Palestinian youth in Lebanon. To listen to as they shared with me their knowledge and wisdom, their doubts, their humanity. The hub gives us that space, both literal and spiritual, to resist the competitiveness, the narrowness, the isolation that we have experienced as students. It's given us a space to struggle with our identities and futures as scholars in an institution that most days makes those decisions for us. We are remaking academia in our image in this space. This to me feels like revolutionary resistance. Princess Leia would be proud.

Juan (response to Lucia, prompt 1)

Lucia, you make me think of this academic year, the ups and down at UNC. We are living a year where there are attacks and surveillance of students during protests, the fear of liberatory "truth," and the dismantling of space for the voices that fight for social justice is ongoing. Depending on the week when I read the university paper, some social justice oriented center or another is being shut down. The absurdity of adults going after good deeds is a bizarre pill, a tonic, and bittersweet rhapsody of emptiness. Yet, here we are, in the hub space narrating our links to Spain, Compton, New York, Oak Cliff, Texas, here we are. It is powerful to hear your familia's story, as so much of what you mentioned links to the stories of what others have told me when meeting in the hub space. And here we are going to be. Here we will narrate a curriculum of place that clears up the sore throat. No matter what.

Lucia (response to Juan, prompt 1)

Juan, thank you for sharing more about the legacy and groundwork for the hub. It doesn't surprise me that it comes from your family, your past—that which, and those whom, you love. That is evident in the spirit, and feeling, of the space. It also brings me some comfort to know that the hub was in response to the same feelings of detachment and frustration that I've been experiencing; that I'm not alone in these feelings. That I'm also not alone in hoping for something more. What you, and the hub, help me envision is a way through—a path that is illuminated by mentors like you, peers like those I've met in that space, and by ideas and passion that give this work meaning. I agree: the hub is definitely a speaking point; a space that values and amplifies our voices and then helps us take action against these imposed silences, against these othering, dehumanizing perspectives we encounter so often. I just got off the phone with a hub compañero. He listened while I told him how last night my peers—those who call themselves critical scholars—silenced and dismissed the stories that other colleagues from New Zealand, India, Ecuador, Vietnam, India had shared during class; commenting that *they didn't really say anything we didn't already know.* In between online shopping and messaging their friends as they sat in class, my peers decided that these peoples' stories were not worth their time. I'm still upset as I write this, partly because I wasn't surprised at their reaction. But my friend listened to my rant, and then told me to go to the hub to reclaim my hope. That's where I'm headed.

Prompt 2: How has LERH helped you in producing critical work?

Juan

The work at the hub space has provided conversations, friendships, laughs, and really a hope to address the tensions that we feel in these spaces sometimes—like where is the critical work? In the south, sometimes I do face isolation as it relates to some of the critical education scholarship related to Latinx communities. By convening and sharing and acting on our ideas, it really has been influential in my own work. I also appreciate the national level critical researcher affiliate program. I learned so much from inviting them to give talks. After each talk, I leave energized and it helps with my theorization and action related work. The organic nature of things also reminds me of Freirian principles of love, dialogue, critical consciousness, and solidarity around working on the side of those in the margins. I can feel the genuine commitment. From these conversations, I am able to think about my own scholarship. Additionally, I developed courses that address issues of intersectionality and critical perspectives on Latinx communities and students. So much of the momentum around that work is also triggered by engaging with students and others in the hub space.

Lucia

One of the first things I noticed about LERH was the bookshelf, housing books not otherwise often seen in our School of Education—the works of Anzaldúa, Valenzuela, so many other scholars that have paved the way for critical scholarship in education. So, in many ways, LERH has been the library for this critical work. Which is interesting to think about now that I write this, because one of the recurring themes that I noted in our readings in your class this semester (fall 2017) was how the library was a place of sanctuary for so many of the young men we read about. Which was familiar because books have always been home for me. *Anna Karenina, Beloved, Sons and Lovers, To the Lighthouse*—those were my teachers. But while a library can be a solitary place, and books such an escape, LERH is a vibrant, loud *comunidad* where ideas flow as freely as jokes about someone's taste in music. I want to share a story from last year that hopefully will get at this question:

One afternoon in March of last year, we were all hanging out in the "Hub" doing our work. C (a friend and graduate school peer) had a meeting scheduled in the Hub with one of our peers—since it was an informal meeting to discuss a paper, RR (a graduate school peer) and I sat quietly on the couch while C met with her. A few minutes into the meeting, I began to feel a shift in the room, an energy between C and this woman that felt unfamiliar and uncomfortable in the Hub. I was uneasy with her tone and demeanor, a stance that to me indicated some sort of defensiveness or impatience with C. I put in my headphones to remove myself from the dynamic, and T (friend and graduate school peer) did so as well.

When the woman left a short while after, the three of us looked at each other, befuddled, and then tried to examine what had just happened— why we had all shared a similar sense of discomfort. C perhaps summed it up best when he remarked that the Hub had been "white-jacked"—that is, that the space had been taken over by the whiteness that our peer carried with her. With that whiteness, our sacred space of the Hub had been questioned, taken away from us.

This led us to a long conversation and reflection on our own identities (I, after all, am not Latinx, but Spanish, and white), what the Hub meant to us, and why we felt so strongly that the space needed to remain ours.

These questions have stayed with us—so much so that we are writing about it. And for me and C especially, it's pushed us into the world of critical educational research—Chicana feminist scholarship, third world feminisms, border pedagogies, among others. Of course, the first place we turned to was the bookshelf in the hub. But these books, these ideas, these theories have come to life for me because of C and T, because of our conversations about them, the perspectives we each bring to this work. It's convinced me that it's in the spaces between us where knowledge is generated; it's those bridges we build for each other that makes critical work, radical.

Juan (response to Lucia, prompt 2)

It is great to read your response and reflect on the moments when I brought some of the books you mentioned into the hub space. I appreciate the way you link the readings to critical scholarship, the way it all wraps around to doing critical work and resisting and naming moments where Whiteness may try to alter the space and the work. It is true, the library, both the physical work that is in the space, but also our conversations, that library of connection can push the critical and elevate the critical. I was thinking today that when I was a graduate student, books came to me. At bookstores. A poet from the neighborhood would chat with me and share his/her work. A few years ago, I attended a writer's workshop taught by the the Chicano poet, Jimmy Santiago Baca. At night, in the mountains of New Mexico, he gave me connection, a book. I cherish these transactions. We resist curricular genocide in the LERH space. We talk about our future publications, we name the gaps, we enter North Carolina narratives around Latinx communities in critical ways. I even design classes with a critical lens in that space. The books that I see in the LERH space name power. We also name the silences in the curriculum of our university and shape projects and work and courses around pushing back against that.

Lucia (response to Juan, prompt 2)

Your words make me think a lot about how important it is to consider and feel 'love' in our work. How often in our professional settings, emotions—particularly love—are posed as something to be controlled, measured, regulated by the mind. Emotions are something we quantify with ease, but rarely do we actually genuinely allow them into our classes, papers, conversations. Whereas in the hub, it seems to me that emotion is at the center of everything—*cariño, amor, amistad*—and also that excitement that you mention after leaving talks given by other professors doing this work. I've felt it too, and wonder where else that exists in our school. But in those moments when we've had the Latinx presence centered and celebrated in our school—through presentations, courses, the coffee hour with Julio Cammarota last year—the power has been undeniable, and it's come from that same place of love and solidarity you talk about. The hub brings that to our school; we need it.

Prompt 3: What role does LERH have in producing a community and sense of belonging at a Predominantly White Institution (PWI)?

Juan

I can hear Tracy Champan's song, "Fast Car." Here are some of the lyrics:

> You got a fast car
> I want a ticket to anywhere
> Maybe we make a deal
> Maybe together we can get somewhere
> Anyplace is better
> Starting from zero got nothing to lose
> Maybe we'll make something
> Me, myself I got nothing to prove. (Chapman 1988)

I think of the "fast car"—about the desire to leave. I hear it from students and faculty. This nothing new. I heard about this since I moved to NC in 2011. Some leave. Some stay. Latinx-related social pain is so thick here. Where should we take our fast car? When we go the basement, the physical space where the hub is, I actually do feel like we "leave" even as we stay. In that space, I often get to work with students from across the university that want to do critical work in education policy, Latino urbanism, and other areas. As the state continues to have demographic shifts, I think this is one space, one place where we can come together and push back against silence and address issues of identity and self-determination in our communities. It is "allowed." Sometimes the university or our school of education may send a different message, but here, it is go time. Let's do it. We do it. I see it. That spirit, that community, that love really, leverages a certain courage in the midst of some red lights that are all around us.

Lucia

It's hard to write about community and belonging because it feels like these are words that are thrown around so carelessly. I've heard those words often at our University; used so cynically they've lost meaning. Sometimes I can almost see the person giving me a knowing wink when they talk about these concepts—like I'm in on the joke. I should say though, belonging and community have always felt elusive to me. I've never been American enough; never spanish enough; never straight enough ... but just enough to pass; never quite sure the knowledge I'm looking for is found within the walls of higher education.

It's not lost on me that I'm a white woman and Education is a field of white women so really I do *belong* in this *community*. But so often it feels like those words have been constructed by others who then decide who belongs and what the community values and if you don't like it there's something wrong with you. And there's an intervention for that. I'm not sure I even want to belong here.

So what role does a space like the hub have at a PWI in constructing community and belonging? I'm not sure. I'm tempted to say it takes those words and stomps them under its boot. And then, *con cariño*, remakes them into something damaged, but beautiful. I can tell you that it is a *refugio* from meaningless words and stilted, forced dialogues, from the almost fetishtic regard for diversity and social justice and equity (but we'll threaten to charge you with vandalism if you hang up posters at school demanding that we address the white supremacy on our campus and in our *community*).

The beauty of the hub is that it exists within a PWI and is the home of a struggle to take back the meaning of these words and reclaim our humanity. Its very presence feels like a battle won, or at least fought. And I say this because I think ultimately this is a fight worth fighting, because I truly believe education (in its many forms) can be liberating. I've seen this come to life at a refugee camp in Lebanon, and I feel it happening to me when I am in the Hub with my colleagues, with my professor, with my compañeros. Education through vulnerability, trust, compromiso, radical love, through each other. That is the community of belonging that the LERH is building, at least for me.

Juan (response to Lucia, prompt 3)

I agree with you, Lucia. The word community is thrown around so much. It is commodified, it enters into the professional realm of opportunity. So, when I think about the apartments where I grew up in working-class Los Angeles, I wonder how local universities used some themes related to my pain to get resources even if I saw little if any of them. Here, at the hub, and in our university, it also a challenge. But yes, we are taking back this word and others and smiling back at the context that seems to want a notion of community that is often violent and full of silences and gaps. Every moment, every single time we talk, we create curriculums of hope, Anzaldúan-type bridges that narrate something more beautiful, organic, and emancipatory.

Lucia (response to Juan, prompt 3)

Maybe together we can get somewhere. I'm reading this and wondering how you have navigated these spaces with such grace and vulnerability (and humor); and what you've lost and gained in the process. What you've given of yourself to stay here for so long, to ride along with us in this fast car. To let us, as students, take the steering wheel and help us make something out of whatever we've brought to the car, the hub, the classroom. Sometimes it does feel like the red lights surround us. Or that we've taken a wrong turn and the street signs are in a language we don't understand. So, leaving is the best option. Seeking refuge is necessary. Do we find that refuge in each other, in our compañeros/as? In the communities that we write for, with, and to? How do you find the energy to keep pushing back against the silences that follow us like shadows through the hallways and classrooms of 'our' school?

Visible Narratives, Southerness, and Resistance

It is often the case that the New Latinx south is framed as a place devoid of agency. Through LERH, we resist not only this perspective, but the idea that Latinx communities and spaces in North Carolina are bound to nonnegotiable subtractive demands of the neoliberal university- and state-level policies that often move away from social justice goals, and even close down centers that are doing equity work. As such, LERH is a site where we meet, where we engage in discussions around developing community work, and we advocate for social justice courses and programming. Often inspired by discussions in LERH, we create classes at the graduate and undergraduate level that focus on Latinx issues. We also bring in Latinx speakers to discuss their work. While we don't claim to have it all figured out, we build narratives and curricular demands that center our stories. As such, we become visible in a university space that often sells a diversity narrative that is compliant with status quo narratives around access, civility, and one-sided branding opportunities.

CONCLUSION

According to Freire (2006), "In order for the oppressed to unite, they must first cut the umbilical cord of magic and myth which binds them to the world of oppression; the unity which links them to each other must be of a different nature" (175). At the Latin@/x Education Research Hub, we push back against being a commodity for one story. Often, this story is the savior, assimilationist, or watered-down narrative of metrics created by the academy to keep conversations in safe zones that are conducive merely for grant funding and colloquia. We acknowledge that we are part of this structure, but naming its limits and "magic" also has helped to nurture curriculum of dissent of place making outside of these confines.

In North Carolina, part of the struggle is related to narratives of "newness" that provide curiosity but often uncritical analysis is at relates to Latinx communities, identity, curriculum, and schooling. This is the *visibility narrative* (Au, Brown, & Calderon 2016). The technocratic university often frames spaces like LERH as esoteric spaces that don't bring in value unless economic resources come in or if tokenism can be exploited. We recognize that Latinxs are moving into North Carolina, and we also argue that we are not just bounded by the visible narratives of the state, but we lead a project of curricular self-determination. In other words, we write, speak, teach, engage in activist work, and develop Latinx-centric courses that center our lenses and stories in critical ways. In this context, we continue to create as we go, dream as we wake, and push for visibility on our terms.

REFERENCES

Au, W., Brown, A., & Calderon, D. 2016. *Reclaiming the multicultural roots of the U.S. curriculum: Communities of color and official knowledge in education.* New York: Teachers College Press.

Beverley, J. 2000. Testimonio, subalternity, and narrative authority. In Norman Denzin & Yvonna Lincoln (eds.), *The Sage handbook of qualitative research* (pp. 547–558). Thousand Oaks, CA: Sage.

Byrd, S. 2014. "The collective circle": Latino immigrant musicians and politics in Charlotte, North Carolina. *American Ethnologist, 41,* 246–260. doi:10.1111/amet.12073

Carrillo, J. F. 2016. I grew up straight 'hood: Unpacking the intelligences of working-class Latino male college students in North Carolina. *Equity & Excellence in Education, 492,* 157–169. https://doi.org/10.1080/10665684.2015.1086247

Carrillo, J. F., & Rodriguez, E. 2016. She doesn't even act Mexican: Smartness trespassing in the new south. *Race Ethnicity and Education, 19*(6). https://doi.org/10.1080/13613324.2016.1168547

Cervantes-Soon, C. 2012. Testimonios of life and learning in the borderlands: Subaltern Juárez girls speak. *Equity & Excellence in Education, 45*(3), 373–391. https://doi:10.1080/10665684.2012.69818

———. 2014. A critical look at dual language immersion in the new Latin@ diaspora. *Bilingual Research Journal, 37*(1), 64–82. https://doi.org/10.1080/15235882.2014.893267

Cervantes-Soon, C., & Turner, A. 2017. Countering silence and reconstructing identities in a Spanish/English two-way immersion program: Latino mothers' pedagogies in El Nuevo Sur. In Xue Lan Rong & Jeremy Hilburn (eds.), *Immigration and education in North Carolina: The challenges and responses in a new gateway state* (pp. 195–220). Rotterdam: Sense Publishers.

Chapman, T. 1988. *Tracy Chapman.* David Keshenbaum. Elektra. CD.

Cuadros, P. 2006. *A home on the field: How one championship team inspires hope for the revival of small town America.* New York: Harper Collins.

De Guzmán, M. 2017. Latinx: ¡Estamos aquí!, or being "Latinx" at UNC-Chapel Hill. *Cultural Dynamics, 29*(3), 214–230. https://doi.org/10.1177%2F0921374017727852

Duncan-Andrade, J. 2009. Note to educators: Hope required when growing roses in concrete. *Harvard Educational Review* 79, no. 2, 181–194. https://doi.org/10.17763/haer.79.2.nu3436017730384w

Espino, M., Vega, I., Rendón, L., Ranero, J., & Muñiz, M. 2012. The process of reflexión in bridging testimonies across lived experience. *Equity & Excellence in Education*, 45(3), 444–449. https://doi.org/10.1080/10665684.2012.698188

Freire, P. 2006. *Pedagogy of the oppressed*, 30th anniversary ed. New York: Continuum.

González, N. 2006. Testimonios of border identities: "Una mujer acomedida donde quiera cabe." In Dolores Delgado Bernal, C. Alejandra Elenes, Francisca E. Godinez, & Sofia Villenas (eds.), *Chicana/Latina education in everyday life: Feminist perspectives on pedagogy and epistemology* (pp. 197–214). Albany: State University of New York Press.

Green, M., Perreira, K., & Ko, L. 2017. Schooling experience of Latino/a immigrant adolescents in North Carolina: An examination of relationships between peers, teachers and parents. In Xue Lan Rong & Jeremy Hilburn (eds.), *Immigration and Education in North Carolina: The Challenges and Responses in a New Gateway State* (pp. 53–81). Rotterdam: Sense Publishers.

Hate group protests in Troy; residents say they're embarrassed. *Fox8 News* (Greensboro, NC). August 9, 2014.

Lennon, P. UNC students united and outraged over DACA announcement. *Daily TarHeel* (Chapel Hill, NC). September 19, 2017.

McDaniel, P., Harden, S., Smith, H., & Furuseth, O. 2017. Increasing immigrant settlement and the challenges and opportunities for public education in Charlotte, North Carolina. In Spencer Salas & Pedro Portes (eds.), *US Latinization: Education and the New Latino South*. New York: State University of New York Press.

Menchú, R., & Burgos-Debray (eds.). 1984. *I, Rigoberta Menchú: An Indian woman in Guatemala* (A. Wright, Trans.). London, England: Verso.

Murrillo, E. 2002. How does it feel to be a problem?: "Disciplining" the transnational subject in the American south. In Stanton Wortham, Enrique Murillo, & Edmund Hamann (eds.), *Education in the new Latino diaspora: Policy and the politics of identity* (pp. 215–240). Westport, CT: Greenwood.

Poniatowska, E. 1971. *La noche de Tlatelolco [The night of Tlatelolco]*. México, DF: Ediciones Era.

Portes, P., & Salas, S. 2015. Nativity shifts, broken dreams, and the new Latino south's post-first generation. *Peabody Journal of Education: Issues of Leadership, Policy, and Organizations*, 90(3). https://doi.org/10.1080/0161956X.2015.1044296

Rong, X. L., & Hilburn, J. 2017. Immigration, demographic changes and school in North Carolina from 1990 to 2015: Transformations to a multiethnic, global community. In Xue Lan Rong & Jeremy Hilburn (eds.), *Immigration and education in North Carolina: The challenges and responses in a new gateway state* (pp. 3–24). Rotterdam: Sense Publishers.

Shofer, S. 2017. The lost years of opportunity for North Carolina's ESL students. In Xue Lan Rong & Jeremy Hilburn (eds.), *Immigration and education in North Carolina: The challenges and responses in a new gateway state* (pp. 25–49). Rotterdam: Sense Publishers.

Smith, L. T. 2012. *Decolonizing methodologies: Research and indigenous peoples*. New York: Zed Books.

Soja, E. 2010. *Seeking spatial justice*. Minneapolis: University of Minnesota Press.

The Latina Feminist Group. 2001. *Telling to live: Latina feminist testimonios*. Durham, NC: Duke University Press.

Valenzuela, A. 1999. *Subtractive schooling: US Mexican youth and the politics of caring*. Albany: State University of New York Press.

Villenas, S. 2002. Reinventing educación in new Latino communities: Pedagogies of change and continuity in North Carolina. In S. Wortham, E. G. Murillo, & E. T. Hamann (eds.), *Education in the new Latino diaspora: Policy and the politics of identity* (pp. 17–35). Westport, CT: Greenwood.

FIVE
"Illegality" and the Curriculum

Making New Civics with Undocumented Activists

Jesús A. Tirado

Undocumented activists suffer a great injustice from the mechanisms of immigration policy. Borderlines divide them from their families, and the criminalization of being on the wrong side of the border limits their choices.[1] These mechanisms make the concept of "illegality" an important lens for seeing and understanding the work that these activists do and how they are reimagining our nation. "Illegality" not only shapes the facets of their daily life but also how they challenge the matrix of oppression that targets them. Undocumented activists reimagine a new way of being and acting that resists how "illegality" shapes them but also inspires the ways that they seek to improve their community and decrease these ill-effects. This chapter will introduce the concept of illegality and how undocumented activists live with it and use it to reimagine a new civics curriculum.

As we attempt to understand and examine "illegality" and how it shapes these activists' lives, we need to examine how they live and how they move through the world. It is hard for someone not shaped by "illegality" to understand how deep of an influence it is. The rhetoric and symbols of "illegality" can be found in several places, but harder to understand is how "illegality" shapes the daily lives of the undocumented community. Astrid, one of my participants, tells the story about getting sick in college and due to not having access to a doctor, she had to return home for a few days. This lead to missed classes; she could not get a doctor's note for her absences, and she ended up explaining to each of her professors why she had missed class and did not have a note.[2] While every professor was sympathetic, they could only come to understand through interactions with Astrid. These interactions, while fruitful, took a toll on Astrid as she had to come out and talk about her status, health, and progress in the class at great length. "Illegality" both prevented her from having health care and from obtaining the doctor's note that would have eased the conversations with her professors.

This chapter attempts to address the question: how are undocumented activists affected by illegality changing the curriculum and schooling? This work will not only talk about their experiences but also their ideas for how to change the curriculum to create a more fair and engaging curriculum. These changes, these challenges, represent better ways to think about and imagine a better, more inclusive curriculum and classroom. As "illegality" exists in big and small facets, their new vision for what a civics class should be is also big and small. They don't reimagine new standards, but new ways of being in the classroom.

SIGNIFICANCE

The experiences and ideas of these undocumented activists stand out because their perspectives and experiences in America position them to offer critiques and insights into how the mainstream positions, and culture maintains, dangerous attitudes. Standpoint theory, according to Jaggar, privileges the positions and experiences of those who face oppression as needing to be heard because they aren't as inculcated with the mainstream as others.[3] My participants, both undocumented men and women, live and thrive without many of the benefits that the privileged among us experience. Understanding how these participants see and experience the effects of the mainstream provides a perspective of how curriculum can challenge the mainstream.

This kind of challenge can help people feel less alienated by schooling. Salinas and Jaffee have both identified problems with curriculum that is alienating to Latinx and immigrant students. Both works exemplify that the curriculum, and other aspects of schooling, alienate students and limit their capacity to learn.[4] This harkens to many discussions and works in education. Valenzuela's seminal work described how schooling disrupts students' learning and interferes with their growth.[5] While this work does not focus on the specific aspects of subtractive schooling and alienation, this work wants to offer an entry into how undocumented Latinx activists would rewrite the curriculum.

"ILLEGALITY"

There are several concepts in this chapter that are needed to contextualize "illegality" and Latino education. Both concepts illustrate the limits that the system places on these activists and their community. "Illegality" was described by De Gevona as a process by the state affecting the lives of the undocumented.[6] These processes create limitations that shape how these activists move through the world. "Illegality," according to Menjívar and Kanstroom, goes beyond legal status and encompasses the processes that shapes many of the daily experiences of these students.[7] For undocumented activists, the concept of illegality is extremely important and one that defines much of the way they see the world and their place in society. Gonzales describes illegality as not just the state of being undocumented but how being undocumented affects every single aspect of their lives.[8] Butler writes about how precarity forms important aspects for our lives, and for the undocumented community, this concept of illegality is at the heart of it.[9] Fears over deportation make communities unsafe even here in Georgia. Illegality comes from the rhetoric that targets this group and how they move through society. Understanding the role of illegality means understanding the role that the border plays for this community, their families, and their livelihoods.

Illegality becomes clear when we examine the experiences of these activists. Astrid's earlier anecdote is one example of this. Maria tells another story. She told me:

> I know that that my mom she got stopped back then she didn't have a drivers license and lucky her she went to jail for that she stayed there for 2 days and Immigration didn't come that day so you know she was very lucky to not get deported.[10]

Maria's story illustrates the capriciousness that many undocumented people live under. This story illustrates that her mother was so close to being deported and how she felt about it. When telling the story, Maria's voice became animated, and she felt lucky to still have her mother. This event, and others, help her see her own work as needing to protect the whole community from these problems. For her, "illegality" provides a reminder that communal action and organization can challenge these damaging structures.

It is important to place the power of knowledge and meaning-making not in the hands of the researcher but in the hands of the people in the field. While orientating this theory to work for those in the field, it is important to make sure they are getting appropriate access to their power. For social studies, this means recognizing that there is not only power being valued and distributed in the classroom pedagogy but also in the curriculum. As different experiences need space and prioritizing, that changes and transforms the classroom.

LATINA/O CRITICAL RACE THEORY

Latina/o Critical Race theory is particularly useful as it calls special attention to issues that oppress and stigmatize the Latina/o population and groups. Issues like "bilingualism, immigration, citizenship, ethnicity, culture, identity, phenotype, sexuality, and history"[11] are particularly important to recognize as significant because of the way they affect the Latina/o community and the undocumented community. There are many overlapping concerns with curricular studies that LatCrit can provide a new perspective on several areas and how Latina/o students, in general, interact with content, teachers, and their community.

We need to consider the considerable work that has been done to incorporate Latina/o Critical Race Theory (LatCrit) into the classroom. Salinas, Vickery, and Franquiz point out that "LatCrit encourages the deconstruction of majoritarian tales, defined as a mindset of positions, perceived wisdoms, and shared cultural understandings."[12] The challenging of hegemonic ideas and methods of knowledge production and reification is important work. Solórzano and Yosso point out that not only is there a decentering of hegemonic ideals, but there needs to be a reinforcing of the traditions and knowledges that challenge them.[13] The idea that "they can build community among those at the margins of society by putting a human and familiar face to educational theory and practice"[14] needs careful examination and thought. Finding ways to not only challenge the hegemonic ideals but also build strong communities needs to be done and can transform how schooling works.

THE STUDY AND THE PARTICIPANTS

The two activists I worked with embody many aspects of their work and their community and their struggles. Like seen in Gonzales's *Lives in Limbo*, many times the struggles and legal problems of undocumentedness can present certain limitations, but these two activists never let that slow them down.[15] While the descriptions below will show that the two participants share many things in common, location and place are also omnipresent factors that are shaping their lives. Before the interviews, I corresponded with both activists via email and I became Facebook friends with them. This allowed them to get to know me and my perspective. It is important they got to see something about me beyond our conversations so they could know my role and interest in the issues we were talking about. Since we were talking over the phone, it was important we have personal contact.

Maria

Born in Mexico City, Maria grew up in Georgia. We were introduced through a mutual friend who also works on issues of immigration and migration. Maria could not attend college due to the laws in Georgia, but she has worked and done many things. Even though she knew she was going to be blocked from having access and affordable access at that, she still pushed herself in high school and pursued a robust education. Even though she has struggled with her lack of access to higher education, she has continued to work and hopes to help her community as much as she can. Over the course of our interviews, Maria switched jobs from working from as a classroom assistant to joining a law firm that serves the Latino community in the Atlanta Metro Area. Besides her job, Maria also has been an activist since she graduated high school. She worked with Freedom University, an undocumented activist group in Atlanta, and has attended, planned, and spoken at their events and rallies.

Astrid

Astrid is from Central Mexico and has lived in the United States for many years, calling Connecticut home. Now she calls the University of Connecticut home. She started as a performing arts major and now is a politics major. We met while I was teaching in Connecticut, so Astrid and I know each other well. Since leaving high school, Astrid has joined an activist group that is pushing for undocumented issues in Connecticut and at the universities around the state; she is majoring in political science as well so that she can become even stronger and more active in these issues. She became active in this group and other political rallies in Storrs and has been working hard to make sure that her issues are at the forefront of her college experience.

THE METHOD

This project was designed with the tenets of LatCrit and interviewing.[16] Maria and Astrid and I talked on the phone about a variety of topics. I was interested in how they approached the culture of activism and what has, and hasn't, influenced them and their vision of civics. Spradley, in his work on ethnographic interviewing, notes that this work should seek to uncover how people use their culture, meaning their "acquired knowledge that people use to interpret experience and generate social behavior."[17] These interviews sought to tap into the experiences of these undocumented activists and ask them about their craft, their involvement, and what sustains them.

Using the interviews as the main source of data collection was an effort to see how activists thought about their work and how they saw themselves being activists. I knew that we shared some identity groups, and I hoped that would help them feel comfortable talking to me. The works of Roulston and Kirkland stress how being an insider/outsider affects how we talk about and see people.[18] Roulston refers to how differences between you and your participants influence the relationship.[19] Kirkland adds that as researchers, we must work to ensure that we do not take over for our participants, but let them speak for themselves.[20] As I can never fully share the undocumented identity or experience with my participants, and it would be faulty to think that our shared Mexican identity allows us to share everything, it does allow us to share something. I know that it would be faulty thinking that the differences did not matter at all since we talked mainly about issues that they confront on a daily basis and make up a considerable part of how they move through the world.

Once the three interviews were done, the work was transcribed by the researcher, me, and organized into different topics and coded. Codes and the quotations that were paired with them were organized and grouped together. After making a collection, the quotations were read again and themes emerged from the collected codes. Analytic memos were written on these quotations and codes, and they formed the basis for the data and analysis below. The memos helped focus the analysis and helped generate the themes and incorporate the theoretical perspectives of LatCrit.

The theme regarding the counterstory was placed at the center of this article due to the nature of LatCrit's emphasis on the counterstory. As discussed above, the writings about the counterstory have emphasized the challenges to hegemonic ways of knowing, but I was struck with the element of how counterstorytelling was also important to building community and unity for the activists. This lead to more writing and thoughts about the role of the counterstory and counterstorytelling for these activists. After this writing, it became clear that this needed to be the focus of some further writing. The memos helped frame the analysis sections and became the main exercise that generated themes.

ILLEGALITY AND NEW CURRICULUM

I asked these activists about their life and how they would change the civics curriculum. Maria started off with a call to "definitely change the curriculum from like what I learned is that we always put the white race as the superior as the best race."[21] Challenging white supremacy took several forms from both activists. Their challenge needs to be contextualized and understood from their position and how "illegality". Their resistance to these forces, and the curricular ideals they evoke, provide an entry into how they understand how "illegality" shapes experiences of schooling. Understanding and exploring their ideas and experiences around being political and aware allow us to understand how they would change and manipulate the curriculum.

Being Political

For both participants, they want a curriculum that reflects the political nature of their existence. Both Astrid and Maria verbalized this in different ways, but both emphasized that people need to take part in politics instead of just ignoring these issues. "Illegality" plays a role in this as the activists' call to action is also a call for their struggle for recognition and to involve people in the reform or end of these structures. Reforming these structures takes more than just one person, and both activists discussed the dangers of being ignored. Both discuss the power of being paid attention to and having their voice heard, it's creating and taking part in a political space that engages all people and does not allow those who have the privilege to ignore issues, to do just that.

Maria voices this drive of people to be political by emphasizing awareness. She emphasized that awareness about the situation can help address the structural problems. Maria told me that:

> not only my goal but our goal, within the Hispanic community is that we have the same rights as everyone else, just like everyone else we are human, and, like, especially in Georgia, attacking the policies are against undocumented students that are banned from attending the top 5 universities so have it overturn and educate others about what is happening in Georgia and have more voices with us and that people should be allies and informing them of what is happening here.[22]

The combination of goals, rights, and education reflect a different set of values for our participants. Maria's goal is about gaining rights owed her community. At the center of this statement, creating awareness is the key action step. She wants people to know that policies that are targeting and harming people in her community can be overturned. Awareness of the political ongoings, for Maria, leads to action. Awareness does not always lead to engagement, but a lack of awareness will never lead to action. While there may be faith here on Maria's part, it isn't a naïve faith. Being aware of what is happening in your state can lead to action. Maria's call to awareness is a call to engage in being political.

Astrid took a similar approach when we talked, although she stressed how people opt out more than getting people to opt in. Astrid expressed concern about how people ignore politics. She told me:

> I think when people hear politics they like dismiss stuff um but when like we explain to them why it is important to like get involved but also how that can change socially getting educated socially go hand in hand.[23]

Like Maria, educating and building awareness go hand in hand with action and change. Astrid talked about being confronted with people reluctant to become political and how that lead them to "dismiss stuff." Like Maria, Astrid takes issue with the orientation of those who are unaware, but Astrid wishes to engage those are unaware. Having this as a tenet for education leads to thinking about how people engage with politics and are aware of the different struggles around us.

Becoming and being political may seem like an odd tenet for a civics curriculum, but it connects to how we move through the world. Both Astrid and Maria, although from different vantage points, illustrate how dangerous it can be to remain unpolitical and unaware of one's society. They did not want people to leave civics classes feeling limited or closed off to the world around, but connected to it. Both Maria and Astrid make calls for being political, but they are also calls for people to be connected to their community in ways that go beyond voting. They want people to leave civics classrooms being better informed about the world beyond the classroom and then being a part of that world.

Schooling

For schooling, Maria and Astrid call attention to the structures and pedagogies that could transform schooling, especially civics classes. Their transformations aim to make schooling a more effective space at helping students realize their own power. Through challenging representation and the pedagogies, Astrid and Maria outline two powerful ways to change how schools work and educate students. While these challenges cannot solve the issues that plague schooling, they represent how "illegality" shapes their schooling and how they attempt to overturn these oppressive forces. The issues of representation within learning and curriculum can change schooling and students inside; it deeply matters for those who are learning a curriculum.

Maria addressed representation and how even if schools were diverse, they were not representative at all levels. Maria told me about how she had to fight to get into AP classes at her school, classes she succeeded in. Most of these decisions about classes occurred through scheduling, and parents could appeal the process afterward. She told me:

> Oh yea I definitely well I took a lot of AP classes and I always noticed that most of you know the kids around me were white so I feel like if I could go back and talk to teachers and administrators I should tell them to definitely give a chance to Hispanic students.[24]

Her school, which she spoke about positively at other times, did not have a good representation of its student body in its AP classes. Often this was due to a variety of factors but one was allowing parents to change students' schedules. Hispanic parents, according to Maria, did not have the same opportunities, or comfort level, to just call the school and demand schedule changes for their kids. Maria pushed to get into the class and did well. This issue of representation matters because it pertains to access, who gets access and how is that mitigated and negotiated in schooling. Maria wants Hispanic students in those upper level classes and not just having to fight for them. While *Plyer v. Doe* shields schools from the impact of "illegality," this is not the case.[25] Fear, language, and other issues complicate schooling, and instead forced parents and students to react to the sorting that had occurred. By aiming to make representation a more present value in schooling, Maria challenges how students move through the school and the classrooms. Issues of representation matter a great deal in classrooms as we think that classrooms must become diverse places in order for students to maximize their learning.

Astrid takes on a different challenge as she talks about pedagogy. While also a successful student, one aspect that Astrid challenged was learning in social groups and situations. Her school did not have clubs to help students learn as part of the curriculum, and she spoke for a more social pedagogy. She told me she wanted schools to have:

> clubs definitely clubs and interest groups and what I would like is like an office that has stuff in there for undocumented students but also other students and one other thing like a social justice type of office more like a resources.[26]

Astrid's desire for clubs and a resource office reflects a pedagogy that engages students, gets them outside of the classroom and learning for themselves. Astrid found the current structures of schooling to be inadequate to begin social change and helping students become aware and active in their community. Her emphasis on clubs and a social justice office represent a shift in how schooling could reach students and engage the community. Both ideas emphasize interactions instead of specific content. For Astrid, changing the pedagogy would transform how schooling would treat students and value them. Instead of placing content or standards at the forefront of the civics classroom, Astrid wants students, their interests, and their interactions with others, to be at the forefront of what schools do. Classes should get outside and explore their community and directly address the concerns of their students.

Changing the pedagogy from how students enter and exist in the classroom and how the classroom works would transform the civics classroom into something very different. While there is definitely power in knowing the structures of government and politics, people also need to know that they have power in this process.[27] Astrid and Maria both present democratic challenges to the way that classrooms work and how they respond to their students.

A Start for a New Curriculum

Maria and Astrid both emphasize new ways to have schools and curriculum work and affect students. Far from standards-driven or content-driven learning, they want students to be at the center and they want students to learn about the world around. Being political and challenging the structures of schooling present some challenges that both activists encountered as "illegality" shaped their schooling. They are challenging being ignored; not finding themselves and their communities and experiences valued in school are all a part of this. Through their challenges with "illegality," some new curricular ideas and pedagogies emerge that can transform schooling, not just for other undocumented students, but all students.

THOUGHTS AND QUESTIONS

When "illegality" shapes your world, it may seem odd that the challenges to it are small, but they only feel small. Becoming political and challenging the structures of schooling are in fact massive challenges to how "illegality" shapes these activists and their lives. "Illegality" only works because it isolates the undocumented population and targets them. Astrid and Maria present us with two small ways to consider changing how schooling, even if not involved with creating and sustaining "illegality," does just that. There is a long-standing critique of schooling as being harmful to students and what they carry with them to the classroom. Valenzuela's work on subtractive schooling illustrates this better than I ever have.[28] By promoting values of being political and schooling that has representational and pedagogical roots in the school and the community, Astrid and Maria have reimagined a new way for schooling to work and look that challenges these problems and the problems brought about by "illegality."

NOTES

1. Roberto Gonzales, *Lives in Limbo* (Berkeley, CA: University of California Press, 2016); Hiroshi Motomura, *Immigration outside the Law* (New York: Oxford University Press, 2014); Susana Muñoz, *Identity, Social Activism, and the Pursuit of Higher Education: The Journey Stories of Undocumented and Unafraid Community Activists* (New York: Peter Lang, 2015).
2. Astrid, in discussion with the author, July 2016.
3. Alison Jaggar, *Just Methods: An Interdisciplinary Feminist Reader* (Boulder, CO: Paradigm, 2014).
4. Cinthia Salinas, "Educating Late Arrival High School Immigrant Students: A Call for a More Democratic Curriculum," *Multicultural Perspectives*, 8, no. 1 (2009): 20–27; Ashley Taylor Jaffee, "Social Studies Pedagogy for Latino/a Newcomer Youth: Toward a Theory of Culturally and Linguistically Relevant Citizenship Education," *Theory & Research in Social Education*, 44, no. 2 (2016): 147–183.

5. Angela Valenzuela, *Subtractive Schooling: US-Mexican Youth and the Politics of Caring* (Albany, NY: State University of New York Press, 1999).
6. Nicholas P. De Genova, "Migrant 'Illegality' and Deportability in Everyday Life," *Annual Review of Anthropology, 31* (2002): 419–447.
7. Cecilia Menjívar and Daniel Kanstroom, "Introduction—Immigrant 'Illegality': Constructions and Critiques," in *Constructing Immigrant 'Illegality': Critiques, Experiences, and Responses*, ed. Cecilia Menjívar and Daniel Kanstroom (New York: Cambridge University Press, 2014).
8. Gonzales, *Lives*, 2016.
9. Judith Butler, *Frames of War: When Is Life Grievable?* 2nd ed. (Brooklyn, NY: Verso, 2016.)
10. Maria, in discussion with the author, August 2016.
11. Dolores Delgado Bernal and Enrique Alemán, *Transforming Educational Pathways for Chicana/o Students: A Critical Race Feminista Praxis* (New York: Teachers College Press, 2017), 23.
12. Cinthia Salinas, Amanda E. Vickery, and Maria Franquiz, "Advancing Border Pedagogies : Understandings of Citizenship through Comparisons of Home to School Contexts," *The High School Journal, 99*, no. 4 (2016): 326.
13. Daniel G. Solorzano and Tara J. Yosso, "Critical Race Methodology: Counter-Storytelling as an Analytical Framework for Education Research," *Qualitative Inquiry, 8*, no. 1 (2002).
14. Daniel G. Solorzano and Dolores Delgado Bernal, "Examining Transformational Resistance through a Critical Race and Latcrit Theory Framework: Chicana and Chicano Students in an Urban Context," *Urban Education, 36*, no. 3 (2001): 327.
15. Gonzales, *Lives*, 2016.
16. Soyini Madison, *Critical Ethnography: Method, Ethics, and Performance*, 2nd ed. (Los Angeles: Sage, 2011); Kathryn Roulston, *Reflective Interviewing: A Guide to Theory and Practice* (London: Sage, 2011); Solórzano & Yosso, 2002; Spradley, *The Ethnographic Interview* (New York: Holt, Rinehart and Winston, 1979).
17. Spradley, *Ethnographic*, 1979, 5.
18. Roulston, 2011; and David Kirkland, "Why I Study Culture, and Why It Matters: Humanizing Ethnographies in Social Science Research," in *Humanizing Research: Decolonizing Qualitative Inquiry with Youth and Communities*, eds. Django Paris and Maisha T. Winn (Thousand Oaks, CA: Sage, 2014), 179–200.
19. Roulston, *Reflective*, 2011.
20. Kirkland, "Why I Study," 2014.
21. Maria, in discussion with the author, August 2016.
22. Maria, in discussion with the author, August 2016.
23. Astrid, in discussion with the author, July 2016.
24. Maria, in discussion with the author, September 2016.
25. *Plyler v. Doe*, 457 U.S. 202 (1982).
26. Astrid in discussion with the author, August 2016.
27. Gert JJ Biesta, *Learning Democracy in School and Society: Education, Lifelong Learning and the Politics of Citizenship* (Rotterdam: Sense Publishers, 2011).
28. Valenzuela, *Subtractive Schooling*, 1999.

REFERENCES

Astrid, interview by Jesus A. Tirado, July 14, 2016, interview 1, transcript.
Astrid, interview by Jesus A. Tirado, August 21, 2016, interview 2, transcript.
Astrid, interview by Jesus A. Tirado, September 12, 2016, interview 3, transcript.
Biesta, G. J. J. 2011. *Learning democracy in school and society: Education, lifelong learning and the politics of citizenship*. Rotterdam: Sense Publishers.
Butler, J. 2016. *Frames of war: When is life grievable?* 2nd ed. Brooklyn, NY: Verso.

De Genova, N. P. 2002. Migrant "Illegality" and Deportability in Everyday Life. *Annual Review of Anthropology*, 31, 419–447. https://doi.org/10.1146/annurev.anthro.31.040402.085432

Delgado Bernal, D., & Alemán, E. 2017. *Transforming educational pathways for Chicana/o students: A critical race feminista praxis*. New York: Teachers College Press.

Gonzales, R. G. 2016. *Lives in limbo: Undocumented and coming of age in America*. Berkeley, CA: University of California Press.

Jaffee, A. T. 2016. Social studies pedagogy for Latino/a newcomer youth: Toward a theory of culturally and linguistically relevant citizenship education. *Theory & Research in Social Education*, 44(2), 147–183. https://doi.org/10.1080/00933104.2016.1171184

Jaggar, A. M. 2014. *Just methods: An interdisciplinary feminist reader*. Boulder, CO: Paradigm.

Kirkland, D. 2014. Why I study culture, and why it matters: Humanizing ethnographies in social science research. In Django Paris & Maisha T. Winn, *Humanizing research: Decolonizing qualitative inquiry with youth and communities* (pp. 179–200). Thousand Oaks, CA: Sage.

Levinson, M. 2012. *No citizen left behind*. Cambridge, MA: Harvard University Press.

Madison, D. S. 2011. *Critical ethnography: Method, ethics, and performance*, 2nd ed. Thousand Oaks, CA: Sage.

Maria, interview by Jesus A. Tirado, August 2, 2016, interview 1, transcript.

Maria, interview by Jesus A. Tirado, August 16, 2016, interview 2, transcript.

Maria, interview by Jesus A. Tirado, September 16, 2016, interview 3, transcript.

Menjívar, C., & Kanstroom, D. 2014. Introduction: Immigrant "illegality": Constructions and critiques. In Cecilia Menjívar and Daniel Kanstroom (eds.), *Constructing immigrant "illegality": Critiques, experiences, and responses* (pp. 1–36). New York: Cambridge University Press.

Motomura, H. 2014. *Immigration outside the law*. New York: Oxford University Press.

Muñoz, S. M. 2015. *Identity, social activism, and the pursuit of higher education: The journey stories of undocumented and unafraid community activists*. New York: Peter Lang.

Roulston, K. J. 2011. *Reflective interviewing: A guide to theory and practice*. Thousand Oaks, CA: Sage.

Salinas, C. 2009. Educating late arrival high school immigrant students: A call for a more democratic curriculum. *Multicultural Perspectives*, 8(1), 20–27. https://doi.org/10.1207/s15327892mcp0801_4

Salinas, C., Vickery, A. E., & Franquiz, M. 2016. Advancing border pedagogies: Understandings of citizenship through comparisons of home to school contexts. *The High School Journal*, 99(4), 322–336.

Solórzano, D. G., & Delgado Bernal, D. 2001. Examining transformational resistance through a critical race and Latcrit theory framework: Chicana and Chicano students in an urban context. *Urban Education*, 36(3), 308–342. doi:10.1177/0042085901363002

Solórzano, D. G., & Yosso, T. J. 2002. Critical race methodology: Counter-storytelling as an analytical framework for education research. *Qualitative Inquiry*, 8(1), 23–44. doi:10.1177/107780040200800103

Spradley, J. 1979. *The ethnographic interview*. New York: Holt, Rinehart and Winston.

Valenzuela, A. 1999. *Subtractive schooling: US-Mexican youth and the politics of caring*. Albany: State University of New York Press.

SIX
Radical Literacy

Building Curriculum on Mexican American Youths' Lived Experiences

Stacy Saathoff

The above epigraph serves as the inspiration behind this chapter. The present practice-oriented chapter explores using literature and writing within a critical pedagogical framework to allow students, Mexican American students specifically, to highlight their own voices and integrate their lived experiences into the language arts and social studies curriculum. Yosso explains that "traditional curricular discourses distort, omit, and stereotype Chicana/o, Latina/o, African American, Asian American/Asian Pacific Islander, and Native American experiences."[1] Therefore, youth of color being able to include their voices in the curriculum is of utmost importance.

This work is significant in two major ways. First, new perspectives are necessary for examining how and if the curriculum students are learning is relevant to their lived experiences. I define relevant by distinguishing whether or not students see themselves reflected in the curriculum's learning materials. This means intentionally examining to see if there is a reflection between the curriculum and students. Asking questions such as, Are the materials students exposed to authentic? Does the curriculum portray realistic daily experiences or is the material representative of stereotypes based on larger society's view of a particular group of people?

Gay[2] and Ladson-Billings[3] have constructed a solid foundation on which curriculum studies can build. As leading scholars in the field their work has been groundbreaking in regard to critically analyzing curriculum and proposing teaching practices that consider students' cultural backgrounds. Gay recommends culturally responsive pedagogy which uses the cultural orientations of students to teach students from diverse backgrounds who are not performing well in content areas. Ladson-Billings's work on culturally relevant pedagogy offers not only applications to practice but also theory that affirms cultural identities of students as they develop critical perspectives to challenge inequities in society. These two pedagogies offer an asset-based alternative that challenges the discourses of inferiority and deficit thinking often repeated in school settings.

Cammarota[4] observes how curriculum for youth of color is focused on standardized test preparation, remediation, and memorization of skills. Within this curriculum students are immersed in a "master script" that privileges Eurocentric ideologies, values, and practices in ways that reinforce white hegemony.[5] A disconnection exists between what students of color learn and how it applies directly to their lives. There is also a lack of students' own history and stories represented accurately in the curriculum.[6] In fact a form of deculturalization is "curriculum content that reflects [the] culture of [society's] dominant group."[7]

Viewing the experiences of Mexican Americans in the United States through a historical lens is the second way this discussion is significant. Mexicans, when compared to other Latinx communities, have the longest history in America and were a part of America long before the arrival of Europeans.[8] The education of Mexicans and Mexican Americans in the United States has been plagued by deficit discourses, racism, segregation, and Americanization programs.[9] Early 20th-century Anglo Americans faced two contradictory points of view.[10] First, Mexican labor was essential to the survival of farms which meant that children attending school would not be able to work in the fields. On the other hand, farmers and other public officials used education as a form of social control and wanted Mexican children to attend school so that they could be Americanized.[11] By educating Mexicans it was believed that they would leave the farms which depended on their cheap labor. Deculturalization of Mexican students was through Americanization. Spring states "similar to the Indians isolated in Indian Territory and boarding schools, the deculturalization program was designed to strip away Mexican values and culture and replace the use of Spanish with English."[12] Deficit discourses continue to affect Mexican and Mexican American students in the United States.

The curriculum design presented in this chapter provides students with an opportunity to read and interact with books that reflect the Mexican American experience as they develop their own autobiographical creative projects. Students are encouraged to create materials in the language of their choice (i.e., Spanish, English, or both), which adds another dimension to the social studies and language arts curriculum in middle or high school classrooms. The chapter is divided into three main sections. The first section highlights a sociocultural perspective on defining literacy and literacies. The theoretical frameworks of Critical Race Theory (CRT), intersectionality, and Freire's notion of dialogue are underscored in the second section to situate the curriculum's approach. The third and final section of the chapter describes the curriculum design.

DEFINING LITERACY AND LITERACIES

A definition of literacy that most people agree on is that literacy is "a set of basic reading and writing skills possessed by an individual."[13] Literacy is a set of these reading and writing skills; however, this understanding of literacy is narrow and does not speak to how larger society plays a role in literacy and one's worldview. This chapter assumes a sociocultural approach to literacy meaning that literacy events (reading, writing, speaking, and thinking) are situated within a sociocultural context.[14] Pérez states a sociocultural approach to literacy "seeks to understand how children interpret who they are in relation to others, and how children have learned to process, interpret, and encode their world."[15] Literacy inherently cannot be separated from the sociocultural context. Pérez further describes this view:

> All literacy users are members of a defined culture with a cultural identity, and the degree to which they engage in learning and or using literacy is a function of this cultural identity. Literacy cannot be considered to be content free or context free, for it is always used in service of or filtered through the culture.[16]

A sociocultural approach to understanding literacy further expands what is used to define literacy. For example, using the term literacies provides space to view different types of literacy such as financial literacy, school literacy, digital literacy, visual literacy, and so on. Each of these literacies requires different types of knowledge, skills, and abilities. I define school literacy as the skills needed to succeed in literacy events that take place within the school environment. These events may be timed reading passages, locating specific answers to respond to comprehension questions, and completing worksheets. School literacy is often viewed as a school subject and a learning tool.[17] Teachers, administrators, and school boards dictate what materials will be used, how, and the purposes of those materials. O'Brien declares, "By the time students reach adolescence, their experiences with reading materials and practices in school have taught them to dislike school literacy activities."[18] Within the school environment students also have other forms of literacy occurring through their social practices that students define within their own parameters.

Outside school settings students engage in other literacies which may include oral storytelling with family, translating important documents for parents, or writing poetry. In nonacademic contexts literacy events occur between students and their peers such as writing notes to each other,[19] sending text messages, and posting content on social media such as Facebook and Instagram—all are forms of literacy. In these instances students define the purpose of the literacy event and make the decisions regarding what materials will be used and how. The examples highlight how students in fact are knowledgeable and able to use a multitude of literacies in varying sociocultural settings during their everyday lives. Students are also able to move in and out of these literacies to serve the purpose of that particular event. An added element to understanding literacies is that bilingual youth have access to literacies in two languages both Spanish and English. Shifting the focus of literacy beyond mastering a set of skills highlights the multitude of literacies youth practice. Collins and Blot argue that "we must conceptualize literacy as *literacies*, that is, as embedded in a multiplicity of social practices, rather than as a monolithic technology or tradition."[20]

THEORETICAL UNDERPINNINGS

The theories that structure this chapter are Critical Race Theory (CRT), intersectionality, and Paulo Freire's concept of dialogue, which is a component within critical pedagogy. This section outlines these areas and is revisited after explaining the curriculum design to demonstrate how the theories and curriculum are connected. First, I provide a brief outline of CRT and the specific aspects that this curriculum design addresses. Second, I explore intersectionality and how it serves as a foundation for interpreting and making sense of social identities. Lastly, the notion of dialogue, a component of critical pedagogy, is discussed. Together these frameworks provide a basis for the curriculum design that follows.

Critical Race Theory—A Brief Overview

Broadly speaking Critical Race Theory (CRT), as defined by Yosso, is "a framework that can be used to theorize, examine, and challenge the ways race and racism implicitly and explicitly impact on social structures, practices and discourses."[21] The theoretical basis of CRT lies in internal colonialism, feminism, cultural nationalism, and Marxism. The CRT movement began with the early work of legal scholars Derrick Bell and Alan Freeman. Scholars such as Richard Delgado, Charles Lawrence, Mari Matsuda, Patricia Williams, Kimberlé Crenshaw, and others built and expanded critical law studies of the 1970s and 1980s. CRT scholars were influenced by the continued civil rights struggles of the 1960s and used fundamental ideas from both the Chicano and Black Power movements of the time. Many lawyers, legal scholars, and activists recognized that the promises of civil rights had been left unfulfilled and sought new ways to understand the centrality of race itself in society.[22] CRT extends critical legal studies concepts and insights from feminism such as examining the relationships of power, patriarchy, and diverse forms of domination.[23] CRT is further guided by the work of European theorists such as Michel Foucault, Jacques and Antonio Gramsci, and important thinkers in the United States such as W.E.B. Du Bois, Sojourner Truth, and Frederick Douglass to name a few.

CRT rests on five assumptions: race, history, voice, interpretation, and praxis.[24] Although race is a social construction,[25] it is endemic in the United States and as such race is embedded in larger societal structures such as law, education, and housing, and it is present in intimate relationships such as marriage, for example.[26] Delgado and Stefancic highlight the social construction thesis and maintain that "race and races are products of social thought and relations."[27] These products are "not objective, inherent, or fixed, they correspond to no biological or genetic reality; rather, races are categories that society invents, manipulates, or retires when convenient."[28] In other words race has permeated every aspect of society. CRT recognizes the crucial role that historical practices, such as colonization and slavery, have played in the creation of ideologies about race and how these ideologies were and continue to be utilized to distinguish between the binary of people being either white or nonwhite.

CRT was introduced into the education field in 1995 by education scholar Gloria Ladson-Billings and social scientist William F. Tate who wrote a foundational piece in which they proposed that race in education was untheorized as a tool for comprehending and making sense of school inequity in the United States. It is beyond the scope of this chapter to provide a complete history of CRT and its underlying tenets. However, two aspects of CRT explored in this chapter are voice and intersectionality as both are embedded within the curriculum design described in this chapter.

Voice

CRT's tenet of voice is crucial in terms of voice being the foundation of this curriculum design. Voice is "the centrality of experiential knowledge."[29] Voice asks questions such as, Who is doing the speaking? The act of speaking and who does the speaking is a vital part of the theoretical framework. The voices of people of color in particular are validated and their experiences counter society's dominant narrative. Society's dominant narrative is not neutral; individuals and groups in power create and disperse the narratives as if they are Truth[30] and representative of all people's experiences. Through schooling most people are taught to accept these dominant narratives. Zamudio, Russell, Rios, and Bridgeman argue "schools represent one of the major modes for disseminating the truths or master narratives of the dominant group and in doing so often silence alternative truths or narratives."[31]

The curriculum design described in the upcoming pages is rooted in voice and the lived experiences of youth. I refer to their stories as counternarratives or counterstorytelling. Counterstorytelling centers the experiences of students of color and how they navigate the U.S. educational system.[32] Counterstorytelling allows youth to use their own words to describe their life experiences and experiential knowledge specifically on their social identities of gender, race, ethnicity, socioeconomic status, and language. Youth's voices speak of their experiences which are usually ignored, marginalized, or essentialized in the curriculum. Counterstorytelling in the curriculum provides students with a space to additionally challenge and question whose knowledge is regarded as valuable.[33]

Intersectionality

The importance of youth's overlapping social identities, such as language, citizenship status, race, gender, socioeconomic status, and ethnicity, provide a platform from which curriculum can be developed. The CRT framework recognizes intersectionality and how various social identities serve as sites of multiple oppressions in daily life. Intersectionality allows for an analysis of the complexities of human experiences.[34] Delgado and Stefancic assert intersectionality is "the examination of race, sex, class, national origin, and sexual orientation, and how their combination plays out in various settings."[35] For example, a student may be female, speak two languages, be a U.S.-born citizen, and identify as Mexican American. When examining identities, this particular student is not only female or a U.S-born citizen or bilingual. She identifies with all of these identities not just one. Intersectionality allows educators to acknowledge, support, and value students' multiple identities.

Intersectionality began with the work of a Black feminist group known as the Combahee River Collective who gathered in April 1977 and authored a statement calling for the need to theorize the multiple forms of oppression they faced and how to respond to this oppression.[36] They declared that an individual first develops a critical consciousness that they can use to characterize their personal shared experience. Intersectionality was expanded further by a collection of essays and poems written by feminists of color. The anthology entitled *This Bridge Called My Back: Writings by Radical Women of Color*, first published in 1981, explores the conversation of understanding multifaceted identities and provides insight into the lived experiences of women of color in the United States—a living testimony and coming into consciousness. The anthology serves as a testament of writing as liberation, healing, and solidarity among women of color around the world.

Legal scholar Kimberlé Crenshaw is credited with bringing intersectionality into the larger academic discourse.[37] She examines the use of how a single-axis framework is implemented in the analysis of Black women's experiences. Crenshaw notes how discrimination cases in the United States focus on either race or sex as separate issues but not how race and sex interact in Black women's experiences. Gender discrimination cases, for example, erase Black women's experiences because the focus is on white women's experiences and is framed within their experiences. Within this emphasis white privilege is seen as inherent and there is a normalization of the white race. Crenshaw argues "yet often they [Black women] experience double-discrimination—the combined effects of practices which discriminate on the basis of race, and on the basis of sex."[38]

The notions of double-discrimination and multiple identities lead to an ability to view life through different lenses at the point of intersectionality. Du Bois's notion of double consciousness also helps to situate the concept of intersectionality and partly provides a historical understanding of the origins of intersectionality.[39] Du Bois was a scholar, historian, sociologist, and activist who was and is still considered one of the leading figures in the struggle for Civil Rights during the first half of the twentieth century. He provided insight into the Black experience and dilemmas facing African Americans. Du Bois was first in conceptualizing and writing about double consciousness. Double consciousness is the idea of being able to see oneself through one's own lens and at the same time being able to see oneself as society does. Du Bois eloquently stated:

> It is a peculiar sensation, this double-consciousness, this sense of always looking at one's self through the eyes of others, of measuring one's soul by the tape of a world that looks on in amused contempt and pity. One ever feels his two-ness,—an American, a Negro; two souls, two thoughts, two unreconciled strivings; two warring ideals in one dark body, whose dogged strength alone keeps it from being torn asunder.[40]

This notion of double consciousness applies to other communities of color, such as Mexican American youth in this case. An undercurrent of Gloria Anzaldúa's work is double consciousness and looking at oneself through multiple lenses. She speaks of these two worlds—Anglo and Mexican—in which there is constant negotiation and a dichotomy that does not fully embrace one's complex identities.[41] Anzaldúa expanded the notion further from which a *mestiza consciousness* can emerge, creating a new space, allowing for contradictions, encompassing dualities, and generating new ways of thinking and being in the world.

When applied to curriculum, Mexican American students face two worlds that they are constantly navigating and often times these worlds are contradictory. Latinx parents hold family values such as bilingualism (i.e., using both Spanish and English), collectivity, and interdependence. Yet within a school setting independence, promptness, and individualism are held in high regard,[42] and instruction in English furthers the Eurocentric view of education. Thus, cultural values of Mexican and Mexican American students may be in stark contrast to the values that are more respected in a school setting where importance is placed on competition and individualism instead of collectivity and community. Vázquez García, García Coll, Erkut, Alarcón, & Tropp note that the largest contrast between white and Latinx culture is the concept of individualism versus collectivism.[43] While individualism is more focused on individuals achieving personal goals and being separate from a group, collectivism is centered on the well-being of the group as a whole.

Dialogue

Dialogue is an aspect within a larger pedagogical approach known as critical pedagogy. Critical pedagogy comes from the scholarship of Brazilian educator Paulo Freire. Freire's most prominent work is *Pedagogy of the Oppressed* published in 1970 which details the main components of critical pedagogy. In his literacy programs with adult peasants he encouraged learners to read beyond the word, meaning beyond what is merely written on a page. In this case, learners began to develop a critical consciousness which allowed them to build a new awareness about the society in which the learners lived. This connects with the sociocultural approach to literacy described earlier in which reading, writing, speaking, and thinking events are situated within larger sociocultural contexts.

Critical pedagogy acts against traditional teaching methods which Freire referred to as a banking education model. A banking model assumes students to be passive objects that come into the classroom with little to no knowledge. The teacher's role is to fill students up with knowledge. Students are later tested on this knowledge they absorbed and then discard it.[44] According to Freire, the banking model is not true education because it lacks dialogue. Teachers *name* the world for their students instead of students *naming* the world for themselves, which is a focal point of critical pedagogy.

In contrast, Freire proposed a problem-solving model to education. This model encourages students to ask questions or problem-pose issues that are relevant to their lives and communities, which allows students to take action. Students are provided a space to develop their sense of self and analyze the world around them. One of the main components of critical pedagogy is dialogue which consists of both action and reflection. Freire believed dialogue was "an act of creation."[45] In this classroom space all voices have value and no one speaks over another; speaking is a right of everyone. hooks (2010) asserts that "genuine conversation is about the sharing of power and knowledge; it is fundamentally a cooperative enterprise."[46]

In critical pedagogy students are treated as humans and not merely as objects absorbing information where the act of teaching is one-directional. Instead students are viewed as coming to the classroom with experiences and knowledge. Teachers recognize that students are "holders and creators of knowledge."[47] Students' experiences and histories are acknowledged and validated in the classroom as places to be used in order to begin and expand on learning opportunities. Students and their families are seen as possessing resources which González, Moll, and Amanti term *funds of knowledge*.[48] A classroom space that further recognizes humanity creates an opportunity for trust to grow through dialogue. Darder addresses the notion of humanizing education when she states:

> Accordingly, a humanizing vision of pedagogy nurtures critical consciousness and social agency, in ways that move students away from instrumentalized forms of learning and replaces these with pedagogical activities that ignite both their passion for learning and their creative engagement with the world around them.[49]

By viewing students on a human level, reciprocal relationships between students and their teachers are developed. For Mexican American youth, these reciprocal relationships with their teachers are significant to their education. Valenzuela confirms the importance of these relationships through her study of Mexican and Mexican American high school students in Houston, Texas.[50] Teachers conformed to an *aesthetic* type of caring which is more focused on academic success and achievement, whereas as students prefer an *authentic* form of caring which is concerned with reciprocal and respectful relationships built on mutual trust. Given the mismatch in definitions of what constitutes caring, Valenzuela declares that teachers view "students as not sufficiently *caring about* school, while students see teachers as not sufficiently *caring for* them."[51]

Critical pedagogy also offers individuals a way to develop a sense of community as teachers and students work together in partnership.[52] Critical pedagogy provides us with a connection to others, and hooks highlights that "it [critical pedagogy] teaches us how to create community."[53] Critical pedagogy furthers this sense of community as students and teachers dialogue and learn together while also developing power and solidarity in community. The current focus on high-stakes testing emphasizes the individual over what students can accomplish collectively. Critical pedagogy allows for students to make deep human connections with their peers and teachers based on mutual trust and respect.

CURRICULUM DESIGN

Students lived experiences and the elements of voice, intersectionality, and dialogue are the roots of this curriculum design. The curriculum contains four main components: reading, journaling, meeting in dialogue groups, and completing autobiographical creative projects. This curriculum design can be used with both middle and high school students and be modified to meet students' needs. The content areas this student-centered curriculum design addresses are language arts and social studies. The role of the instructor in this design is to act as a facilitator and guide.

There are two overall objectives for this unit. The first objective involves students exploring their identities through materials reflecting their own life experiences and demonstrating this knowledge through an autobiographical creative project. Students use their own voices to tell their counternarratives and select the best medium through which to share their stories is the second objective. There is a great deal of flexibility to allow for the curriculum design to be adapted or modified to meet students' specific needs. For example, a student may need practice with how to provide evidence when making a statement. The student writes that her cultural identity has always been an important part of her life. At this point her peers and instructor prompt her to tell a story that demonstrates how cultural identity plays a role in her life. Using this prompt, she writes a brief story about how her grandmother often uses natural remedies when anyone in the family is sick. This experience has always been prominent in the student's mind because she wondered why her grandmother used natural remedies instead of medicines that could be easily purchased at a pharmacy. With this information she interviews her grandmother to find out that through generations the use of natural remedies has always been a part of her family's daily cultural practices. The student then includes this evidence using quotes from the interview to support her statement in the story she writes. In this example the curriculum reflects her identity and addresses various elements of writing, such as providing evidence when making a claim.

Exploring Identities: An Introduction to the Curriculum

The introduction to the unit and first component is students reading the same text and analyzing a poem entitled "Yo Soy Joaquín" by Chicano Civil Rights Movement activist Rodolfo "Corky" Gonzales.[54] The poem is available in both Spanish and English which allows students to access the material in both languages and select the language that best meets their needs. In this poem Gonzales expresses a great amount of pride in Mexican and Mexican American culture and history. The poem is descriptive, beautifully written, and powerful. The fact that it was written during the time of the Chicano Civil Rights Movement invites students to explore that particular time in the United States during the 1960s. The first activity has students reflecting in writing to two of the following four questions:

1. What line or lines from Rodolfo Gonzales's poem most resonated with you? Why?
2. If you were to interview Rodolfo Gonzales about his poem, what are five questions you would ask him?
3. Select a passage from the poem and visualize it. Draw what that passage looks like to you. Explain in writing what your picture captures.
4. Which of your identities (gender, race, ethnicity, culture, etc.) is most important to you and why? Did you see this idea expressed in the poem?

Students' responses to these questions are to provide a foundation for discussion. First, students discuss the responses in dialogue groups of three to four students. Each dialogue group writes a five- to seven-sentence summary based on the small group discussion. The students' written summaries are then used to prompt further dialogue as the whole class discusses the poem.

A second activity for students is creating a graffiti board on a large sheet of paper or on a whiteboard. In this activity students include quotes, sketches, images, thoughts, and pictures inspired by the poem. Students can complete this activity while reading or after reading. The graffiti board provides a foundation for later discussion either in a small group or large group setting. Exploring specific aspects of the poem is the third activity for students. Either individually, in partners, or small groups, students choose to research the cultural, historical, social, or political context of the poem. Students then present to the rest of the class about the aspect they explored.

Reading and Journaling

The second component of the curriculum design is students reading one of three book selections and journaling on six themes: resiliency, language, ethnicity, hope, race, and immigration. Students have a choice between three books: *I Am Not Your Perfect Mexican Daughter*,[55] *Two Badges: The Lives of Mona Ruiz*,[56] and *A Place to Stand*.[57] *I Am Not Your Perfect Mexican Daughter* is a work of fiction based on the life of a Mexican American teenage girl with whose experiences students may be able to identify. *Two Badges: The Lives of Mona Ruiz* and *A Place to Stand* are both autobiographical. The three books are written by Mexican American authors, and each book speaks to the larger overarching theme of identity.

I Am Not Your Perfect Mexican Daughter by Erika L. Sánchez is the story of a fifteen-year-old young woman named Julia who lives in Chicago,

Illinois, with her mother and father. Julia's sister, Olga, has recently passed, which leads to Julia's journey of discovering who her sister really was. Julia's family saw Olga as the perfect daughter who stayed at home helping her family while Julia wanted more freedom for herself. Julia wants to pursue a higher education and attend college in New York City. Her relationship with her mother is difficult, and Julia is often compared to Olga. Julia struggles with depression and at one point in the novel attempts to commit suicide. As a result, Julia's mother sends her to Mexico to spend time with her grandmother Mamá Jacinta. The novel addresses complex issues that affect Julia's life such as language, immigration, race, socioeconomic status, and dealing with mental illness as a young person.

In *Two Badges: The Lives of Mona Ruiz* Mona becomes a member of the Troopers gang during high school in Santa Ana, California. Mona's autobiography chronicles the struggles and violence she faced as a gang member. Later she becomes a police officer, which was always her dream, protecting the same community in which she was a gang member. *A Place to Stand* is Jimmy Santiago Baca's memoir about how he was in and out of prison. Baca has since been released but discusses how while serving his time in prison he taught himself to read and began writing poetry, which he is still passionate about to this day. These memoirs and novel address various themes surrounding identity such as race and ethnicity, but resiliency and hope seem to be the most prevailing themes.

Students keep a journal as they read one of the selected books. Each day students journal on three of the following six themes that play a role in shaping youth's identities and perspectives: resiliency, language, ethnicity, hope, race, and immigration. Students provide an example from the book that highlights the given theme and then write about how they have seen this particular theme personally play out in their own lives. For example, while reading *I Am Not Your Perfect Mexican Daughter* a student selects to journal about the themes of immigration, ethnicity, and language. Students provide an example from the text that underscores each of the themes they have selected. First, identifying the theme of immigration a student may write "[the border is] nothing but a giant wound, a big gash between the two countries. Why does it have to be like that? I don't understand. It's just some random, stupid line. How can anyone tell people where they can and can't go?"[58] The student provides a personal example of how she relates to the theme and writes about the negative stories she hears through the media about immigrants in the United States.

Continuing to use *I Am Not Your Perfect Mexican Daughter*, the second theme the student explores is ethnicity. Here the student provides the following passage from the text found on page 174 which is a conversation between the main character, Julia, and Connor, who later becomes a close friend. Connor asks Julia, "But where are you *from* from?" Julia responds by saying, "I'm *from* Chicago. I just told you." Connor then states, "No what I mean is . . . Forget it." In this example, Connor assumes that because Julia looks Mexican American she must not be from the United States. The student, relating the theme to her life, writes a short story about a personal example about when she was asked the same question by someone she had just met.

Third, the theme of language appears in the text on page 71 when Julia meets Ramiro in Mexico while she is visiting Mamá Jacinta. The monologue in Julia's head states, "He only speaks Spanish, which makes me nervous. I speak it fine, of course, but I sound ten times smarter in English. My vocabulary is just not as extensive, and sometimes I get stuck. I hope he doesn't think I'm dumb, because I'm not." This example demonstrates how Julia questions her language abilities and admits to being nervous about speaking Spanish. In response to this theme, a student writes about how she feels when visiting her extended family in Mexico, who only speak Spanish.

Dialogue Groups

The third component of the curriculum design is students meeting weekly in their dialogue groups. Students meet with other students in the class who are reading the same book. Depending on the number of students reading each book, there may be more than one group per book. The dialogue groups are small with three to four students in each. The small number of students in the dialogue groups allows for everyone to share and contribute to the discussion. Students decide how they want to structure the time with their groups. The format for the dialogue groups includes time for each member to share examples from their journals and discuss the book. At the end of each group session, the groups share the main highlights from their dialogue groups with the rest of the class.

Autobiographical Creative Projects

The students' autobiographical creative projects are the final and culminating experience of the curriculum. Students select two themes out of the six mentioned above: resiliency, language, ethnicity, hope, race, and immigration that most resonate with them and use those themes to assist in developing their autobiographical stories through a medium and language(s) of their choice. A few possible options for students include poetry, spoken word, art, photo journals, music, and digital stories. The students' options are endless in the way they wish to present their story. An example of an autobiographical creative project is a student who, inspired by the themes of immigration and hope, decides to draw a map that reflects the migration experience of her family from Mexico to the

United States. She interviewed several family members to understand their stories and as a result also learned about history and the role it played in her family emigrating from Mexico. Along with the student's map she writes a story about her family and their journey to where they are today. In her counternarrative she also includes her perspectives on what it is like to be a Mexican American young person in the United States and the hopes she holds for the future.

When students complete their creative projects, they present to classmates, family, and community members in a format called an Encuentro.[59] An Encuentro, grounded in Freire's pedagogy, acknowledges and appreciates families focusing on their assets instead of deficits which are often portrayed within the larger educational system. Cammarota & Romero affirm that Encuentros can become "spaces for funds of knowledge that rais[e] consciousness around injustices in Latina/o education,"[60] further leading to transformation among students and families. Encuentros provide a community learning environment and are an invitation to dialogue between families and their children.

CONNECTION TO THEORY

The three theoretical frameworks of voice, intersectionality, and dialogue mentioned in the beginning of this chapter are addressed in the curriculum design. First, CRT's tenant of voice is present in the autobiographical creative projects students develop. This project is a counterstory as students give voice to their experiential knowledge and name their reality.[61] Students' stories offer them the opportunity to speak against how they are viewed by larger society. Storytelling has the power to invoke memory and healing. Ladson-Billings asserts "historically, storytelling has been a kind of medicine to heal the wounds of pain caused by racial oppression."[62] Underscoring voice prompts students to tell about their own lived experiences. Allowing students to reflect on their own experiences illustrates the value of their voices and the power of their counter-narratives.

Second, intersectionality is enacted in the reading and creating of the autobiographical creative projects. Students discover how intersectionality is present in their own lives through making personal connections with the themes and exploring their social identities. Collins and Bilge describe how intersectionality can be an analytic tool for anyone seeking to create a new frame that allows them to acknowledge all of the complexities of their identities and the discrimination they face as a result of their social identities.[63] Intersectionality as a tool connects theory to practice and does so in a way that is understandable to youth as a helpful framework to interpret their lived experiences and social identities, which discredits the idea that theory is only available to academics or people in more privileged positions. Theory can in fact be used as an act of healing.[64] Theory for students can provide a way of healing and can be used as a way to comprehend and make sense of their experiences.

Third, dialogue is exhibited through small group and large group discussions, and the Encuentros. Revisiting Freire dialogue is a way to *name* and read one's world using their own experiences and perspectives.[65] In discussing Freire's work, Gee defines dialogue as "both face-to-face conversational interaction and conversation-like interaction at a distance through reflection on what one has heard or read in which diverse viewpoints and perspectives are juxtaposed is, at several levels, essential for learning to 'read the world' and to read the 'word.'"[66] The opportunities and choices students are provided in this curriculum design invite them to talk and share with each other.

As the epigraph at the beginning of the chapter suggests, through this critical pedagogical approach to curriculum, students are "us[ing] their own reality as a basis of literacy."[67] Students are using their life experiences to inform their learning and making deep connections with material that reflects their realities. Examining new ways to define literacy and literacies showcases how it goes beyond the act of reading and writing. Students realize that they in fact have different types of literacies that they apply to a multitude of social situations and contexts. Given the current sociopolitical context, it is challenging to determine what and whose literacies will be acknowledged and used in the future as the foundation for developing engaging curriculum reflective of all youth's experiences.

NOTES

1. Tara J. Yosso, "Toward a Critical Race Curriculum," *Equity & Excellence in Education* 35, no. 2 (2002): 93.
2. Geneva Gay, *Culturally Responsive Teaching: Theory, Research, and Practice,* 2nd ed. (New York: Teachers College Press, 2010).
3. Gloria Ladson-Billings, "Toward a Theory of Culturally Relevant Pedagogy," *American Educational Research Journal* 32, no.3 (1995): 465–491.
4. Julio Cammarota, "A Social Justice Approach to Achievement: Guiding Latina/o students toward Educational Attainment with a Challenging, Socially Relevant Curriculum," *Equity & Excellence in Education* 40 (2007): 87–96.
5. Ellen E. Swartz, "Emancipatory Narratives: Rewriting the Master Script in the School Curriculum," *The Journal of Negro Education* 61, no. 3 (1992): 341–355.
6. Ibid.
7. Joel Spring, *Deculturalization and the Struggle for Equality: A Brief History of the Education of Dominated Cultures in the United States,* 5th ed. (New York: McGraw-Hill, 2007), 106.
8. Juan Gonzalez, *Harvest of an Empire: A History of Latinos in America* (New York: Penguin Books, 2011); Rudy Hernández, Marcelo Siles, and Refugio Rochín, "Latino Youth: Converting Challenges to Opportunities," in *Making Invisible Latino Adolescents Visible: A Critical Approach,* ed. Martha Montero-Sieburth and Francisco A. Villarruel, 1–28. New York: Falmer Press, 2000.

9. See Gilbert G. González, *Chicano Education in the Era of Segregation* (Denton: University of North Texas Press, 1990); Gilbert G. González, "Culture, Language, and the Americanization of Mexican Children," in *Latinos and Education: A Critical Reader*, ed. Antonia Darder, Rodolfo D. Torres, and Henry Gutiérrez, 158–173 (New York: Routledge, 1997), 158–173; Richard R. Valencia, *Dismantling Contemporary Deficit Thinking: Educational Thought and Practice* (New York: Routledge, 2010); Richard R. Valencia, ed., *Chicano School Failure and Success: Past, Present, and Future*, 3rd ed. (New York: Routledge, 2011).

10. Spring, *Deculturalization and the Struggle for Equality*.

11. Ibid.

12. Ibid., 96.

13. Robert P. Yagelski, *Literacy Matters: Writing and Reading the Social Self* (New York: Teachers College Press, 2000), 8.

14. James Paul Gee, "Socio-cultural approaches to literacy (literacies)," *Annual Review of Applied Linguistics* 12 (1992): 31–48; James Paul Gee, *Sociolinguistics and Literacies: Ideology in Discourses*, 4th ed. (New York: Routledge, 2012); Shirley Brice Heath, *Ways with Words: Language, Life, and Work in Communities and Classrooms* (New York: Cambridge University Press, 1983); Brian V. Street, *Literacy in Theory and Practice* (Cambridge, UK: Cambridge University Press, 1984).

15. Bertha Pérez, "Literacy, Diversity, and Programmatic Responses," in *Sociocultural Contexts of Language and Literacy*, 2nd ed., ed. Bertha Pérez, Teresa L. McCarty, Lucille J. Watahomigie, et al. (New York: Lawrence Erlbaum Associates, Inc., 2004), 4.

16. Ibid., 5.

17. David G. O'Brien, "Multiple Literacies in a High School Program for 'At-Risk' Adolescents," In *Reconceptualizing the Literacies in Adolescents' Lives*, ed. Donna E. Alvermann, Kathleen A. Hinchman, David W. Moore, et al. (Mahwah, NJ: Lawrence Erlbaum Associates, Inc., 1998), 27–49.

18. Ibid., 29.

19. David G. O'Brien, "Multiple Literacies in a High School Program for 'At-Risk' Adolescents," In *Reconceptualizing the Literacies in Adolescents' Lives*, ed. Donna E. Alvermann, Kathleen A. Hinchman, David W. Moore, et al. (Mahwah, NJ: Lawrence Erlbaum Associates, Inc., 1998), 27–49.

20. James Collins and Richard K. Blot, *Literacy and Literacies: Texts, Power, and Identity* (Cambridge, UK: Cambridge University Press, 2003), 60.

21. Tara J. Yosso, "Whose Culture Has Capital? A Critical Race Theory Discussion of Community Cultural Wealth," *Race Ethnicity and Education* 8, no. 1 (2005): 70.

22. Richard Delgado and Jean Stefancic, *Critical Race Theory: An Introduction*, 2nd ed. (New York: New York University Press, 2012).

23. Ibid.

24. Ibid.; Margaret M. Zamudio, Christopher Russell, Francisco A. Rios, and Jacquelyn L. Bridgeman, *Critical Race Theory Matters: Education and Ideology* (New York: Routledge, 2011).

25. Michael Omi and Howard Winant, *Racial Formation in the United States*, 3rd ed. (New York: Routledge, 2015).

26. Zamudio et al., *Critical Race Theory Matters*.

27. Delgado and Stefancic, *Critical Race Theory*, 8.

28. Ibid.

29. Tara J. Yosso, *Critical Race Counterstories along the Chicana/Chicano Pipeline* (New York: Routledge, 2006), 7.

30. Zamudio et al., *Critical Race Theory Matters*.

31. Ibid., 5.

32. Daniel Solórzano and Tara J. Yosso, "Critical Race Methodology: Counter-storytelling as an Analytical Framework for Educational Research," in David G. O'Brien, "Multiple Literacies in a High School Program for 'At-Risk' Adolescents," in *Foundations of Critical Race Theory in Education*, ed. Edward Taylor, David Gillborn, and Gloria Ladson-Billings (New York: Routledge, 2009), 131–147.

33. Yosso, "Toward a Critical Race Curriculum," 93–107.
34. Patricia Hill Collins and Sirma Bilge, *Key Concepts: Intersectionality* (Malden, MA: Polity Press Press, 2016).
35. Delgado and Stefancic, *Critical Race Theory*, 57.
36. Combahee River Collective, "A Black Feminist Statement," in *This Bridge Called My Back: Writings by Radical Women of Color*, 4th ed. ed. Cherríe Moraga and Gloria Anzaldúa (Albany: State University of New York Press, 2015), 200–218.
37. Kimberlé Crenshaw, "Demarginalizing the Intersection of Race and Sex: A Black Feminist Critique of Antidiscrimination Doctrine, Feminist Theory and Antiracist Politics," *University of Chicago Legal Forum* (1989): 139–167.
38. Ibid., 149.
39. W.E.B. Du Bois, (1903) 2003, *The Souls of Black Folk* (New York: Barnes & Noble, Inc.).
40. Ibid., 9.
41. Gloria Anzaldúa, (1987) 2007, *Borderlands/La Frontera: The New Mestiza*, 3rd ed. (San Francisco: Aunt Lute Books).
42. Concha Delgado-Gaitan, *Involving Latino Families in Schools: Raising Student Achievement through Home-School Partnerships* (Thousand Oaks, CA: Corwin Press, 2004).
43. Heidie A. Vásquez García, Cynthia García Coll, Samru Erkut, Odette Alarcón, and Linda R. Tropp, "Family Values of Latino Adolescents," in *Making Invisible Latino Adolescents Visible: A Critical Approach to Latino Diversity*, ed. Martha Montero-Sieburth and Francisco A. Villarruel (New York: Falmer Press, 2000), 239–264.
44. bell hooks, *Teaching Critical Thinking: Practical Wisdom* (New York: Routledge, 2010).
45. Paulo Freire, *Pedagogy of the Oppressed* (New York: Continuum, 1970), 89.
46. hooks, *Teaching Critical Thinking*, 45.
47. Dolores Delgado Bernal, "Critical Race Theory, Latino Critical Theory, and Critical Raced-Gendered Epistemologies: Recognizing Students of Color as Holders and Creators of Knowledge," *Qualitative Inquiry* 8, no. 1 (2002): 105–126.
48. Norma González, Luis C. Moll, and Cathy Amanti, *Funds of Knowledge: Theorizing Practices in Households, Communities, and Classrooms*, ed. Norma González, Luis C. Moll, and Cathy Amanti (New York: Routledge, 2005).
49. Antonia Darder, *Freire and Education* (New York: Routledge, 2015), 64.
50. Angela Valenzuela, *Subtractive Schooling: U.S.-Mexican Youth and the Politics of Caring* (New York: State University of New York Press, 1999).
51. Ibid., 61.
52. bell hooks, *Teaching Community: A Pedagogy of Hope* (New York: Routledge, 2003).
53. Ibid., xv.
54. Rodolfo Gonzales, *I Am Joaquín/Yo Soy Joaquín* (New York: Bantam Books, Inc., 1972).
55. Erika L. Sánchez, *I Am Not Your Perfect Mexican Daughter* (New York: Alfred A. Knopf, 2017).
56. Mona Ruiz, *Two Badges: The Lives of Mona Ruiz* (Houston, TX: Arte Público Press, 2005).
57. Jimmy Santiago Baca, *A Place to Stand* (New York: Grove Press, 2001).
58. Sánchez, *I Am Not Your Perfect Mexican Daughter*, 280.
59. Julio Cammarota and Augustine Romero, "Encuentros with Families and Students: Cultivating Funds of Knowledge through Dialogue," in *Raza Studies: The Public Option for Educational Revolution*, ed. Julio Cammarota and Augustine Romero (Tucson: The University of Arizona Press, 2014), 122–134.
60. Ibid., 123.
61. Richard Delgado, "When a Story Is Just a Story: Does Voice Really Matter?" *Virginia Law Review*, 76 (1990): 95–111.

62. Gloria Ladson-Billings, "Just What Is Critical Race Theory and What's It Doing in a *Nice* Field like Education?" In *Foundations of Critical Race Theory in Education*, ed. Edward Taylor, David Gillborn, and Gloria Ladson-Billings (New York: Routledge, 2009), 24.
63. Collins and Bilge, *Key Concepts*.
64. bell hooks, *Teaching to Transgress: Education as the Practice of Freedom* (New York: Routledge, 1994).
65. Freire, *Pedagogy of the Oppressed*.
66. Gee, *Sociolinguistics and Literacies*, 62.
67. Paulo Freire and Donaldo Macedo, *Literacy: Reading the Word and the World* (Westport, CT: Bergin & Garvey, 1987), 151.

BIBLIOGRAPHY

Anzaldúa, G. (1987) 2007. *Borderlands/La Frontera: The new Mestiza*, 3rd ed. San Francisco: Aunt Lute Books.
Baca, J. S. 2001. *A place to stand*. New York: Grove Press.
Cammarota, J. 2007. A social justice approach to achievement: Guiding Latina/o students toward educational attainment with a challenging, socially relevant curriculum. *Equity & Excellence in Education*, 40, 87–96.
Cammarota, J., & Romero, A. 2014. Encuentros with families and students: Cultivating funds of knowledge through dialogue. In Julio Cammarota & Augustine Romero (eds.), *Raza studies: The public option for educational revolution* (pp. 122–134). Tucson: The University of Arizona Press.
Collins, J., & Blot, R. K. 2003. *Literacy and literacies: Texts, power, and identity*. Cambridge, UK: Cambridge University Press.
Collins, P. H., & Bilge, S. 2016. *Key concepts: Intersectionality*. Malden, MA: Polity Press.
Combahee River Collective. 2015. A black feminist statement. In Cherríe Moraga & Gloria Anzaldúa (eds.), *This bridge called my back: Writings by radical women of color* (pp. 200–218). Albany: State University of New York Press.
Crenshaw, K. 1989. Demarginalizing the intersection of race and sex: A black feminist critique of antidiscrimination doctrine, feminist theory and antiracist politics. *University of Chicago Legal Forum*, 139–167.
Darder, A. 2015. *Freire and education*. New York: Routledge.
Delgado, R. 1990. When a story is just a story: Does voice really matter?" *Virginia Law Review*, 76, 95–111.
Delgado, R., & Stefancic, J. 2012. *Critical race theory: An introduction*, 2nd ed. New York: New York University Press.
Delgado Bernal, D. 2002. Critical race theory, Latino critical theory, and critical raced-gendered epistemologies: Recognizing students of color as holders and creators of knowledge. *Qualitative Inquiry*, 8(1), 105–126.
Delgado-Gaitan, C. 2004. *Involving Latino families in schools: Raising student achievement through home-school partnerships*. Thousand Oaks, CA: Corwin Press.
Du Bois, W. E. B. (1903) 2003. *The souls of black folk*. New York: Barnes & Noble, Inc.
Freire, P. 1970. *Pedagogy of the oppressed*. New York: Continuum.
Freire, P., & Macedo, D. 1987. *Literacy: Reading the word and the world*. Westport, CT: Bergin & Garvey.
Gay, G. 2010. *Culturally responsive teaching: Theory, research, and practice*, 2nd ed. New York: Teachers College Press.
Gee, J. P. 1992. Socio-cultural approaches to literacy (literacies). *Annual Review of Applied Linguistics*, 12, 31–48.
———. 2012. *Sociolinguistics and literacies: Ideology in discourses*, 4th ed. New York: Routledge.
González, G. G. 1990. *Chicano education in the era of segregation*. Denton: University of North Texas Press.

———. 1997. Culture, language, and the Americanization of Mexican children. In Antonia Darder, Rodolfo D. Torres, & Henry Gutiérrez, *Latinos and education: A critical reader* (pp. 158–173). New York: Routledge.
Gonzalez, J. 2011. *Harvest of an empire*. New York: Penguin Books.
González, N., Moll, L. C., & Amanti, C. (eds.). 2005. *Funds of knowledge: Theorizing practices in households, communities, and classrooms*. New York: Routledge.
Gonzales, R. 1972. *I am Joaquín/Yo soy Joaquín*. New York: Bantam Books, Inc.
Heath, S. B. 1983. *Ways with words: Language, life, and work in communities and classrooms*. New York: Cambridge University Press.
Hernández, R., Siles, M., & Rochín, R. I. 2000. Latino youth: Converting challenges to opportunities. In Martha Montero-Sieburth & Francisco A. Villarruel (eds.), *Making invisible Latino adolescents visible: A critical approach* (pp. 1–28). New York: Falmer Press.
hooks, b. 1994. *Teaching to transgress: Education as the practice of freedom*. New York: Routledge.
———. 2003. *Teaching community: A pedagogy of hope*. New York: Routledge.
———. 2010. *Teaching critical thinking: Practical wisdom*. New York: Routledge.
Ladson-Billings, G. 1995. Toward a theory of culturally relevant pedagogy. *American Educational Research Journal, 32*(3), 465–491.
———. 2009. Just what is critical race theory and what's it doing in a *nice* field like education? In Edward Taylor, David Gillborn, & Gloria Ladson-Billings (eds.), *Foundations of Critical Race Theory in Education* (pp. 17–36). New York: Routledge.
Ladson-Billings, G., & Tate, W. F. 1995. Toward a critical race theory of education. *Teachers College Record, 97*(1), 47–68.
Moraga, C., & Anzaldúa, G. 2015. *This bridge called my back: Writings by radical women of color*, 4th ed. Albany: State University of New York Press.
O'Brien, D. G. 1998. Multiple literacies in a high school program for "at-risk" adolescents. In Donna E. Alvermann, Kathleen A. Hinchman, David W. Moore, et al. (eds.), *Reconceptualizing the literacies in adolescents' lives* (pp. 27–49). Mahwah, NJ: Lawrence Erlbaum Associates, Inc.
Omi, M., & Winant, H. 2015. *Racial formation in the United States*, 3rd ed. New York: Routledge.
Pérez, B. 2004. Literacy, diversity, and programmatic responses. In Bertha Pérez, Teresa L. McCarty, Lucille J. Watahomigie, et al. (eds.), *Sociocultural contexts of language and literacy*, 2nd ed. (pp. 3–24). New York: Lawrence Erlbaum Associates, Inc.
Ruiz, M. 2005. *Two badges: The lives of Mona Ruiz*. Houston, TX: Arte Público Press.
Sánchez, E. L. 2017. *I am not your perfect Mexican daughter*. New York: Alfred A. Knopf.
Solórzano, D. G., & Yosso, T. J. 2009. Critical race methodology: Counter-storytelling as an analytical framework for educational research. In Edward Taylor, David Gillborn, and Gloria Ladson-Billings (eds.), *Foundations of critical race theory in education* (pp. 131–147). New York: Routledge.
Spring, J. 2007. *Deculturalization and the struggle for equality: A brief history of the education of dominated cultures in the United States,* 5th ed. New York: McGraw-Hill.
Street, B. V. 1984. *Literacy in theory and practice*. Cambridge, UK: Cambridge University Press.
Swartz, E. E. 1992. Emancipatory narratives: Rewriting the master script in the school curriculum. *The Journal of Negro Education, 61*(3), 341–355.
Valencia, R. R. 2010. *Dismantling contemporary deficit thinking: Educational thought and practice*. New York: Routledge.
———. 2011. *Chicano school failure and success: Past, present, and future*, 3rd ed. New York: Routledge.
Valenzuela, A. 1999. *Subtractive schooling: U.S.-Mexican youth and the politics of caring*. New York: State University of New York Press.
Vasquéz García, H. A., Coll, C. G., Erkut, S., Alarcón, O., & Tropp, L. R. 2000. Family values of Latino adolescents. In Martha Montero-Sieburth & Francisco A. Villarruel

(eds.), *Making invisible Latino adolescents visible: A critical approach to Latino diversity* (pp. 239–264). New York: Falmer Press.

Yagelski, R. P. 2000. *Literacy matters: Writing and reading the social self.* New York: Teachers College Press.

Yosso, T. J. 2002. Toward a critical race curriculum. *Equity & Excellence in Education,* 35(2), 93–107.

———. 2005. Whose culture has capital? A critical race theory discussion of community cultural wealth. *Race Ethnicity and Education,* 8(1), 69–91.

———. 2006. *Critical race counterstories along the Chicana/Chicano pipeline.* New York: Routledge.

Zamudio, M. M., Russell, C., Rios, F. A., & Bridgeman, J. L. 2011. *Critical race theory matters: Education and ideology.* New York: Routledge.

Part III

Latinx Currere, Latinx Curriculum as Autobiographical

SEVEN

Conocimientos Míos

Engaging Possibilities for School Curriculum

Alba Isabel Lamar and Lynette DeAun Guzmán

SOMOS AMÉRICANAS: OUR POSITIONALITIES

I (Alba) am a 33-year-old Latinx woman and a third-year Ph.D. student of Curriculum, Instruction and Teacher Education. *Mi papi*, Líder Manuel, often taught my siblings and me how to read and write in our mother tongue by listening and talking about music with us. During dinner, after we considered our blessings and gave thanks to our *mami*, Elsa Luz, for the nourishment she provided, sometimes we would join hands and sing the intro *La Muralla* (1969) by Chilean group Quilapayún: *Para hacer esta muralla, tráiganme todas las manos los negros, sus manos negras los blancos, sus blancas manos. . . .* The walls we intended to create, as the song states, were made of people of all backgrounds holding hands. As we ate, we'd talk politics. Mami played the role of Language Arts teacher, offering us knowledge about the orthography, grammar, and phonology of Spanish. The folk music played in the background until profound, political pieces such as *Solo le Pido a Dios* (1978) by Argentine Leon Gieco came on. Then my father would ask us to listen for understanding. He would direct us to pay attention to and try to understand the harmonica, acoustic guitar, and the emotional baritone. The song, covered by musicians across the globe, has been translated into more than twenty-five languages, including Quechua, English, Portuguese, Basque, German, Catalan, Persian, Arabic, Armenian, and Hebrew. Papi would teach us that language analysis is a crucial life-skill to have. The line that has become my personal motto in adulthood is "*Solo le pido a Dios que lo injusto no me sea indiferente,*" or "I only ask of God that I'm never indifferent to injustices." As a family, we dissected how Gieco's language expressed his understanding of woes of the world. The lyrics make better sense, Papi would say, if we study the sociopolitical climate of the time in which the song was written. My father situated the folk songs he shared in *Las Américas*, explicating various political events that inspired Gieco and other folk artists in Latin America of the times, such as Mercedes Sosa, Violeta Parra, and Victor Jara. These social studies lessons in my home included learning about Isabel Martínez de Perón of Argentina, the first female to have the title of "President" in any country in the world; we learned about the September 11, 1973, Chilean coup and Salvador Allende; we learned about *La Revolución cubana* led by Fidel Castro's 26th of July Movement and its allies. As homework, Papi would give us books to read such as the *House of Spirits* by Isabel Allende, first cousin once removed of Salvador Allende (president of Chile from 1970 to 1973) and *Cien Años de Soledad* (1967) by Colombian author, Gabriel García Márquez.

In these ways, outside of school, at home, I learned about the violent, beautiful, revolutionary pieces of my culture and ancestry through long, winding conversations with the elders of my family. This is where my story begins. I didn't have the language for it, but I knew by first grade that I was considered different from my peers. My dark, curly hair was just one divider in school. Whereas I loved the coastal Ecuadorian fish, baked platano, and *arroz y menestra* lunches my mother would deliver to school each day and I enjoyed speaking and learning in Spanish, students teased the looks and smells of our food and mocked my bilingualism. As many Latinx learners, I felt subjugated by the prohibition of my mother-tongue in school through overt and structural means (Cobas & Feagin, 2008). What's more, I had zero Latinx teachers from Kindergarten and throughout my undergraduate studies, and the various curricula used in my private and public schools seemed to function as a window into whiteness. The pedagogy of my White teachers contrasted greatly with the nature of my humanity. None of it seemed to match what I was taught at home. My parents did their best to account for our omitted, occluded, misrepresented, or subsumed narratives (Monroy-Miller, 2015, p. 2) by teaching their children our epistemologies, our people, through books, music, food, cultural events, and family vacations. In adulthood, now I realized what a disservice my education has been. Time and (time) again, I wondered if the stories of my people were considered, perhaps, *too* revolutionary to be included or valued in school.

My *Latinidad* is multifaceted. My struggle has been finding a sense of belonging. When I began teaching in 2006, I adapted to White norms, dressing "professionally"; I wore my hair straight, wore a three-piece suit with a Windsor tied tie and heels because I had internalized racial oppression (Bivens, 1995), believing that White cultural norms and ways of life are "advanced and [the] most beneficial way of living for everyone, including non-Whites" (Warren, 2012, p. 199). I soon found, however, that no matter how "White" I acted, I was still racialized and treated as inferior. Treated as inept. Treated as deficient. Called "un-American" by Euro-Americans and "White-washed" by many Latinxs.

I (Lynette) am a 28-year-old Latinx woman and a postdoctoral scholar in mathematics education. As a Tejana—born and raised in San Antonio, Texas—I attended predominantly White schools and was one of a few students of color in advanced placement courses. A huge part of how I grew up was influenced by my parents and their encouragement to assimilate. From my distinct childhood memories, my family never explicitly talked about race in our home—it always seemed largely unspoken. In a more nuanced reflection, though, we never fully assimilated into imperialist white supremacist capitalist patriarchy (hooks, 2013).

My resilience and resistance come from my family; without their advocacy, I would not have had the early opportunity to test into my school's gifted and talented program. From my parents' stories of me as a child in school, I was smart, quiet, and well-behaved in the classroom, and all the White blonde-haired children loved to stroke my beautiful dark hair. I imagine that my visible identity markers became intricately connected to how people in school saw me. I overheard conversations between my parents about my smartness not being recognized. Fundamentally, a major issue with gifted programs is the impact of ability grouping structures within schools (e.g., Noguera, 1995). That is, "gifted" students were afforded more opportunities and access to rich subject area content. My parents knew this and were actively involved in advocating for me to ensure that I was on the advanced tracks and on my path to a college degree.

Both of my parents speak Spanish, but they will tell you they do not. I imagine that this is because much of their Spanish speaking was at home and outside of their homes they were forced to speak English. They grew up in the middle of the Mexican American civil rights movement in Texas (Alemán & Luna, 2013; Orozco, 2009; Treviño, 2016). My sister and I also are not fluent in Spanish, which I think eventually bothered my *tata* as he would make comments about being "an embarrassment" for not knowing the language. I pick up on much of Spanish that I hear, though, because my parents and grandparents would sometimes speak Spanish around me when I was younger. As a child, I was also obsessed with Tejana superstar Selena and sang all her songs even though I did not really understand all the words. I learned a bit of Spanish words through listening to Tejano music. I also would often play Lotería, a Mexican bingo game, with my grandmother and sister and learn some Spanish words from the cards.

In graduate school, I learned about the atrocious complexity of colonizing structures in educational contexts. I began thinking about projects of decolonization from literature in TribalCrit. For example, I was overwhelmed with anger as I read a book chapter about the Sand Creek Massacre (Haynes Writer, 2012)—history that I never learned through my "advanced" schooling. I was angry because these stories are largely not part of anyone's schooling in the United States, stories of slaughter intended to leave "no child left behind." This word choice intentionally linked colonial atrocities to educational policy. When I was younger, my dad used to always tell me, "History is written by the victors." I say no; history is written by the colonizers.

As a woman of color scholar, I am critiqued regardless of how much I talk about race; I either talk about race too much or too little. It is an almost impossible space to navigate. I know that what I know is something to be known, something real, because other people's stories resonate with my stories. For example, *Borderlands/La Frontera* (Anzaldúa, 1987) was published two years before I was born, but the resonance I felt when reading it was powerful and nearly indescribable. It was incredible to read text that told pieces of my life—my racialized experiences, my relationship with Spanish and English (and Spanglish) languages—even before I existed in this world. How was that possible?

The complexities of my language and my culture make up my Latinxness. My struggle has been finding a sense of belonging. With my current critical consciousness, this is a burden; it is something I cannot avoid. No matter how "White" I can try to act, I will always have my visible identities as a woman of color. Assumed to be weak and incompetent by fellow Americans. Assumed to be *not* an American by non-Americans (and some Americans). Seen as "not a real Latina" by many Latinxs because I do not fluently speak Spanish—an embarrassment. From hearing multiple *testimonios*, however, I know that there are people in the world who share similar experiences as I do, never fitting into the labels imposed by societal norms and structures. Our collective strength is built from these stories.

THEORETICAL FRAMEWORK: CRITICAL RACE THEORY AND LATCRIT

> *The truest act in liberation is giving voice to all who suffer, valuing all experiences. I believe it is only in expanding our awareness of the intersectional and regenerating forces of oppression that we can dismantle our current conditioning.* —Monroy-Miller (2016)

Critical Race Theory (CRT) is an examination and transformation of the relationship between race, racism, and power. CRT takes a broad perspective—connected to legacies of economics, history, law, and more—to center issues of civil rights. That is, CRT involves explaining the ways that race and racism (dis)advantages people in multifaceted ways. Tenets of CRT include (Delgado & Stefancic, 2012):

- *Racism is normal*—it is central, endemic, and permanent in the functioning of U.S. society.
- *Interest convergence*—advancements for people of color often occur when benefiting those in power (i.e., White people).
- *Race as a social construction*—it is not objective, inherent, or fixed.
- *Intersectionality and anti-essentialism*—CRT centers race, in relation to other forms of oppression.
- *Voice or counternarrative*—recognizes and privileges experiential knowledge of people of color as legitimate, appropriate, and critical; the counternarrative is meant to counter the dominant, hegemonic deficit narratives about people of color.

Ladson-Billings and Tate (1995) described CRT as a way to challenge claims of neutrality and meritocracy in education. Similarly, we draw on CRT to make visible that structured racial oppression is an educational reality (Carter Andrews & Tuitt, 2013; Ladson-Billings, 1998; Taylor, Gillborn, & Ladson-Billings, 2016).

With CRT, then, we can shift "the center of focus from notions of White, middle-class culture to the cultures of Communities of Color" (Yosso, 2005, p. 77). CRT both names the creation and normalization of race and racism while it also, as a theoretical lens, can be used to reimagine the ways in which education can take up culturally relevant and sustainable education. Today in the United States, it is useful to validate community cultural wealth and to reimagine ways in which education can take up inclusive pedagogical practices.

As a specific thread of CRT, Latinx Critical Race Theory (LatCrit) "is grounded in an ethos of social justice and action for change, and there are major efforts to link scholarship to teaching and higher education to schools and communities" (Oliva et al., 2013, p. 142). LatCrit responds to the invisibility of Latinx people in the United States by reflecting on the conditions of Latinx peoples. Engaging critical race praxis, LatCrit also seeks to improve and elevate the lives of Latinx and other people of color.

LatCrit engages a coalitional Latinx panethnicity and addresses issues such as language, immigration, ethnicity, culture, identity, phenotype, and sexuality (Solorzano & Delgado Bernal, 2001). In turn, this theory elucidates Latinxs' multidimensional identities and can address the intersectionality of multiple forms of oppression. Researchers, then, can use LatCrit to better articulate the experiences of Latinxs specifically, through a more focused examination of the unique forms of oppression this group encounters (Solorzano & Delgado Bernal, 2001). LatCrit centers the intersectionality of race and more specific issues (e.g., immigration status and language) that Latinx students negotiate in their educational careers (Pérez Huber, 2010).

Only relatively recently, ethnographic researchers have been giving "powerful testimony to the cultural strengths and assets of Latino families" (Valencia, 2002, p. 94). Dolores Delgado Bernal (2002) also reiterated some points about empowering and improving the experiences of people of color by decentering Eurocentric epistemologies and centering, instead, critical raced gendered perspectives. Scholars are beginning to produce a collection of work that highlights "how the cultural resources and funds of knowledge such as myths, folktales, dichos, consejos, kitchen talk, autobiographical stories, and pedagogies of the home are indeed educational strengths and strategies found in communities of color" (Bernal, 2002, p. 120).

Critical race theories center relationships among race, racism, and power by centering lived experiences of people of color. We draw on *testimonio* as a methodological approach to produce counternarratives that speak back to deficit framings (e.g., Pérez Huber & Cueva, 2012). *Testimonios*, as stories of our lives, engage critical, intentional reflections on autoethnographic narratives (Blackmer Reyes & Curry Rodríguez, 2012; Latina Feminist Group, 2001). Grounded in these theoretical frameworks, we view stories as intricately connected to theory. Stories—both within academic research and our bodies at home—embody epistemologies and ontologies. We do not want to contribute to deficit narratives about Latinx students and educators; we seek to complicate the narratives. We entered this space by sharing pieces of our own stories in the introduction to this chapter, following scholars who foreground their positionalities as connected to their work (e.g., Espino, 2012).

LATINX STUDENTS AND EDUCATION

The proportion of doctorates awarded to Latinx people in the United States has risen from 3.3% in 1994 to 6.5% in 2014 (National Science Foundation, 2015). According to the Pew Research Center (2012), "over the past four decades, the number of Hispanics graduating with either an associate or a bachelor's degree has increased seven-fold." However, these huge strides in accomplishments, which should be celebrated, are commonly unknown. This data is purposefully absent from major media outlets and, more importantly, discourse about Chicanx and Latinx populations in education.

Monumental Chicanx Latinx Studies (CLS) texts such as "The Chicano Studies Reader," emerged from wanting to question how knowledge gets produced and what forms of knowledge are reproduced in the university system; further, it spoke to inherent social and cultural inequities propagated by institutions of higher learning and various realms of academia. For example, in CLS we point to and name language hierarchies that have been created by the subordination of other languages. CLS identifies the Eurocentric hegemonic ideologies that are pushed in society at many levels, which proliferates white supremacy ideology:

> It has been noted by several family scholars (Mindel & Haberstein, 1976; Rodman, 1968; Staples, 1970, 1971a, 1976) that much of the research and theory on both majority group and ethnic minority group family life proceeds on the basis of the undocumented assumption that the norms established by Anglo families are somehow the "best" and the "most desirable" for all families in the United States regardless of their ethnicity or cultural background. The logical consequence of such an assumption is that families (and, by implication, cultures) which vary from this majority norm are thereby inferior. (Cromwell & Ruiz, 1979, p. 355)

This notion is replicated in education, pedagogy, and schooling around the world. As Freire (1970) argued, education is political and schools are never neutral institutions because schools often function to maintain and reproduce the existing social order rather than empower people to transform themselves, their community, and/or society. In this chapter, we are not interested in discussions of "social pathology" or "social deviance" theories because these arguments often aim to homogenize the Chicanx and Latinx population. In education, for example, Paris and Alim (2014) note that deficit approaches to teaching and learning view the languages, literacies, and cultural ways of being of many learners and communities of color as deficiencies to be overcome if they are to learn the dominant language, literacy, and cultural ways of being demanded in schools.

Schools "teach" three curricula: the explicit, the implicit, and the null (Eisner, 1985). Explicit curriculum is commonly what we see in textbooks, on worksheets, and the publicly announced programs of study (i.e., English Language Arts, Mathematics, Science, Social Studies). Hidden/implicit curriculum imparts values and expectations in a general way; in public schools, for example, the teacher is often seen as the knowledge authority and decides what is "excellence" and "failure," which is measured and attributed with the letters A, B, C, D, and F. Null curriculum encompasses all the cultural and political statements that are made about what matters in society by excluding content (i.e., multicultural epistemologies and ontologies) (Lamar, forthcoming). In schools, curriculum can function as "a culturally specific artifact designed to maintain a White supremacist script" (Ladson-Billings, 1998, p. 10) by entirely excluding and/or misrepresenting people of color.

In the United States, schools are places where Chicanx, Latinx, and other racialized groups are often minoritized and invalidated. In the ways race is constructed for population counts, Latinx/Hispanic is referred to as an ethnicity. In other words, Latinx people can be of any race; however, "their experiences in the United States have undoubtedly been racialized, and they have been the target of individuals as well as institutional manifestations of racism" (Irizarry, 2017, p. 95). Latinx people become racialized, in part, by hegemonic discourses. That is, imperialist modes of domination are effective through "domination of the mind, of the worldviews and ways of life of people" (Villenas & Deyhle, 1999, p. 417).

One way that Latinx people are forced to comply with the imposition of White ways of knowing in school is what Villenas and Deyhle (1999) call "a cultural assault" (p. 420). Through the analyses of seven ethnographic studies, Villenas and Deyhle (1999) used CRT to unpack how children are raced in school and to explain how the subordination and marginalization of people of color is created and maintained in the United States. This is coupled with harsher disciplinary consequences if Latinx students stray from demands of White society, emphasizing particular ways of being (i.e., submissiveness, assimilation, English-only) to maintain a place in U.S. society (Murillo Jr., 1997). In U.S. public schools, Latinx students are being taught to repress their own knowledges and culture and are pushed to take up whiteness, instead, simultaneously while being punished for deviating in any way.

Villenas and Deyhle (1999) deconstruct the notion that Latinx students simply perform badly compared to their White peers by analyzing how schools operate under societal hierarchies and institutionalized racism. The consequences of white supremacist ideologies become apparent in legislation, policies, and school practices. Villenas and Deyhle explain that it is pivotal for education to take up Latinx knowledges and values in schooling because "the goal of Latino educational success is linked to goals of self-determination, linguistic and cultural human rights, and the right to a history and education based on community-identified terms" (p. 441).

TOWARD LATINX REVITALIZING PEDAGOGIES

To expose the truths of our people—Chicanx and Latinx communities—is to deliver alternative ways of thinking and knowing about the world; it is also to expose "competing universalities" (Butler, 2000, as quoted by Flores & Rosaldo, 2007). In this chapter, we purposefully draw from our experiences as students and educators and intentionally applied assets/strength-based analyses to affirm and promote Latinx epistemologies, which we believe is beneficial for humanity as a whole. The truth cannot be obfuscated. Like Acuña (2011) stated:

> Stereotypes and myths thrive because of ignorance and fear. Without the structure to study Mexican Americans and other Latinos, they remain marginalized. The role of Chicana/o Studies is to organize and systemize the knowledge of people of Mexican descent, as well as to

serve as a pedagogical tool to educate and motivate the massive numbers of Mexican Americans and Latinas/os in the United States. (p. xxi)

Traditionally, pedagogy has involved delivery of and promotion of standardized patriarchal, cisheteronormative, English-monolingual, ableist, classist, xenophobic, Judeo-Christian content-knowledge with western models of discipline and classroom management (Paris & Alim, 2017). As CRT reminds us that race is a socially constructed and racism is not aberational (Delgado & Stefancic, 2012), in this chapter we intend to de-center any dehumanizing epistemology and center the experiences of people not traditionally revered in U.S. curriculum. Researchers have noted, "When the cultural diversity of our students is embraced, appreciated, understood, and honored, students will respond in favorable ways that many never knew they could respond" (Romero & Arce, 2009). This positive emphasis is meant to highlight a sense of resilience, success, and sustainable ideologies within Latinx culture. That is, when curriculum materials reflect students' values and cultures they are more apt to succeed academically than students who don't see themselves in lessons and topics covered in school (Cabrera, Milem, Jaquette, & Marx, 2014). Our goal is to *thrive*, not just survive in our hostile society.

To preserve our *raices* (cultural roots) means revisiting our stories and de-centering the "Americanization" mission, obsessed with erasing the Spanish language and any historical connections to Latin America (Garcia, 2001). As we reflected on our positionalities, we understood the efforts of our families in teaching us about our culture and histories as grounding us in *Latinidad*. De-centering whiteness also means reframing issues of access and equity (Paris & Alim, 2017) and shifting *culture of power* (Delpit, 1988). We recognize that we must assert that our knowledges are valid and crucial not only for our own sustainability but also for the sustainability of all living things and *La Pachamama*, or Mother Earth. As we recognize that we need restorative practices to nurture our knowledges, we understand that the work shouldn't be solely on working families. To this end we promote and build on culturally relevant pedagogies (CRP) (Ladson-Billings, 1995), culturally sustaining pedagogies (CSP) (Paris, 2012; Paris & Alim, 2014, 2017), and culturally revitalizing pedagogies (CRP) (Ladson-Billings, 2014).

Paulo Freire (1970) proposed Critical Pedagogy, which suggests that we create new forms of knowledge through the dismantling of old disciplines. Furthermore, Critical Pedagogy suggests that society should raise questions between the margins and centers of power in society and school; rewrite history in order to reclaim power and identity, particularly around areas of race, gender, class, and ethnicity; and reclaim a curriculum knowledge that is responsive to the everyday experiences of people (Freire, 1970). Just as we learned about our histories from the testimonios of our elders in our communities, we push the proliferation of Latinx

Revitalizing Pedagogies (LRP) in schools through curriculum that is by, for, and with Latinx folks.

One way to advance sustaining and revitalizing Latinx knowledges, is through intersectionality. Coined by Kimberlé Crenshaw, intersectionality emphasizes complexities in the lived experiences of women of color that cannot be captured by examining race or gender alone (Crenshaw, 1991). Intersectional paradigms remind us that oppression cannot be reduced to one fundamental type, and that oppressions work together in producing injustice (Collins, 2009). For example, Spanish is a gendered language in which nouns ending in an "a" are generally feminine and those ending in an "o" are masculine. People have resisted this linguistic patriarchy by replacing "o" endings with "a/o" or "@" (Reichard, 2017). To subvert linguistic imperialism and allow for the Spanish language to move beyond gender binaries, "Latinx" is now used widely by folks in and out of academia. The -x replaces the standard a/o ending in Spanish.

These revolutionary changes of language do not occur without backlash, however. Linguistic policies have commonly been governed by ideologies that normalize and romanticize dominant languages as well as proliferate ideas of linguistic homogenization being part of modernization. Only within the last 30 years has the area of linguistic human rights started crystallizing as a multidisciplinary research area (Skutnabb-Kangas, 2008, p. 108). Mar-Molinero and Paffey (2011) use common economics concepts of supply and demand when discussing the global linguistic market. Globally, language is treated as a commercial commodity and English, for example, is seen as serving to push imperialistic ideas. If the Real Academia de la Lengua Española (theRAE) and the Instituto Cervantes are the gatekeepers and the power-holders, is maintaining one's mixed Latinx and U.S. American-influenced Spanish a way of subverting authority and challenging linguistic hegemony?

In the struggle to subvert language policing, sometimes there are conflicting ideas within the Latinx peoples. For example, Swarthmore College students, Gilbert Orbea and Gilbert Guerra, wrote an article arguing against "Latinx" calling it a form of "reverse appropriation," stating "they are putting a distinctively American—and really, it's mostly found at elite college institutions—viewpoint into a language without appreciation or reverence for it" (Reichard, 2017). In other words, the "x" does not fit the phonology of Spanish. Orbea and Guerra propose "Latine" as the gender-inclusive umbrella term, which is already used in various countries around Latin America.

We need to be united in the struggle toward liberation in many ways. Like the example above, we must validate language claims such as the word "Latine" because it can be equally effective as "Latinx" when attempting to challenge the imperialist white supremacist capitalist patriarchy (hooks, 2013). It is clear that we must draw on each other for support. We must listen to our communities as they are our primary sources.

What we truly mean when saying "by, for, and with Latinx people" is that in order to help ameliorate some of the woes of the world, we must start by trying to understand those that are most marginalized in society first. Better yet, we need to pay extra close attention to our youth. In this chapter we hope to focus our discussion on education and, more specifically, Latinx youth and their knowledges.

This chapter emerged from the authors' desire to transform systems that did not give us a sense of belonging, inspired by our right to be in spaces freely without having to change ourselves to be accepted as fully human. In sharp contrast to the competitive, individualist ideologies fostered in school, we aim to center community in our scholarship. In our youth, we felt that our experiences with language, namely Spanish, was part of belonging to a community, which is part of our *Latinidad*. Yet, it is commonly forgotten that "one of the most important yet most devalued resources, available to youth of color is their language" (Bucholtz, Casillas, and Lee, 2017, p. 44).

In "Language and Culture as Sustenance," Bucholtz, Casillas, and Lee (2017) offer a narrative about two Latina high school students—Isabel and Elisa—who participated in a program titled "School Kids Investigating Language of Life and Society" (SKILLS), in Santa Barbara, California, in 2014. The authors explain that culture is produced primarily through language and that it "endows experience with meaning, and provides a deeply held sense of identity and social belonging" (p. 45). The SKILLS program group aims to achieve CSP in the following ways:

1. By supporting and developing the full repertoire of cultural and linguistic practices that young people engage in with their communities, families, and peer groups.
2. By facilitating students' access to the language and culture of institutional power.
3. By guiding students to critically scrutinize and directly challenge social inequalty or exclusion, whether in the practices that perpetuate institutional power or in those that they themselves employ and encounter in their everyday lives. (Bucholtz, Casillas, and Lee, 2017, p. 46; also see Paris & Alim, 2014)

From this narrative, Isabel and Elisa's language repertoires exemplify the higher order thinking skills supposedly valued in U.S. schooling of which we have much to learn. The bilingual students of Mexican American heritage highlight the way youth can help us unlearn notions of linguistic imperialism such as the supremacy of English-monolingualism. Their narratives serve as *testimonio* to uplift the experiential knowledge of people of color.

One of the skills discussed through these narratives of Latinx youth is what García (2009) coined as the process of *translanguaging*. Defined as "the act performed by bilinguals of accessing different linguistic features or various modes of what are described as autonomous languages, in order to maximize communicative potential" (García, 2009, p. 140), translanguaging centers communication over language. With this in mind, the Latinx youth Elisa and Isabel are, indeed, dismantling "the artificial boundaries that exclude their language from public spaces, bringing 'informal' language into formal settings and introducing bilingual practices into monolingual domains" (Bucholtz, Casillas, and Lee, 2017, p. 55). Through the exposure of multiple varieties of English and Spanish, the youth named above exemplify how it is an asset to have multicultural skills and use language variations, which, we argue and demand exposure of as we move toward an education that sustains. The stories of Isabel and Elisa serve to identify and document cultural wealth (Yosso, 2005).

Now and again, scholars may say that it is insufficient for people to come together in only dialogue in order to gain knowledge of their social reality. Freire (1970) proposed praxis, "reflection and action directed at the structures to be transformed" (p. 126). Through praxis, oppressed people can reach a critical awareness of their own condition and struggle for liberation in solidarity. One community-centered group that is committed to liberation through social change is the New York Collective of Radical Educators (NYCoRE), "a group of current and former public school educators and their allies committed to fighting for social justice in our school system and society at large, by organizing and mobilizing teachers, developing curriculum, and working with community, parent, and student organizations" (retrieved from http://www.nycore.org/nycore-info/mission/). Since its inception, NYCoRE has joined other organizations and founded a multitude of intersectional social justice projects such as NYQueer, The New Teacher Underground, and, most recently, they have teamed up with thousands of educators in about a dozen other cities to enact the first National Black Lives Matter in Our Schools Week of Action starting February 5, 2018.

Almost a decade ago, when I (Alba) was teaching in New York City, I became involved in several transformative projects with NYCoRE such as cofacilitating an Inquiry to Action Group (ItAG) and researching social justice curriculum for the group's *Planning to Change the World: A Plan Book for Social Justice Teachers 2017–2018*, which is edited by the Education for Liberation Network with the support of Rethinking Schools (Brion-Meisels, Nikundiwe, and Shalaby, 2017). We assert that the plan book is an extraordinary resource, providing users with important information about social justice activists, events, and movements as well as links to lesson plans and resources for elementary, middle, and high school students and educators. The plan book emphasizes intersectionality in the struggle for liberation. One featured resource in NYCoRE's plan book (2017–2018 edition) useful to teach about the intersection of race and sexuality is a series of essays called *Queer Brown Voices: Personal Narratives of Latina/o LGBT Activism* (Quesada, Gomez, & Vidal-Ortiz, 2015). The plan book provides a link to the essays which chronicled the experiences of 14 Latinx LGBT activists along with middle and high school teacher resources (p. 174).

The above example of strides being made in social justice curriculum theorizing is facilitated by the rapid-growing resource sharing online via social media. Another clear example of technology amplifying our voices is evident by NYCoRE's plan book. The power of social media is sometimes understated in academia, and we argue that, instead, collaboration and knowledge production in social media spaces should be welcomed. Through these mediums we might challenge traditional access to knowledge that often marginalizes the lives and histories of people of color.

During the summer of 2017, when part of Latin America was devastated by Hurricane Maria, now regarded as the worst natural disaster on record, many took to hashtags to share resources. A hashtag is a tool that facilitates the connection with others to easily find messages with a specific theme or content. Myslewski (2014) explained that "hashtag" was born on August 25, 2007, in a Twitter posting and was added to the OED due to it being "extremely widespread." In the case of Puerto Rico's current crises, activists took on creating online fund-raising opportunities to help with basic survival items and then, almost simultaneously, created the #PRSyllabus to couple the aid with often untold histories of Puerto Rico. This project materialized "to raise critical questions about the role of debt in contemporary capitalism; the relationship between debt, migration, and violence; and the emergence of new political and cultural identities" from cooperation between the Unpayable Debt working group at Columbia University convened by Frances Negrón-Muntaner and Sarah Muir, and syllabus project leaders Yarimar Bonilla, Marisol Lebrón, and Sarah Molinari (https://puertoricosyllabus.com/).

Adding to other collective projects of intellectual community building such as the #StandingRockSyllabus, #ImmigrationSyllabus, and #IslamophobiaIsRacismSyllabus, the #PRSyllabus serves as Latinx currere. Currere prompts educators and learners to undertake an autobiographical examination of themselves (Pinar, 1975). Educational materials gathered and shared online encourage discussion and analysis of the Puerto Rican debt crisis which affects the current and future lives of millions of Puerto Ricans across the territory and in the diaspora (https://puertoricosyllabus.com/).

Educators, students, and anyone interested in advancing culturally revitalizing practices can turn to technology such as the hashtag model described above. The importance of CSL, for example, is catching up with mainstream culture. For instance, last year, during Latinx History Month (which is celebrated from September 15 to October 15), in partnership with 50 organizations across the globe, Google launched one of the largest digital collections of Latinx art and history. The project was created "to preserve and share stories and exhibits related to Latino history in the United States, went live today" with more than 4,300 archives in Spanish and English; there are artworks in the digital exhibit related to the Latinx experience in the United States, multimedia exhibits and virtual tours of historic sites, as well as profiles of key Latino figures (Villafañe, 2017).

CONOCIMIENTOS MÍOS: ¿Y DÓNDE ESTÁ MI GENTE?

It is time we honor our *mamis, papis, tatas* and our *gente* by having structural conversations and establishing spaces (physically and symbolically) for our knowledges. We understand that the role of civility racism as "ideology" is also material and consequential. Even though "race is a socially produced classification scheme, races are meaningful categories because they are "real in their consequences" (Bonilla-Silva, 1997, p. 472; Thomas & Thomas, 1928, p. 571). We must be actively antiracist with our work above all and we must commit to reproduce our knowledges wherever and whenever, particularly in educational institutions.

Paris and Alim (2017) discuss the purpose of schooling compared with with schooling in pluralistic societies. They write, "while it is crucial that we work to sustain Black, Latinx, Asian, Pacific Islander and Indigenous languages and cultures in pedagogies, we must be open to sustaining them in ways that attend to the emerging, intersectional, and dynamic ways in which they are lived and used by young people" (Paris & Alim, 2017, p. 9). Schools have created an environment that allows for only moments of success for students of color insofar as they deny or lose their cultures, histories, languages, and literatures. CSP aims to accept, support, and sustain pluralism on cultural and linguistic levels. Paris and Alim (2017) assert that "the goal is to move beyond assimilationist goals for Black, Brown and impoverished youth to create and use curriculum and pedagogy with, for, and by youth themselves (p. 267). Teachers play a critical role in the education and academic trajectory of Latinx learners, though we know most teachers are discouraged from using schooling practices or pedagogies that misalign with their particular school's mandated curricula (Romero, Arce, and Cammarota, 2009).

As Friere (1970) wrote, "Liberating education consists in acts of cognition, not transferals of information." So should we ask, as Paris and Alim (2014) ask, "What if, indeed, the goal of teaching and learning with youth of color was not ultimately to see how closely students could perform White middle-class norms but to explore, honor, extend, and, at times, problematize their heritage and community practices?" (p. 86). In a world that centers people of color and our knowledges, there is collaboration instead of competition, there is restorative justice in the place of punitive systems, and there is unrelenting love of all living things. One method we suggest to conceive the new reality where our ideas sprout into society is *guerilla gardening*. Guerilla gardening consists of volunteers, individually or collectively, "who, without permission operate to target public and private spaces of neglect and unlawfully transform the environment through the planting of flora without the landowner's consent" (Flores, 2006). *Tu lucha es mi lucha.*

They tried to bury us. They didn't know we were seeds. —Mexican Proverb

REFERENCES

Acuña, R. F. 2011. *The making of Chicana/o studies: In the trenches of academe*. New Brunswick, NJ: Rutgers University Press.
Alemán, E. Jr. (executive producer), & Luna, R. (producer and director). 2013. *Stolen education* [Documentary movie]. United States: Alemán/Luna Productions.
Anzaldúa, G. 1987. *Borderlands/La Frontera: The new Mestiza*, 4th ed. San Francisco: Aunt Lute Books.
Bernal, D. D. 2002. Critical race theory, Latino critical theory, and critical raced-gendered epistemologies: Recognizing students of color as holders and creators of knowledge. *Qualitative Inquiry*, 8(1), 105–126. http://dx.doi.org/10.1177/107780040200800107
Bivens, D. 1995. *Internalized racism: A definition*. Boston, MA: The Women's Theological Center.
Blackmer Reyes, K., & Curry Rodríguez, J. E. 2012. Testimonio: Origins, terms, and resources. *Equity and Excellence in Education*, 45(3), 525–538.
Bonilla-Silva, E. 1997. Rethinking racism: Toward a structural interpretation. *American Sociological Review*, 62(3), 465–480. http://dx.doi.org/10.2307/2657316
Brion-Meisels, G., Nikundiwe, T., & Shalaby, C. 2017. *Planning to change the world: A plan book for social justice teachers 2017–2018*. New York Collective of Radical Educators.
Bucholtz, M., Casillas, D. I., & Sook Lee, J. 2017. Language and culture as sustenance. In Django Paris and H. Samy Alim (eds.), *Culturally sustaining pedagogies: Teaching and learning for justice in a changing world* (pp. 43–59). New York: Teachers College Press.
Cabrera, N. L., Milem, J. F., Jaquette, O., & Marx, R. W. 2014. Missing the (student achievement) forest for all the (political) trees: Empiricism and the Mexican American studies controversy in Tucson. *American Educational Research Journal*, 51(6), 1084–1118. https://doi.org/10.3102/0002831214553705
Carter Andrews, D. J., & Tuitt, F., eds. 2013. *Contesting the myth of a "post racial" era: The continued significance of race in U.S. education*. New York: Peter Lang.
Cobas, J. A., & Feagin, J. R. 2008. Language oppression and resistance: The case of middle class Latinos in the United States. *Ethnic and Racial Studies*, 31(2), 390–410. https://doi.org/10.1080/01419870701491945
Collins, P. H. 2009. *Black feminist thought: Knowledge, consciousness, and the politics of empowerment*. New York: Routledge.
Crenshaw, K. 1991. Mapping the margins: Intersectionality, identity politics, and violence against women of color. *Stanford Law Review*, 43(6), 1241–1279. http://dx.doi.org/10.2307/1229039
Cromwell, R. E., & Ruiz, R. A. 1979. The myth of macho dominance in decision making within Mexican and Chicano families. *Hispanic Journal of Behavioral Sciences*, 1(4), 355–373. https://doi.org/10.1177/073998637900100404
Delgado, R., & Stefancic, J. 2012. *Critical race theory: An introduction*, 2nd ed. New York: New York University Press.

Delpit, L. 1988. The silenced dialogue: Power and pedagogy in educating other people's children. *Harvard Educational Review*, 58(3), 280–298. http://dx.doi.org/10.17763/haer.58.3.c43481778r528qw4

Eisner, E. W. 1985. *The educational imagination: On the design and evaluation of school programs*. New York: Macmillan.

Espino, M. M. 2012. Seeking the "truth" in the stories we tell: The role of critical race epistemology in higher education research. *The Review of Higher Education*, 36(1), 31–67. http://dx.doi.org/10.1353/rhe.2012.0048

Flores, H. C. 2006. *Food not lawns: How to turn your yard into a garden and your neighborhood into a community*. White River Junction, VT: Chelsea Green Publishing.

Flores, J., & Rosaldo, R., eds. 2007. *A companion to Latina/o studies*. Malden, MA: John Wiley & Sons.

Freire, P. 1970. *Pedagogy of the oppressed*. Translated by Myra Bergman Ramos. New York: Continuum.

Garcia, E. E. 2001. *Hispanic education in the United States: Raíces y alas*. New York: Rowman & Littlefield Publishers.

García, O. 2009. Racializing the language practices of U.S. Latinos: Impact on their education. In José A. Cobas, Jorge Duany, and Joe R. Feagin (eds.), *How the United States racializes Latinos: White hegemony and its consequences* (pp. 101–115). New York: Taylor & Francis.

Haynes Writer, J. 2012. The savage within: No child left behind—again, and again, and again. In Beverly J. Klug (ed.), *Standing together: American Indian education as culturally responsive pedagogy* (pp. 55–70). Lanham, MD: Rowman & Littlefield.

hooks, b. 2013. *Writing beyond race: Living theory and practice*. New York: Routledge.

Irrizary, J. G. 2017. "For us, by us": A vision for culturally sustaining pedagogies forwarded by Latinx youth. In Django Paris and H. Samy Alim (eds.), *Culturally Sustaining Pedagogies: Teaching and Learning for Justice in a Changing World* (pp. 83–98). New York: Teachers College Press.

Ladson-Billings, G. 1995. Toward a theory of culturally relevant pedagogy. *American Educational Research Journal*, 32(3), 465–491. http://dx.doi.org/10.3102/00028312032003465

———. 1998. Just what is critical race theory and what's it doing in a nice field like education? *International Journal of Qualitative Studies in Education*, 11(1), 7–24. http://dx.doi.org/10.1080/095183998236863

———. 2014. Culturally relevant pedagogy 2.0: A.k.a. the remix. *Harvard Educational Review*, 84(1), 74–84. http://dx.doi.org/10.17763/haer.84.1.p2rj131485484751

Ladson-Billings, G., & Tate, W. F. IV. 1995. Toward a critical race theory of education. *Teachers College Record*, 97(1), 47–67.

Lamar, A. I. Forthcoming. Understanding why teachers leave: An autoethnographic methodology with critical race theory analysis. In Carol R. Rinke and Lynnette Mawhinney (eds.), *Opportunities and challenges in teacher recruitment and retention*. Charlotte, NC: Information Age Publishing.

Latina Feminist Group. 2001. *Telling to live: Latina feminist testimonios*. Durham, NC: Duke University Press.

Mar-Molinero, C., & Paffey, D. 2011. Linguistic imperialism: Who owns global Spanish? In Manuel Díaz-Campos (ed.), *The handbook of Hispanic sociolinguistics* (pp. 747–764). Oxford, UK: Wiley-Blackwell.

Monroy-Miller, M. 2015. History indexes in a U.S. textbook: Exploring the existence and omission of Chicano narratives as an opportunity for growth. Unpublished manuscript.

———. 2016. CRT Brief #3. Unpublished manuscript.

Murillo, E. Jr. 1997, November. Those damned Mexicans! Resisting alien discourses in rural North Carolina. Paper presented at the annual conference of the American Anthropological Association, Washington, DC.

Myslewski, R. 2014. "Hashtag" added to the OED—but # isn't a hash, pound, nor number sign. *The Register.* June 13, 2014. http://www.theregister.co.uk/2014/05/23/the_internet_of_things_help s_insurance_firms_reward_punish/.

National Science Foundation. 2015. Doctorate recipients from U.S. universities: 2014. Report. December 2015. https://www.nsf.gov/statistics/2016/nsf16300/digest/nsf16300.pdf

Noguera, P. A. 1995. Educational rights and Latinos: Tracking as a form of second generation discrimination. *La Raza Law Journal, 8*(1), 25–41.

Oliva, N., Pérez, J. C., & Parker, L. 2013. Educational policy contradictions: A LatCrit perspective on undocumented Latino students. In Marvin Lynn and Adrienne D. Dixson (eds.), *The handbook of critical race theory in education* (pp. 140–152). New York: Routledge.

Orozco, C. E. 2009. *No Mexicans, women, or dogs allowed: The rise of the Mexican American civil rights movement.* Austin: University of Texas Press.

Paris, D. 2012. Culturally sustaining pedagogy: A needed change in stance, terminology, and practice. *Educational Researcher, 41*(3), 93–97. http://dx.doi.org/10.3102/0013189X12441244

Paris, D., & Alim, H. S. 2014. What are we seeking to sustain through culturally sustaining pedagogy? A loving critique forward. *Harvard Educational Review, 84*(1), 85–100. http://dx.doi.org/10.17763/haer.84.1.982l873k2ht16m77

———, eds. 2017. *Culturally sustaining pedagogies: Teaching and learning for justice in a changing world.* New York: Teachers College Press.

Pérez Huber, L. 2010. Using Latina/o critical race theory (LatCrit) and racist nativism to explore intersectionality in the educational experiences of undocumented Chicana college students. *Educational Foundations, 24*(1–2), 77–96.

Pérez Huber, L., & Cueva, B. M. 2012. Chicana/Latina testimonios on effects and responses to microaggressions. *Equity & Excellence in Education, 45*(3), 392–410. http://dx.doi.org/10.1080/10665684.2012.698193

Pew Research Center. 2012. College graduation and hispanics. August 20, 2012. http://www.pewhispanic.org/2012/08/20/iv-college-graduation-and-hispanics/

Pinar, W. F., ed. 1975. Currere: Toward reconceptualization. In William Pinar (ed.), *Curriculum theorizing: The reconceptualists* (pp. 396–414). Berkeley, CA: McCutchan Pub. Corp.

Quesada, U., Gomez, L., & Vidal-Ortiz, S., eds. 2015. *Queer brown voices: Personal narratives of Latina/o LGBT activism.* Austin: University of Texas Press.

Reichard, R. 2017. Latino/a vs. Latinx vs. Latine: Which word best solves Spanish's gender problem? *Latina Magazine.* March 30, 2017. http://www.latina.com/lifestyle/our-issues/latinoa-latinx-latine-solving-spanish-gender-problem

Romero, A. F., & Arce, M. S. 2009. Culture as a resource: Critically compassionate intellectualism and its struggle against racism, Fascism, and intellectual apartheid in Arizona. *Hamline Journal of Public Law and Policy, 31,* 179–217.

Romero, A., Arce, S., & Cammarota, J. 2009. A Barrio pedagogy: Identity, intellectualism, activism, and academic achievement through the evolution of critically compassionate intellectualism. *Race, Ethnicity and Education, 12*(2), 217–233. http://dx.doi.org/10.1080/13613320902995483

Skutnabb-Kangas, T. 2008. Human rights and language policy in education. In Stephen May and Nancy Hornberger (eds.), *Encyclopedia of language and education: Language policy and political issues in education,* 2nd ed. (pp. 107–119). New York: Springer.

Solorzano, D. G., & Delgado Bernal, D. 2001. Examining transformational resistance through a critical race and LatCrit theory framework: Chicana and Chicano students in an urban context. *Urban Education, 36*(3), 308–342. http://dx.doi.org/10.1177/0042085901363002

Taylor, E., Gillborn, D., & Ladson-Billings, G., eds. 2016. *Foundations of critical race theory in education,* 2nd ed. New York: Routledge.

Thomas, W. I., & Thomas, D. S. 1928. *The child in America: Behavior problems and programs.* New York: A. A. Knopf.

Treviño, L. 2016. Forgotten futures: The benign existence of Mexican Americans in Texas. *Barrio Intellect* (blog). January 5, 2016. https://www.barriointellect.com/forgotten-futures.html

Valencia, R. R. 2002. "Mexican Americans don't value education!" On the basis of the myth, mythmaking, and debunking. *Journal of Latinos and Education, 1*(2), 81–103. http://dx.doi.org/10.1207/S1532771XJLE0102_2

Villafañe, V. 2017. Google launches massive digital history, culture and arts project for Hispanic heritage month. *Forbes.* September 7, 2017. https://www.forbes.com/sites/veronicavillafane/2017/09/07/google-launches-massive-digital-history-culture-and-arts-project-for-hispanic-heritage-month/#5ffb1fec3ba4

Villenas, S., & Deyhle, D. 1999. Critical race theory and ethnographies challenging the stereotypes: Latino families, schooling, resilience and resistance. *Curriculum Inquiry, 29*(4), 413–445. https://doi.org/10.1111/0362-6784.00140

Warren, C. A. 2012. The effects of post-racial theory on education. *Journal for Critical Education Policy Studies, 10*(1), 197–216.

Yosso, T. J. 2005. Whose culture has capital? A critical race theory discussion of community cultural wealth. *Race Ethnicity and Education, 8*(1), 69–91. http://dx.doi.org/10.1080/1361332052000341006

EIGHT
"Un Puño de Tierra"
Curriculum and Pedagogy Theorizing along the U.S./Mexico Border

Ganiva Reyes

When I think of my childhood, I remember walking through the mercado in Matamoros, Tamaulipas—right across the border from Brownsville, Texas. I reveled in the lively colors all around me coming from produce, artesenias, bright dresses, piñatas, birds, everything and anything you can imagine in a market. I also savored the smell of tacos, gorditas, grilled onions, carne asada, and tamales traveling through the air from restaurants and food stands. But, what always stood out the most to me from the visits to the mercado was the music radiating out of booths and stores selling cassette tapes. The beats and rhythm of cumbias, the tantalizing chords and runs of the accordion, and melodramatic lyrics of romantic music in Spanish flowed throughout the open air along with the scent of food cooking on the grills. The places that radiated the music were where my dad would stop to buy the latest cassette from the hippest grupo or conjunto of the time. That music carried knowledge, stories, generations of experiences, history, emotion, and truth. That music carried the cultural DNA of the border community I grew up in, as well as the lived realities of working-class Latinx people across Las Americas. This music also played in weddings, quinceañeras, birthdays, and other celebrations or pachangas in local salones and the front yards of our neighborhoods. This was part of my curriculum from the education I received in these communal spaces of joy, parties, and everyday life. Although this curriculum was part of my everyday life outside of school, when I stepped into the classroom, the familiarity of the melodies and lyrics seemed like they were from a different world that did not belong in the formal school curriculum.

The message was that these cumbias, corridos, musica Norteña, and Tejano music were uncultured and low-class and didn't belong in a U.S. school.

I start this chapter with a portrait of my own story growing up along the U.S./Mexico border in deep South Texas to position myself as a researcher and paint a picture of the borderland context. Although this region is rich in dynamic, cultural resources and knowledge, in my formal schooling experiences, this joyful and lively curriculum was rarely tapped into by my teachers—many of whom were also of Mexican origin and part of the border culture. Growing up, it seemed like we were all living double lives: (1) our Mexican border lives in spaces like family, the home, parties, and the mercado, and (2) our Americanized selves who met whitestream standards (Urrieta, 2010). Students who left their Mexicanness, or Mexican ways of knowing, outside the school door and spoke mostly English were rewarded with the "good student" status and tracked into college-bound classes. I learned that is was best to shapeshift into my Americanized self in order to excel in school. It was too messy to acknowledge my border ways of knowing. Rather than building bridges between my different identities and experiences, I was encouraged to perfect my white, middle-class performance and master the "official" school curriculum for social mobility. The border culture was just too messy for teachers and students to bring into the classroom. It was far more neat and orderly to validate state standards and textbooks as curriculum, rather than our everyday lives and stories from our own border community. I now wonder: What if our borderland stories and experiences were validated as curriculum in school? What if my teachers, peers, and I had been more open about our Mexicanness in the classroom?

I have shared my experiences in order to contextualize my classroom observations in an alternative school in the Rio Grande Valley (RGV). I engaged with portraiture methodology (Lawrence-Lightfoot & Davis, 1997) to present a portrait of one science classroom in which music invoked stories about family and community. The central question(s) that guide this chapter are the following: What does it look like when the messiness of the U.S./Mexico borderlands enters the classroom space? What happens when an environment of authentic care (Noddings, 2013; Valenzuela, 1999) enables a teacher and her students to embrace their border identities and Mexicanness to create a sense of belonging? I use engaged pedagogy (hooks, 1994; Berry, 2010), the concept of nepantla (Anzaldúa, 2007), and an ethic of care (Noddings, 2013) to make sense of how a science teacher and her students of Mexican-origin engaged in mutual interactions of vulnerability and storytelling through music. By centering this portrait, this chapter analyzes what it took to facilitate an organic use of regional music as curriculum in a science classroom. The teacher did not plan a lesson using regional music, but rather her caring pedagogy allowed her students to coconstruct this learning experience. This shows how caring pedagogical interactions allowed Latinx students to use their own border identities, experiences, and memories to coconstruct curriculum in the classroom.

THE RIO GRANDE VALLEY AND LATINX STUDENTS IN U.S. SCHOOLS

According to Kearney, Gómez Arguelles, and González's (1989) work, President Porfirio Diaz once remarked, "Poor Mexico, so far from God and so close to the United States!" One might alter the saying for the Rio Grande Valley of South Texas to read, "Poor border area, so far from both Mexico and the United States!" (Kearney, Gómez Arguelles, & González, 1989, p. 1). While the towns and small cities that make up the RGV are cut off from "their respective heartlands by large stretches of arid landscape on both north and south" of the Rio Grande River (Kearney, Gómez Arguelles, & González, 1989, p. 1), it is nonetheless "one of the most dynamic cultural areas in the United States" (p. 16). This fertile land is often referred to as the "Magic Valley" (particularly Hidalgo and Cameron counties), but it is known to some as the "Valley of Tears" (Madsen, 1973). The multiple layers of colonialism and war that occurred in this region make up a complicated history.

The Spanish government colonized this region, which was home to indigenous people (Maestas, 2003). After Mexico became independent from Spain, RGV became part of the Mexican province of Tamaulipas (Madsen, 1973). Before the Rio Grande River (or Rio Bravo as it is called in Mexico) ever became an international border, it was a natural resource that supplied farms and ranches that sat on both sides of the river. However, in 1836, Texas declared independence from Mexico, and the Rio Grande River became the new boundary between Texas and Mexico (Madsen, 1973). Once Texas joined the Union in 1845, the Treaty of Guadalupe-Hidalgo was enforced by the United States after the Mexican-American War to ensure the Rio Grande River as an international border between Mexico and the United States (Madsen, 1973). This transformed a natural resource into a border dividing families and communities that are deeply connected. This colonialist/imperialist legacy has created a common saying among the locals, "We did not cross over the border, the border crossed us" (Mier et al., 2004, p. 16).

Although an international border now exists, cultural exchange with Mexico in RGV occurs at all levels of society, both formally and informally. Part of this dynamism also comes from the high rate of border crossing by shoppers, tourists, workers, and students. It is distinguished for its "one-of-a kind amalgam of the culture and commerce of Texas and Mexico" (Mier et al., 2004, p. 16). There is also a continual flow of people in the region as seasonal visitors and workers spend their summers in the northern United States and their winters in the valley. Gloria Anzaldúa

(2007) calls the borderlands an open wound "where the Third World grates the first and it bleeds ... the lifeblood of two worlds merging to form a third country—a border culture" (p. 25). This border culture is socially fluid and multifaceted, as many families have members on both sides of the border. The familiar code switching between Spanish and English is a "linguistic manifestation of the cultural interconnection" between both sides of the border (Kearney, Gómez Arguelles, & González, 1989, p. 1). RGV is also home to a unique cultural exchange of musical influences and genres like cumbias, musica Norteña, Banda, corridos, and Tejano music (a unique cultural production from Tejanos or Texans of Mexican descent). This music informs the everyday lives of the students who grow up in this region, yet this kaleidoscope of musical and cultural productions seldom enters the classroom as a legitimate form of knowledge.

In fact, the in-between cultural ways of knowing from the youth and their families in this region has long been ostracized in U.S. schools. A large part of the historical trajectory and legacy of U.S. schooling for students along the U.S./Mexico border has been one of exclusion through racist practices, such as school segregation, cultural marginalization, and linguistic elimination (Young, 2010). Stories of students being punished for speaking Spanish and feeling like they have to "Americanize" in order to meet teachers' expectations are typical for people who grew up in the borderlands (Martínez, 1994). More recently, Mexican youth in Texas often attend schools that are poorly funded, overcrowded, English-only, and highly segregated (Valenzuela, 1999). Mexican students and their families are typically not validated and instead are perceived in "deficit ways" by school administration, teachers, and counselors (Valencia, 2002). For instance, parents and students of Mexican origin are often accused of not caring about getting an education, so they are positioned as culturally and morally deficient vis-à-vis a white, middle-class norm. It is no wonder that refraining from speaking Spanish in school is a strategy that youth of Mexican-origin along the border often employ in order to fit into white, middle-class norms to excel in school (Martínez, 1994). Not only are the assets and sources of knowledge from Mexican-origin students devalued, but they are also stripped away to instill behaviors and practices that are sanctioned by white, middle-class values (Valenzuela, 1999). Hence, mainstream schooling has also been referred to as "whitestream schooling" because it is structured around the knowledge base, practices, culture, and norms of the white middle class (Urrieta, 2010).

Despite this discrimination, Mexican-origin students find ways to resist whitestream schooling. Critical race scholars like Solórzano & Yosso (2002) have pointed out that Latinx students may "act up" in school not because they want to be evil or because they are lazy, but rather as a way to resist oppressive structures, pedagogies, and judgments from teachers who do not understand them. Resistance can sometimes be self-defeating in that students may select to reject schooling completely and be pushed out of school. Such is the case with the student population that attends RGV School, the alternative school where I collected data for the study that informs this chapter. Many of the students who attend RGV School may be either teen mothers, caught up in the criminal justice system, or face a combination of complicated circumstances in their personal lives. Moreover, some of the students resisted teachers who they felt did not care about them in their prior school and were consequently pushed out due to "behavior problems." Others may just have trouble attending school every day, so they fall behind in their school credits. In the following section, I will discuss the particular context of RGV School that fosters a different schooling environment in which these students who were once labeled as "bad" students are able to renegotiate their student identities in a different kind of schooling space.

CONTEXT: RGV SCHOOL

RGV School (pseudonym) is a small alternative school located in the lower Rio Grande Valley near the U.S./Mexico border. It is a small campus for students who are struggling academically or behaviorally in their home schools. Rather than adhering to an abstract system of accountability that traditional schools usually espouse (Valenzuela, 1999), RGV school is organized around a "nurturing culture of caring" (specifically outlined in the RGV School newsletter), with the goal of ensuring that students' emotional and personal needs are met first, followed by academics. Thus, the school has flexible schedules, peer counseling, and support services like childcare and homebound teachers for parenting students. The number of students fluctuates throughout the year, because some students may attend the school for a couple of weeks to catch up on their credits, or they may choose to stay and graduate at RGV School.

The supportive school structure and the teachers' positive outlook on students fuel the students' sense of belonging at RGV School. During interviews and informal conversations in hallways, during class, and in the cafeteria, many of the students pointed out that they could depend on their teachers for academic guidance and mentorship. Moreover, the school embraces the borderlands culture of the surrounding region of the school. The front entrance displays artwork in which students painted familiar landscapes from the community. Some of the art pieces have splashes of colors from the U.S. and Mexican flags, signaling the bicultural identities embodied by the students. The school hallways also display student-of-the-month bulletin boards in which pictures of students were rotated to celebrate particular accomplishments and positive traits about the students in the school. One of the students I interviewed confessed that she couldn't believe she was recognized as student of the month, especially because she felt like teachers in her prior school did not respect or care about her. She used to talk back to her teachers and walk out of class in her prior school, but in this alternative space, she got along well with her teachers and was excelling in class. In a caring space, she felt mutual respect with her teachers, which fostered a different set of interactions with them altogether.

THEORETICAL FRAMEWORK

In this chapter, I utilize woman-centered ways of knowing, including engaged pedagogy (Berry, 2010; hooks, 1994), the concept of nepantla (Anzaldúa, 2007), and an ethic of care (Noddings, 2013) to make sense of how a science teacher and her students of Mexican origin engaged in mutual interactions of vulnerability and storytelling through music. Given that RGV School is organized around care and support, Nel Noddings (2013) work is helpful to make sense of the immediate school context that sets the stage for the interactions I observed in the classroom. According to Noddings's (2013) work, an ethic of care in education includes: intimate interpersonal interactions between teachers and students, coconstruction of knowledge in the classroom, and the sharing of experiences. Caring is always a situation- and person-specific act, so there is no model of caring, but rather it is relational and context based.

Like ethics of care, engaged pedagogy (hooks, 1994) is also relational and context specific. However, stemming from a critical feminist lens, engaged pedagogy takes into account the experience of students of color to charge educators with the responsibility of challenging white, Eurocentric ways of knowing more directly. Engaged pedagogy "incorporates passions, dialogue, and interaction through the entrance of lived experiences" of students of color in the classroom (Berry, 2010, p. 22). As discussed previously, whitestream schooling harms Mexican-origin youth because their lived experiences are rarely acknowledged in traditional school curricula. With little recognition in the curriculum comes little opportunity for students to engage in dialogue that centers their experiences in the classroom. In short, "these students suffer a curriculum of oppression" (Berry, 2009, p. 747). Thus, engaged pedagogy encompasses mutual vulnerability in which the teacher and students reveal personal stories in connection with the subject at hand. Berry (2010) states that, "life experiences, when permitted into the classroom and given voice, can call to task the established" curriculum (p. 21). From this vantage point, an ethic of care necessitates engaged pedagogy in order to meet the needs of students of color in a transformative way. It is not enough for students to feel cared for by the teacher; they must also feel a mutual sense of vulnerability in which the teacher and her students learn from one another in a way that challenges the official curriculum.

The last part of my theoretical lens is Gloria Anzaldúa's (2007) concept of nepantla, a cornerstone of Chicana feminist theory. Nepantla is a "Nahuatl word/concept for that ambiguous, tentative, ever-changing space we all inhabit" (Pérez, 2005, p. 1). It is the in-between space where permeable identities overlap to break down fixed categories of identity. This is the space where the subaltern resides, a "decolonial imaginary—that space between colonial and postcolonial . . . where [one] makes sense of [one's] agency" (Pérez, 2005, p. 4). Nepantla is a useful Chicana feminist theoretical tool that allows me to articulate issues of identity, experience, the body, and the permeability of social structures. From this epistemological standpoint, although Latinx students from the borderlands live with ambiguity and contradictions throughout their educational lives, their embodied knowledge can serve as a site for social critique, countervoices, and change.

RESEARCH DESIGN AND METHODS

This chapter is derived from a larger qualitative study that examines the pedagogical interactions of care and support that unfold between teachers and mothering students (or teen mothers) within RGV School. The study was conducted by: (1) completing classroom observations three times a week over the course of one scholastic year in three different classrooms and (2) conducting in-depth interviews with the three teachers whose classrooms I observed and five teen mothers between the ages of 15 and 19. I used portraiture methodology (Lawrence-Lightfoot & Davis, 1997) in my research design to assemble portraits that zoom in on the detailed pedagogical strategies teachers used to connect with students.

Although my larger study focuses on mothering students and includes three different classrooms, the data for this chapter is based on one co-ed classroom that serves parenting and nonparenting students. While I conducted in-depth interviews with teachers and mothering students of all of the classrooms that I visited, for the purposes of this chapter, I focused on the data from the interview with Ms. Luna (the teacher whose classroom is featured here). I also drew upon the interviews that I conducted with two of the teen mothers who were taking or had taken Ms. Luna's class. These voices helped shape and inform my analysis of the events that unfolded in the classroom. Even though this study has a limitation for not interviewing young men or nonparenting students, this was beyond the scope of my original study. In sum, this chapter features a portrait of one science teacher and a certain set of interactions that unfolded between her and her students during one of my visits.

I obtained IRB approval for my study after I secured approval from the school district and the school principal. Before I began the interviews, I observed the classrooms for about 2 to 3 weeks and then analyzed the notes from those visits in order to identify preliminary themes. The themes went through further transformation as more patterns were noted. Preliminary themes were used to construct interview protocols for the teachers and the students; I did this in order to contextualize the interview protocols and provide opportunities for the participants to shed further insight on patterns that I was noticing. I integrated a grounded theory approach in analyzing my data (Charmaz, 2006). I conducted a highly selective process of coding—starting with initial coding followed by focused coding (Charmaz, 2006)—to identify themes.

I conducted the interviews at the same time as I engaged in classroom observations. Because this happened over a long period of time, coding the observations allowed me to reveal new themes and modify pre-existing ones. This enabled me to modify the interview protocols according to these new trends and patterns. Each interview session was tape-recorded and immediately transcribed before I conducted the subsequent interview. Once all the interviews were conducted, I went through more rounds of selective coding of the interviews and all of my field notes. I also kept self-reflexive notes about my own positionality and relationship to the study (Harding, 1988).

Why Portraiture Methodology

Portraiture draws from case study protocol, narrative inquiry, stories, and ethnographic methods (Lawrence-Lightfoot & Davis, 1997). It generates images fashioned by thick descriptions of events and contexts that bring the reader into the lives of the research participants (Dixson, Chapman, & Hill, 2005). Moreover, rather than walking into a site asking what is wrong, the researcher enters the field asking, "What is good here?" There is a long tradition in the social sciences of documenting "pathology and disease rather than . . . health and resilience" (Lawrence-Lightfoot and Davis, 1997, p. 8). This tendency is especially prominent in education research, where investigators most often document failure instead of describing examples of success. I decided to use portraiture methodology to humanize Latinx students and provide a counterstory (Solórzano & Yosso, 2002) of the joy that can be felt if their knowledges and experiences are embraced in the classroom.

However, the aim of portraiture is not to romanticize research settings and subjects; weaknesses and vulnerabilities are always present in any given context (Lawrence-Lightfoot & Davis, 1997). Instead, the contradictory and counterpoint workings of weaknesses and strengths are central to the project. The narrative, aesthetic style of portraiture allows for the demonstration of the complexities and contradictions that encompass everyday life, interactions, and relationships among teachers and students in the classroom. This attention to complexities and contradictions enabled me to: (1) reflect on the messiness I encountered in the field, (2) engage in deep analysis, and (3) compose a portrait that engages with emerging contradictions as opportunities for the reader to imagine other possibilities for improving the pedagogical practices and curricular possibilities that are discussed.

RESULTS

Before I share the following portrait, I will provide context of the typical interactions that occur in Ms. Luna's class, as well as the positionality of the teacher in relation to her students. First of all, Ms. Luna is from Matamoros, a city located immediately on the Mexican side of the U.S.-Mexican border, and she was on a work visa at the time of my study. She also speaks English with a strong, northern Mexican accent. Ms. Luna's Biology class was highly structured because of the fast-paced curriculum she was charged to cover in each class. As part of the accelerated program, Ms. Luna had to cover a year's worth of Biology material in one semester, so it was important for her to maintain order to ensure that students didn't fall behind. She avoided talking about her personal life, especially when it came to her Mexicanness, because she didn't want students to "waste" time. Although she tried to keep her personal life private, her accent betrayed the boundaries she tried to maintain. Students noticed her accent and mispronunciation of words in English, and they often poked fun at her, but the result was not maliciousness but rather connection. From where I sat during classroom observations, it seemed like her imperfection in speaking English was actually a point of connection with which her students could identify. They openly joked to signal a sort of relief that their teacher was a lot like them, thereby forging a sense of belonging and community.

Ms. Luna, however, seemed unaware of this sense of community building. Her preoccupation with time and keeping her students on track seemed to block her view of how students connected with her personal identity. Despite her inclination to be "strict," she nonetheless exhibited care by incorporating flexibility. For instance, *behind the scenes*, she provided students with plenty of opportunities for makeup work, and she typically considered their personal lives and emotional states when she planned her lessons and activities. *On stage*, however, she enacted a "mean" teacher persona to keep her students from "wasting time." The students, however, saw through this act and understood she was "tough" on them because she cared about them. I found it compelling how the students exhibited agency by constructing her teacher identity through their playful interactions with her. Although Ms. Luna usually refrained from exhibiting her Mexicanness with her students, in the following portrait, I show how music changed this common scenario.

"This was a quiet and smooth day!": Ms. Luna Opens Up to Her Students

It was around eleven in the morning when I walked into Ms. Luna's fourth period Biology class. As I settled into my usual place in the back of the room, I noticed that several students were absent that day, and only five students were present. One of the absent students was Susana, who had given birth to her baby and was being homeschooled for a couple of weeks while she recovered from the delivery. The only mothering student present was Esperanza who was pregnant at the time, and as usual, she was focused on her work. She liked to sit in the desk that was right by Ms. Luna's desk. She didn't have a laptop in front her, so I assumed that she was done with the bell ringer (warm-up) for the day. While Esperanza was working on her main assignment, Fernando and Teresa had their laptops open. Ms. Luna then asked them whether they were done with their bell ringers.

As usual, Ms. Luna was sitting at her desk clicking away at her desktop computer and sorting through papers and folders as she called out student names to update them on what assignments they were missing. Suddenly, Josh, out of nowhere, exhibited frustration when he complained that people kept texting him. Ms. Luna responded to his frustration by telling him to, "Stop texting!" But, his thumbs kept bouncing off the screen as he responded to the texts. Ms. Luna then lifted her head as she announced to the class that, on the following day, they were going have a quiz about biomes based on the notes on which they were currently working. A high-pitched ringing sound came out of Josh's phone after Ms. Luna finished her announcement, and Fernando turned to tell Josh that he should look up "the dog whistle." Ms. Luna asked Fernando not to give Josh any ideas.

I was expecting more whistling sounds to come from Josh's phone, since he had successfully attracted Fernando's attention, but instead, a more pleasant sound flowed out of another direction. The soothing sound was music coming from Ms. Luna's computer. She seemed to mark the beginning of a subtle competition with Josh in providing background sounds for the class. The music sounded familiar. The lyrics were in Spanish, and it reminded me of the kind of music my mother enjoyed, which she called música romántica (romantic music) or música internacional (international music). Many of the artists of this music genre are from various Latin American countries and even European countries like Spain and Italy (many Italian artists also sing their songs in Spanish to find success among Spanish-speaking audiences). Although young people may not often listen to música romántica, the sound of music flowing from Ms. Luna's desktop was enough to spark Josh's curiosity and trigger the following dialogue:

Josh: Miss, are you into Gilberto Quintanilla?

Ms. Luna: This is a romantic track.

Josh: But you don't like him?

Ms. Luna: I do, but I don't want to hear him right now, only when I'm dancing.

Josh began playing one of Quintanilla's songs anyway, while Ms. Luna assisted Fernando with one of the questions on his assignment. As the sound of música romántica flowed out of Ms. Luna's desktop computer and Quintanilla's electrifying music blasted out of Josh's phone, Ms. Luna continued to walk from one student to the next to check on their work and answer their questions. These contrasting sounds clashed and created disjointed rhythms with odd-fitting melodies, so Ms. Luna turned to Josh to tell him that she didn't mind him playing his own music as long as he finished his work for the day. She then proceeded to walk to Josh's desk to give him further instructions on how to complete the assignment.

Gilberto or Beto Quintanilla is a famous local artist that is highly respected and admired by people of all ages who live along the U.S.-Mexican border in south Texas. He is notorious for making corridos about Mexican drug cartels, but he also composes corridos about the common experiences of people (especially men) who live in south Texas or northern Mexico. Corridos are a type of Mexican music that is characteristic of the southwest in the United States and northern Mexico. The accordion is the defining instrument and sound of corrido music. In fact, polka music greatly influenced the cultural production of corridos among Mexicans along the U.S.-Mexican border. German settlements and the introduction of the accordion gave rise to different kinds of regional music that dominate the southwestern region of the United States. and northern Mexico today.

After Ms. Luna finished orienting Josh on his assignment, she walked up to Marianna, a very reclusive and quiet student who usually sat away from the rest of the students, to ask her if she needed any help. Mariana shook her head, but Ms. Luna proceeded to help her out anyway as she pointed out parts of the worksheet where it seemed Mariana could benefit from extra assistance. After helping Mariana, Ms. Luna walked up to Fernando to check on his progress. Teresa's voice then redirected Ms. Luna's attention, "Ma'am, I don't get it!" The teacher walked over to Teresa's desk and began a line of questioning through which the student's prior knowledge was accessed little by little, eventually leading Teresa to the correct answer to the question. As Ms. Luna weaved her way around the room to check on students, I took note that this was the most movement I had seen from her since I began the classroom observations. In the midst of feverishly typing my observations of her high energy, constant movement, and long line of questioning, I soon forgot that there were two different kinds of music playing at the same time. Eventually, however, Ms. Luna stopped the music that was playing from her desktop, thereby formally dubbing the corrido music, coming from Josh's phone, as the official backdrop music for the class.

As a new song from Beto Quintanilla began to play, Josh momentarily stopped working to share out loud that he played the same song for his father during his birthday party. Josh explained that his father cried because the lyrics were about growing older and times changing. Esperanza then asked Ms. Luna a question, followed by Josh. After Ms. Luna finished helping Josh, he finished telling his story about his father's birthday party, and Ms. Luna listened intently before she moved on to help Teresa again. Suddenly, the music changed to another genre; Josh began playing Banda music. Banda music in Mexico is characterized by brass instruments and the tuba is the main instrument that maintains the beat and base of the music. This style of music originated in the state of Sinaloa in Mexico.

While the steady tuba sound flowed out of Josh's phone and punctured the space, Esperanza opened up a bag of Hot Funyuns and began to draw them out of the bag one by one with one hand, while her other hand steadily worked to fill up the study guide. Josh soon began playing another set of songs from another music genre. This time música Norteña began to fill the air as melodies from the accordion re-entered the scene. Música Norteña is a more general style of music from the northern region of Mexico. The name música Norteña literally means music from the northern region, particularly from the Mexican state of Tamaulipas. Like corridos, música Norteña is also characterized by the accordion, but the lyrics tend to be thematic, rather than the narrative style that is typical of corridos. Ramón Ayala is a prime example of a Norteño artist. In fact, the first song that Josh began playing was from Ramón Ayala, called *Un Puño de Tierra*. As the song played, Teresa excitedly turned around in her seat to tell Josh, in a voice loud enough for everyone to hear, that the song was played during her father's funeral. She turned back around to keep working as she sang along with the main chorus of the song:

El día que yo me muera,
No voy a llevarme nada,
Hay que darle gusto al gusto,
La vida pronto se acaba,
Lo que pasó en este mundo,
Nomás el recuerdo queda,

Ya muerto voy a llevarme . . . nomás un puño de tierra.
(The day that I die, I'm not going to take anything with me, you must enjoy life while you can [not a direct translation], *life will be over soon, what happened in this world, only memories will remain, when I die I will only take, only a handful of soil.)*

Teresa continued to talk about her father, her brothers, and the rest of her family as the song played, but even in the midst of sharing her stories, she kept working, and while Ms. Luna continued to move about the room assisting students, she periodically looked Teresa's way. More Norteño songs flowed out of Josh's phone. Suddenly, Ms. Luna let out a small grito when a song she really liked began to play. A grito is an expression of joy similar to a yeehaw for U.S. cowboys. It can be a long drawn out "aaahh" or "aaayyeee" that can resemble a laugh. It is typical to hear it in Musica Norteña or Tejano music (the regional music of Texas). In shock upon hearing Ms. Luna's grito and witnessing her dancing, Esperanza and Teresa giggled with amusement. However, Josh changed the song, and Ms. Luna exclaimed, "Why you change it [sic]? I really like that song!" Esperanza then shared, "My dad would play these songs in barbeques to get drunk." Teresa agreed with Esperanza and shared that her family did the same in parties too. Esperanza then asked Ms. Luna, "Miss, how do you know these songs?" Ms. Luna explained that she knew the music because of bailes (dancing parties). The young women seemed surprised again as they giggled and stared at Ms. Luna.

Ms. Luna began singing along with the lyrics of another song that Josh began to play. Her eyes lit up, and she exclaimed, "Oh! I like that song!" Ms. Luna began to sing along, but then paused and said, "That's true! Don't look for someone that's just pretty, because after the years pass by the pretty goes away!" Ms. Luna was referring to the lyrics of the song. Esperanza took another bite out of her Hot Funyun as she looked at Ms. Luna and listened to her advice, incited by the lyrics of a regional Mexican song. More songs steadily flowed out of Josh's phone as he picked out songs that so far had struck up stories, memories, and even advice among the students *and* from Ms. Luna. The students continued to work diligently, including Josh who would intermittently picked up his phone to change the songs or the type of music. There were momentary gaps between songs as Josh would be a little late in picking up his phone to play the next song. In fact, Ms. Luna jokingly remarked, "Where's the DJ? There should be no silent space between songs!" Josh then asked Ms. Luna, "Ma'am, do you know this song?" Another Norteño song began to play, and the teacher exclaimed "YES!" She began dancing in her seat with a huge smile. Teresa began laughing as Esperanza asked another question about the assignment. More questions emerged out of the students as they scrambled to finish as much of the classwork as they could.

When the class began to wrap up, Ms. Luna asked the students to finish at home and study for the quiz. Josh stood up and talked to Ms.

Luna about the kind of music his mother likes, and Fernando shared his success stories with promoting music events on social media like Facebook. In the midst of Fernando sharing his future plans to become a successful events promoter, the bell rang, and the students packed up their belongings and made their way out of the classroom. After all the students left, Ms. Luna looked at me and said:

> Ms. Luna: This was a quiet and smooth day!
>
> I: Why do you think that is?
>
> Ms. Luna: (chuckles) I don't know. I think it can be many things. The weather, even what they ate.
>
> I: I guess there are many variables!

I found it interesting that Ms. Luna named variables that were out of her control to help explain what seemed like a quiet and smooth class time with her Biology students. However, there was so much that she did differently this time. This yielded a different set of results in which she had more control of the flow of the classroom, even though she allowed Josh to play music from his phone out loud for the class. She had a much stronger presence in the room this time as she moved from student to student to help them with their study guide. In fact, she was proactive in providing assistance to the students, instead of the students crowding around her desk or calling her over so that she could help. Ms. Luna's voice also filled up the room much more than usual as she used scaffolding strategies with students. Her pedagogical interactions with students became more cheerful as she smiled, laughed, and even joked with them. Ms. Luna eventually let Josh become the official "DJ" of the class, as he played music that was familiar to the students because it reminded them of their families, especially their fathers, given the patriarchal nature of the music (popular regional Mexican music is usually about the experiences of men). Although Ms. Luna surrendered her música romántica to the regional and even local music (Beto Quintanilla), it actually opened up opportunities for her to expose herself more fully to her students by expressing her joy through singing and even dancing. The students were greatly amused with getting to know Ms. Luna on a more personal level, and in turn, the students also exposed their personal lives to one another and the teacher through the music that invoked a collective Mexicanness that is specific to the region. When she opened up and embraced her cultural roots along with a proactive demeanor in helping students, Ms. Luna's classes became a mutually orchestrated set of interactions between the teacher and students that fostered deeper connections and relationships.

CONCLUSION

In this chapter, I have shown what it looks like when: (1) the messiness of the U.S.-Mexican borderlands enters the classroom space, and (2) a teacher and her students embrace their border identities and Mexicanness to create a sense of belonging. Despite the fast-paced Biology curriculum, Ms. Luna opened up the classroom to music that was characteristic of the surrounding border community. This music invoked engaged pedagogy (Berry, 2009; hooks, 1994) in which stories and memories of home, family, death, and advice were exchanged between the students and Ms. Luna. It took the personal disclosure of Ms. Luna's Mexicanness to foster mutual vulnerability (Berry, 2009) with her students. Her personal self-disclosures about a fun topic like music and dancing may seem small, but for her, it was a big deal to disclose her personal life in relation to her students. Her positionality as a non-U.S. citizen with a Mexican accent complicates the usual teacher-student power dynamic that is more clear-cut for white, U.S.-born teachers. Ms. Luna was aware that students made fun of the way she spoke, so being open about going to bailes and singing along to corridos could be interpreted as risky moves for an educator who wants to solidify a clear power divide with students. The students also took risks in telling stories about family members getting drunk at parties. Because educators may espouse deficit thinking about Latinx students and their families, there is a chance that a teacher could interpret those kinds disclosures in a way that could reinforce stereotypes. The students also talked about death and funerals, which are deeply emotional life experiences. Given the caring schooling structure and classroom (Noddings, 2013), the students felt comfortable with sharing intimate stories about their families with one another and with Ms. Luna.

One limitation, however, is that, even though a different kind of border curriculum entered the scene, students were nonetheless working on a study guide to complete the requirements of the formal curriculum. A critical pedagogue may rightfully wonder what might happen if students were engaged in problem-based learning or a youth participatory action research project about a community problem related to Biology. How can student experiences, stories, and memories be validated in ways that incite social change? While the event in this particular portrait does not draw upon student knowledge in this way, it does show how the cultural resources of Latinx students *and* teachers can rupture whitestream schooling and curriculum in ways that open up possibilities for further transformative change.

The contradiction between the coconstructed border curriculum and the formal curriculum in this portrait helps me think about everyday classroom life as a "third space." Based on the concept of nepantla (Anzaldúa, 2007), third spaces are fleeting moments in which multiple discourses, scripts, and dialogues can overlap, clash, and contradict in ways that can disrupt institutionalized roles of teacher and student in classrooms. These fleeting moments present oppositional instances in which institutional scripts are interrupted and a different set of discourses and interactions momentarily emerge, in which student and teacher roles must change to traverse unexplored territory. For instance, by embracing her Mexicanness, Ms. Luna went against white Eurocentric expectations of keeping her private life out of the classroom—an expectation that she had internalized. This shakes up the institutional expectation that teachers are supposed be in control of their composure in the classroom at all times. Rather than keeping her rational composure, Ms. Luna followed her students' lead in letting the borderlands seep into the classroom and imbue their interactions and relationship building. Thus, a different kind of curriculum emerged out of this rupture in which the students' border identities and experiences were validated and celebrated.

Another way in which the interactions in this portrait work against whitestream schooling is through authentic care. Through an ethic of care (Noddings, 2013), Valenzuela (1999) has made the case that students of Mexican-origin need authentic care from their teachers in order for learning and student engagement to happen. Authentic care (Valenzuela, 1999; Noddings, 2013), which is based on mutual respect and validating the knowledge of students, works against the usual aesthetic care, or impersonal care, that often occurs in U.S. schools (i.e., standardized testing and classroom objectives). Embracing the messy borderland culture and identities of the students through authentic care and engaged pedagogy is an indispensable step toward working in opposition to the curriculum of oppression (Berry, 2010) that students along the border face.

In sum, on the one hand, the Rio Grande Valley is a space where multiple ways of knowing and histories converge to form a border culture. On the other hand, RGV School is an alternative space in which traditional, impersonal schooling structures are decentered through a culture of care and support that the faculty, staff, and administrators collectively espouse. Within these interstitial contexts, I witnessed music bridge the Mexican/American divide that I discussed at the beginning of this chapter. Through a caring schooling environment, engaged pedagogy, and the acceptance of always being in-between worlds, Ms. Luna and her students coconstructed a localized border curriculum. This shows that it is possible for borderland students to seamlessly merge their identities; however, it takes mutual vulnerability between teachers and students and a supportive school community to make this happen.

This study has implications for teacher preparation programs, as well as strategies for expanding notions of curriculum. We must prepare teachers to create an environment of care that allows students to bring in their cultural ways of knowing into the classroom. Increasing participation of Latinx students in curriculum coconstruction can result in rigorous learning experiences in which students not only engage in academic learning, but also transformative education.

REFERENCES

Anzaldúa, G. 2007. *Borderlands/La Frontera: The new Mestiza*, 3rd ed. San Francisco: Aunt Lute Books.
Berry, T. 2009. Women of color in a bilingual/dialectal dilemma: Critical race feminism against a curriculum of oppression in teacher education. *International Journal of Qualitative Studies in Education*, 22(6), 745–753.
———. 2010. Engaged pedagogy and critical race feminism. *The Journal of Educational Foundations*, 24(3/4), 19–26.
Charmaz, K. 2006. *Constructing grounded theory: A practical guide through qualitative analysis*. London: SAGE Publications.
Dixson, A., Chapman, T., & Hill, D. 2005. Research as an aesthetic process: Extending the portraiture methodology. *Qualitative Inquiry*, 11(1), 16–26.
Harding, S., ed. 1988. *Feminism and methodology: Social science issues*. Bloomington: Indiana University Press.
hooks, b. 1994. *Teaching to transgress: Education as the practice of freedom*. New York: Routledge.
Kearney, M., Arguelles, A. G., & González, Y. 1989. *A brief history of education in Brownsville and Matamoros*. Brownsville: The University of Texas-Pan American Brownsville.
Lawrence-Lightfoot, S., & Davis, J. 1997. *The art and science of portraiture*. San Francisco: Jossey-Bass.
Madsen, W. 1973. *The Mexican-Americans of south Texas*, 2nd ed. Fort Worth, TX: Holt, Rinehart and Winston.
Maestas, E. 2003. Culture and history of Native American peoples of South Texas. PhD diss., University of Texas at Austin. https://repositories.lib.utexas.edu/handle/2152/752
Martínez, O. 1994. *Border people: Life and society in the U.S.-Mexico borderlands*. Tucson: University of Arizona Press.
Mier, N., Flores, I., Robinson, J., & Millard, A. 2004. Cultural, demographic, educational, and economic characteristics. In R. Sue Day (ed.), *Nourishing the future: The case for community-based nutrition research in the lower Rio Grande Valley* (pp. 15–24). Houston: The University of Texas School of Public Health.
Noddings, N. 2013. *Caring: A relational approach to ethics and moral education*. Berkeley: University of California Press.
Pérez, E. 2005. Gloria Anzaldúa: La Gran Nueva Mestiza theorist, writer, activist-scholar. *NWSA Journal*, 17(2), 1–10.
Solórzano, D., & Yosso, T. 2002. Critical race methodology: Counter-storytelling as an analytical framework for education research. *Qualitative Inquiry*, 8(1), 23–44.
Urrieta, L. Jr. 2010. *Working from within: Chicana and Chicano activist educators in Whitestream schools*. Phoenix: University of Arizona Press.
Valencia, R. 2002. "Mexican Americans don't value education!" On the basis of the myth, mythmaking, and debunking. *Journal of Latinos and Education*, 1(2), 81–103.
Valenzuela, A. 1999. *Subtractive schooling: U.S. Mexican youth and the politics of caring*. Albany: State University of New York Press.
Young, E. 2010. Challenges to conceptualizing and actualizing culturally relevant pedagogy: How viable is the theory in classroom practice? *Journal of Teacher Education*, 61(3), 248–260.

NINE

Currere from the Borderlands

An Exercise in Possibilities for Latinx Transgender Visibility

Mario Itzel Suárez

I was born to a Mexican father and a Mexican American mother, and assigned female at birth. Eagle Pass, Texas, housed in Maverick County, was and continues to be one of the poorest counties in the state. We did not grow up with luxuries like cable television, barely had electricity, and lived in an underdeveloped subdivision with little to no proper sewage. Some might refer to such a place as a *colonia*, but I just referred to it as my home. I excelled at school and my teachers took notice, particularly in mathematics. Before I knew it, one of the school counselors was helping me apply for colleges and financial aid. I had no idea where these colleges and universities were, what the differences were between them, why there were so many, why they could not just let me go to the junior college at home, or how my family could ever afford such places. Counselors told me that I had the potential to get scholarships, so I trusted them and still applied for every place and everything I qualified for. I opted to go to The University of Texas at Austin, not because of its reputation, but because of the scholarships I received that made it easier for me to choose it. There, I graduated with a Mexican American Studies bachelor's degree and with enough mathematics to be able to get certified to teach at the high school level. The moments I have experienced throughout my life are not isolated in time. They all have had a significant effect on my growth as an educator and researcher. Some moments might have taken longer for me to understand, but nonetheless, they contributed to my identity. As a transgender educator, and someone who advocates for the lives and education of sexual and gender minority youth, particularly those of color, I find it important to remain as visible as I can, and thus, was an openly transgender mathematics teacher when I taught at the high school level.

THE NEED FOR QUEERING EDUCATION

While the attitudes of today's students are evolving with regard to their views on gender and sexuality, that of their teachers might still be stuck in the traditional dichotomous view of gender. That is, gender has been historically thought of as just male or female. Curriculum and textbooks continue to have antiquated information about gender and sexuality and traditional/conservative views of families (Macgillivray & Jennings, 2008, pp. 170–188; Jennings & Macgillivray, 2011, pp. 39–62). In the meanwhile, lesbian, gay, bisexual, transgender, intersex, and queer/questioning (LGBTIQ) youth continue to have negative school outcomes, on average. For example, we know that a hostile school environment and lack of administrative and parental support is associated with higher instances of assault, harassment, discrimination, higher instances of school absences, and lower academic achievement (Kosciw, Greytak, Giga, Villenas, & Danischewski, 2016). That can be reversed, however, by having a supportive school environment that affirms students' gender and sexual diversity. Supportive environments can contribute to a reduction in suicidal ideations for LGBTIQ youth (Hatzenbuehler, Birkett, Wagenen, & Meyer, 2014, pp. 279–286). I contend that preservice teacher education must transition to methodologies that help teachers reflect on their own biases in order to best meet the needs of their students. Representation in curriculum matters, but I believe it is also true that we must have teachers who are aware of how their own education perpetuates certain views of gender and sexuality in order to empathize with a community to which they might not be a part of.

This piece draws from philosophical perspectives in queer theory and queer history, *mestiza consciousness* (Anzaldúa, 1999), my autobiographical reflection, in addition to learning theories in education, and reflects on how all of these have intersected at memorable points in my life as a teacher. Though this chapter is written as a recollection of thoughts from childhood up until adulthood, I weave in pieces of historical and philosophical perspectives that have influenced my personal knowledge base of teaching gender and sexuality within a high school mathematics context. The purpose of this chapter is to provide preservice and in-service teachers with an exercise in reflection via *currere* (Pinar, 2012), as a means to deconstruct their own biases about gender and gender identity. Through my own personal experience and reflection with transgender visibility, it is my hope that preservice and in-service teachers can use *currere* as a means to deconstruct their own biases.

Informed by Schwab's love letter to education, Craig (2013) provides some suggestions as to how different practices can "foster the best-loved self," (p. 267) that is, be the best and capable person they can be for their students. In effecting change through preservice teacher education, Craig uses narratives of the lives of four different teachers' best-loved selves from different walks of life as a means to direct us to the significance the "best-loved self" has with regard to pedagogy. In all the four cases, teachers were able to incorporate what they learned in their pedagogical tool belt. Li and Logan (2017, pp. 137–156) also used narrative inquiry as a means to how a teacher's image of their best-loved self had an effect on their pedagogical knowledge-base. I suggest in this chapter that being a student of *currere* can help foster this best-loved self-image for teachers and thus contribute to the knowledge-base of teaching for gender and sexuality education.

CURRERE AS A METHODOLOGY

Developed by William Pinar, *currere* is a process of self-reflection in which the individual becomes the subject of study (Pinar, 1975a). In describing *currere*, Pinar defines it as the "study of the educational experience" (Pinar, 1975b, p. 400). Historical roots of curriculum are derived from the Latin word *currere*, meaning "to run the racecourse," and when referring to curriculum, is defined as an active process rather than a passive one (Pinar, 2012; Slattery, 2015). Pinar (2012) writes, "The method of *currere* . . . provides a strategy for students of curriculum to study the relations between academic knowledge and life history in the interests of self-understanding" (p. 44). That is, it takes into account the psychoanalytical and the phenomenological, and makes it personal, because it is in our personal journeys that we draw from and construct curriculum. The movies we saw as children, the teachers we had, the places we have been, the books we have read, are all part of our educational journey. We cannot understand teachers and teaching according to Pinar, until we learn to study ourselves and learn from ourselves, or "become students of ourselves" (Pinar, 1975b, p. 412). All these represent our own "knowledge of *currere*" (Pinar, 1975b, p. 402). It is also important to note that if "political analyses" or "anthropological analyses" are not at the root of *currere*, "then we have fallen away from our task, from ourselves . . . " (Pinar, 1975b, p. 406). Pinar then expands:

> This [*currere*], simply enough, involves remembering one's first experience associated with school, and free associating about those early experiences. The task this strategy involves is recording a chronology of associations, beginning with earliest events and continuing to the

present. In both free associative techniques, the aim is to free associate as much as one can, allowing oneself to fall into past experience, to record this experience with as little editing as possible. . . . When sufficient data has accumulated (and the question of when may well be left to the investigator) the analysis begins. . . . But here is the expectation. A sort of model (it's not completely applicable) is the textual analysis practiced by students of imaginative literature. . . . Depending on the nature of the data examined (it might be a series of associations in regard to a book one is reading or it might be historical material from, say, one's first years in school), the questions that guide the analytic process may be the same as or similar to the questions that prompted the free associative process initially. (Pinar, 1975b, pp. 408–409)

Pinar claims that *currere* shifts the curriculum field from a Tylerian prescriptive one and moves toward that of understanding, something that he writes the American educational system does not necessarily subscribe to (Pinar, 1975b). While Pinar cautions us in using *currere* as an instructional tool or strategy for professional development, he mentions that using it as a "sensibility" has numerous possibilities for teachers' and students' transformation and self-reflection.

In this same notion, I would like to preface that my experience as a transgender man of color who was a high school mathematics teacher by trade is different from others. Therefore, my comfort level with reflecting on my experience with gender can be different than other transgender people, or different than other teachers, for that matter. When implementing a methodology as critically reflective as *currere*, it is important to be able to understand that no two experiences will ever evolve in the same manner or at the same pace. It is my hope that my autoethnographical narrative, along with *currere* will be an exercise in self-reflection for teachers that can help unpack their own particular biases or understandings about the world, and in turn, result in a much more empathetic teacher, as evident from empirical work on the best-loved self resulting from Schwab's work notion that the best-loved self can translate into becoming an excellent teacher (Craig, 2013, pp. 261–272; Li & Logan, 2017, pp. 137–156).

Autoethnography and Currere

Autoethnography is a method of qualitative research that takes the personal and makes a contribution to studying the sociocultural (Ellis & Bochner, 2000). Like *currere*, it is a methodology used for self-reflection, usually written in a first-person voice. It weaves the personal and the political, the personal and the cultural, the personal and the social, in a complicated web of connections, using the self as the research subject. As with other types of qualitative research methodologies, concerns of validity, reliability, and generalizability of the research when it comes to doing work on the self comes at play. However, Ellis and Bochner point out the complicated nature of individuals' stories and that no two lives are the same, and therefore, the reader might or might not see themselves reflected in the stories (Ellis & Bochner, 2000, pp. 733–768). However, it might give the reader an insight into a culture or subculture to which they have not been exposed to.

It would be very difficult to find another transgender man from the border that has also been a high school mathematics teacher like myself for a full study. The odds are extremely small. However, there might be some aspects about my autoethnographical account that might resonate with other transgender people or allies, or Mexican Americans from the borderlands, or with other high school mathematics teachers. The point of this is that by using my experience as an exercise in self-reflection, other teachers, particularly preservice and in-service teachers might expose themselves to *currere* and autoethnography, and thus, contribute to becoming their "best-loved self," (Craig, 2013) thereby learning more about gender and sexuality in order to best meet the needs of their LGBTIQ students.

AN EXERCISE IN *CURRERE*

One of the first steps in beginning the process of *currere*, before we even embark in this journey, according to Pinar, is to begin to remember one's own educational experience. To my surprise then, as I was sitting in one of my courses, the professor I had in one of my curriculum and instruction classes began the first class by asking us what the knowledge-base of teaching was, and tasked us with interviewing different teachers we knew concerning their very first recollections of learning something. This assignment included interviewing ourselves. It was in this moment that I tried to delve into my subconscious to pull out the first lesson I was taught as a child. As I have pointed out, I was born and raised in a small town on the Texas-Mexico border named Eagle Pass, Texas. I find it important to note my upbringing because it has been an influential part of my life schooling. I am also a man of transgender experience. That is, my gender identity does not align with the body and gender I was assigned at birth. I did not come to terms with my true identity until I was an undergraduate student in college. Part of the reason for not coming out earlier, I believe, was my lack of exposure to other transgender people living on the Texas-Mexico border. My closest experiences with people who were in some ways gender nonconforming were the drag queens my family and I would go and watch perform at "La Feria del Sol" every year in Piedras Negras, Coahuila, our Mexican sister city. I was mesmerized by the grace and humor in performance that these women had in portraying cisgender female Mexican artists like Gloria Trevi, Maria Felix, Paulina Rubio, and Selena, among many others. I was shaped by those experiences, and continue to evolve as a result of those interactions throughout my life. My hope is that in understanding some of my background, one can understand a little more about the Latinx experience as a transgender person living in the beautiful borderlands, the backdrop for some of Gloria Anzaldúa's writings.

The journey of *currere* for me does not end here. It continues as I continue to evolve, and as I continue to learn not only more about myself but my transgender siblings. I write this with a heavy heart and great awareness of the privilege afforded to me in being able to share my experience in writing and being able to live to tell my story. This is not a story that is afforded to so many of my transgender siblings, particularly transgender women of color, who are year after year the victims of an often transphobic curriculum. As the title of this chapter alludes to, this journey of *currere* for me represents an exercise in the possibilities that can arise when we transgender people are ourselves. This is not to say that my life history has been without challenges and struggles. I have had my share of hardships that I believe have been balanced by the tremendous support I have received from friends and allies. This exercise delves only into the questions that stemmed from asking myself, What is my first memory of having learned something? In this chapter, I go through the four stages of *currere*: the regressive, the progressive, the analytical, and the synthetical moment, which are all explained in each section (Pinar, 2012). In addition, I introduce models of teaching that I engaged with within the lessons learned.

The Regressive Moment

The regressive moment of *currere* entails that the student relive their past. Pinar (2012) writes, "In the regressive step or moment I try to re-experience past 'lived' or existential experience" (p. 45). This step is what helped me re-experience my first vivid recollection of something being taught to me was when I was about 5 years old. I was playing with my older brother, and I really wanted to play with his Star Wars and G. I. Joe figurines. I was very jealous that he had them and I did not. I remember my mom saying, *"Eso es para los hombres! Las tuyas son las Barbies!"* ("That's for boys! The ones that are yours are the Barbies!"). I was confused hearing her say that. I could not understand why I could not have the boys' toys. After all, I was a boy, right? Or was I? Why did I not look like my brother? How was it that my body parts all were distinctly different? I had so many questions for my parents. However, I was never very close to my mother, as she was not one to approach us with heart-to-heart chats. My father was similar. He worked two jobs almost every day and provided for us, but he was hardly ever home. On days he was home, though, he was a jokester. When it was time for me to go through puberty, I did not understand what my body was going through until a talk I had with one of my maternal aunts. However, it took at least two decades from that very first lesson before I could find some answers about the feelings I was having and why my body was physically changing in ways that I did not think they should. As a cisgender female, I was growing breasts, menstruating, and the women around me wanted me to have long hair and to wear women's clothing. I wanted the complete opposite.

That memory probably marked the first time I learned that boys and girls wore different clothing, that boys and girls played with different toys, and more importantly, that boys and girls had distinctly different body parts. To be shown what a girl could do and not do, and what a boy could do and not do (or wear and not wear, for that matter) was a lesson that remained with me all throughout my adulthood. I was learning a very important lesson without being formally taught. In effect, my family engaged in a model known as concept attainment. Concept attainment represents "the search for and listing of attributes that can be used to distinguish exemplars from nonexemplars of various categories" (Bruner, Goodnow, & Austin, 1967, p. 233). I was learning societal norms of what gender meant, and was being reproduced generationally. Without a formal education, I had a lesson in Butler's theory of performativity. Butler argues that gender is a social construction, reinforced by social structures (Butler, 2006). From the time we are born, we are assigned a sex. When friends come to the hospital to see the baby, usually a gendered name is chosen, and gendered-colored clothing and toys are bought. Television feeds into this social construction every day. Parents tell their children what they can and cannot wear, as was my case. Schools tell boys and girls that they have to compete in different sports. Females are taught to "be a lady," while boys are taught to "be a man." It is this consistent repetition that keeps reinforcing gender norms and behaviors, and in turn socially constructs gender, according to Butler.

Historical documentation has shown that definitions of masculinity and femininity and the female/male body have been as ambiguous as they continue to be in current times, as early as 1600s. McClive, Associate Professor of History at Florida State University who specializes in history of gender and sexuality, investigates three cases where the male body was put on trial in France for people who at the time were called hermaphrodites, but are described as what we now understand to be either an intersex or transgender person (McClive, 2006, pp. 45–68). Hermaphroditic genitalia were inspected in order to be judged by someone with power in the town and were deemed as either male or female. To provide a specific definition, an intersex person is someone who was born with chromosomal or physical ambiguities or abnormalities. Throughout U.S. medical history, it was common for intersex people to be surgically transformed to fit into a specific definition of gender, often the decision of the parents at the child's birth (Money & Ehrhardt, 1972). A transgender person is someone whose gender identity does not align with the gender they were assigned at birth. McClive (2009) writes that the trials consisted of "physicians involved in examining the ambiguous bodies, lawyers acting on behalf of the defendants and interested medical practitioners and journalists who published accounts in scientific journals such as *Journal des Scavans* and the *Académie des Sciences* and in foreign lay periodicals such as the *Athenian Mercury*" (p. 47). Another famous historical case that displays the complexity of gender was that of Thomas/Thomasine Hall. Born Thomasine Hall, Thomas caused great controversy in Virginia in 1629 when Thomas would opt to use both male and female clothing at times. When asked, Thomas/Thomasine Hall would say that they were both male and female. One can imagine the stir that such a case caused at the time (Brown, 1995, pp. 171–193). These are just some examples that show that gender complexities have been alive for longer than what media and the current sociopolitical climate would make us believe.

In remembering and reliving the experience I had as a child of my first lesson in differences in gender, I lived the regressive moment of *currere*. In doing so, I was left with some questions. Among them, why was I being treated differently than my brother, and how was it that I could not play with the toys I wanted to? It was not like they had some sort of special power that only boys could understand, right?

The Progressive Moment

Pinar (2012) writes, "In the second or progressive step one looks toward what is not yet the case, what is not yet present. . . . Contemplatively, the student of *currere* imagines possible futures, including fears as well as fantasies of fulfillment" (p. 46). For me, that question that stemmed from the regressive moment when I first learned about gender helped me realize that I did not identify as what society thought about it. I did not fit the mold of what a girl should be. I also did not fit the physical mold of what a boy should look like. That is not to say, though, that the mere reason I transitioned to the male gender was because of the toys I wanted to play with. That would be overly simplistic, and gender and gender identity are much more complex. Many might think that I could have just kept my physical cisgender female body and dressed more "butch." Again, while that fits the gender expression of many cisgender females, it is a misunderstanding of the differences between gender, gender identity, sexual orientation, and gender expression. However, that first lesson in societal expectations of gender resulted in what would become a long process of learning about the potential of a medical and legal gender transition, one that would not have been possible before based on the resources I lacked growing up on the border.

The more and more these doors opened for me, a new world of possibilities came to me. Though extremely risky and potentially deadly, through thorough research, I came to realize that medicine had the ability to help my exterior presentation align with who I knew I was. Again, I feel compelled to say that this is not the case for every transgender person. Not everyone in the community opts to undergo a medical transition, and for different reasons. Some opt out of it because of a lack of financial resources, some for health reasons, and others identify as nonbinary, among numerous other reasons. However, the progressive moment of *currere* left me with several questions in my quest for a further understanding of myself. Was I truly being myself, or was I just buying into the social construction of gender, as Butler writes? Why was I considering a medical and legal transition? Could I just live my life forever in the cisgender female body and gender presentation I was born into? These were all very difficult questions I came across. They had all crossed my mind as an undergraduate, but I reconsidered them again after remembering this one initial episode in playing with my brother's G-I Joes. This progressive moment in my journey through *currere* only brought about many more questions than answers. These questions, I felt, revealed something about my personal philosophy, as I do believe that gender is performative to some extent (Butler, 2006). Nonetheless, I attempted to think it through in the analytical moment.

The Analytical Moment

The analytical stage requires an analysis of both past and the present, as an "attempt to discern how the past inheres in the present and in our fantasies of the future" (Pinar, 2012, p. 46). As I consider my past and present "lives" I live and have lived, I cannot help but realize that I am currently in the analytical moment. I have come to realize that like Anzaldúa, I am an embodiment of the *hieros gamos* (Anzaldúa, 1999, p. 41), a being that contains both female and male characteristics. For me, it comes in the way of having experienced life as a cisgender female, and now as a transgender male. It is this unique experience that has afforded me a very unique view of the world, and of the way that gender and sexuality are taught from the day we are born.

Anzaldúa, in her groundbreaking book *Borderlands/La Frontera: The New Mestiza* writes,

> The U.S.-Mexican border es *una herida abierta* where the Third World grates against the first and bleeds. And before a scab forms it hemorrhages again, the lifeblood of two worlds merging to form a third country — a border culture. Borders are set up to define the places that are safe and unsafe, to distinguish *us* from *them*. A border is a dividing line, a narrow strip along a steep edge. A borderland is a vague and undetermined place created by the emotional residue of an unnatural boundary. It is in a constant state of transition. (p. 25)

My experience as a transgender man of color from the Texas-Mexico border has always resonated with Anzaldúa's work in more ways than one. The very questions I had about why I was opting to medically and legally transition brought me to Anzaldúa's words. While Anzaldúa writes about physical borderlands of the Texas-Mexico border, I started to relate to those words in regard to my medical and legal transition. This "border" between genders, or what our society has constructed as a binary is indeed a wound that has not healed. It is this "border" that has resulted in the othering of transgender, gender nonconforming, gender nonbinary, and intersex individuals. I could relate her work to the physical borderlands where I lived, but also the metaphorical borderlands in which I continue to live my daily life. That is, I have been socialized as a female, and up until I was about 22 years old, I presented myself to the world as a female, and for all intents and purposes, I performed gender as a female (Butler, 2006). As a result, I have experiences in society as a female teacher that I have not had as a male prior to my transition, and vice versa after my transition. Perhaps, as Anzaldúa writes, this physical border is imposed on one's body by medical authorities is in a "constant state of transition" (Anzaldúa, 1999, p. 25), just as borders around nations are dependent on national authorities.

Yet other questions stemmed from this moment in *currere*. If indeed, this invisible border has been socially set up that has historically determined roles and behaviors for girls and boys and if it is in transition, what now? How does that play a part of how I have chosen to live my life? As I have mentioned, not every transgender person chooses to undergo a medical and legal gender transition for various reasons. However, I decided to because I maintained in the core of my being that that was the most authentic option for me. This brings me to the last question in *currere*, though not at the end of my journey. How do I use this knowledge and visibility as a Latinx transgender man?

The Synthetical Moment

The last step of *currere* is known as the synthetical moment and it is, as Pinar (2012) defines it, "the moment in which self-study becomes reconstructed as public service" (p. 47) and is the moment when everything comes together. Slattery refers to these moments as proleptic moments, which synthesize life events. For many teachers, particularly those who see themselves as public servants performing a public service, it is not too difficult to make the leap for public good. In the synthetical moment, I have started to realize that my visibility as a transgender man of color, though dangerous, has possibilities to change people's minds. Thus, a synthetical moment is re-lived every time I "out" myself to different people as a way of educating others about my experience as a transgender man of color. It is in remembering my first lesson with gender that has brought me to this point. What we learn about gender as children can have a tremendous effect on us as adults. Therefore, I have made it my life's task to help in queering gender through my life's story, particularly for preservice and in-service teachers.

Anzaldúa provides us with an insight into how she perceives the new Chicana should be, as she was referring to learning about Mexican Americans' ancestral roots to indigenous cultures in relationship to our colonized European upbringing. However, I feel that it can very well be used in the context of self-reflection and *currere* with regard to gender and sexual diversity. In describing the new mestiza, Anzaldúa (1999) writes,

> She can be jarred out of ambivalence by an intense, and often painful, emotional event which inverts or resolves the ambivalence. I'm not sure exactly how. The work takes place underground—subconsciously. It is work that the soul performs. That focal point or fulcrum, that juncture where the *mestizo* stands, is where phenomena tend to collide. It is where the possibility of uniting all that is separate occurs. This assembly is not one where severed or separated pieces merely come together. Nor is it a balancing of opposing powers. In attempting to work out a synthesis, the self has added a third element which is greater than the sum of its severed parts. That third element is a new consciousness—a *mestiza* consciousness—and though it is a source of intense pain, its energy comes from continual creative motion that keeps breaking down the unitary aspect of each new paradigm. (pp. 101–102)

It is clear that for Anzaldúa, one does not have to conform to the oppressor, nor remain oppressed. It is just fine to remain open to the ambiguity that is the pain that comes from understanding our past, present, and future. While this past can be agonizing for many, it can help toward the path toward liberation, one which Anzaldúa often wrote about. Every time I am outed or out myself, I realize that I may have taken my last breath. The past, present, and future are all aligned at that moment. As the number of transgender individuals that are murdered continues to rise every year, with 26 in 2017 (Adams, 2017), my fears have been confounded by the reality. Many of us who are transgender, gender nonconforming or nonbinary, or intersex, especially people of color, remain in the land of the *atravesados* (Anzaldúa 1999, 25), often not by choice. Continuing to teach gender as a binary construct has some very real and negative implications for the future generations because it perpetuates fear and biases about gender and gender roles.

Continuing the Cycle of Currere

You can see how big of an impact that first lesson about my gender assignment made on me. I continue to go through the stages of *currere* over and over again often in order to resolve that issue. Though the objective is usually the same, the story usually represents small subsections of my life experience that help me understand how I have come up to this point.

By this part of my life story, it might seem easy to understand, then, why I opted to become a high school mathematics teacher. I enjoyed mathematics and I was good at explaining things to my friends that would ask for help, so it was a natural progression. I chose to teach at an urban high school with a large percentage of English Language Learners in Austin, Texas, not because it was one of the lowest-performing schools in the district, but because it felt just like my home. The sea of Black and Brown faces wanting to learn, stuck in a rut of high teacher turnover, provided me with the motivation. Teaching was easy compared to the daily torments of standardization. That pressure and the implications of the standardized test looming over our heads, threatening to fire us in the case that our students did not pass, was a constant reminder. Over the eight years that I was in the classroom, I came to realize that I did not just want to teach mathematics. Sure, I would teach algorithms, functions, graphing, and statistics, among other things, but I wanted to teach my students that mathematics could be an equalizer, that it was the universal language that could potentially get them out of the socioeconomic state they were in, like it had done for me. Best of all, there was something beautiful and artistic at being able to model the chaos that is nature into something as neat as an algebraic function . . . that categories and the axioms we used in mathematics that we take for granted and use so often, that seemed fixed, could potentially change as language, thoughts, humanity evolves. Part of my teaching involved chats talking about how society would not always be fair, that college was not easy, and if it were easy, everyone would have a degree. However, that did not mean it was unattainable for them.

Teaching and learning were not always mutually exclusive. Were my students learning the standards that the state said should be taught in order to pass the tests and graduate? Many did, while many students did not. I do not think that made me a worse teacher, because many of my students learned the material, though not at the pace set forth by standardized tests. Many of my students now as adults have thanked me for trying to teach them that life may be hard, and for being honest with them in telling them that college would not be easy. I asserted there would be people in their lives who would tell the students that they did not belong there, as they did to me, or that they were only in school as a result of affirmative action. I shared what I perceive as true, authentic teaching and I sensed that real learning happened. After all, I think they learned some mathematics in the process. But most of all, my students learned that mathematics could be their way out. It did not matter whether they were an English Language Learner from El Salvador, or one of my several refugees from Burma, or whether they wore an ankle bracelet and had a probation officer. In my classroom, I treated them with the respect that each was due, and with the promise that I did not care whether they were an A+ student or not before they stepped into my classroom. If they gave it their all, I would do the rest to get them where they needed to be, even if that meant me having to stay until 7:00 p.m. and come at 7:00 a.m. every day. If they were willing to come, I would be present to help. Some would call those different learning styles, but to me, that was just being a mindful human being. Overall, I have come to learn over time that my style and perspective of teaching was additive, rather than subtractive, and that caring for my students was often expressed through my actions, not my words (Valenzuela, 1999).

I think that is why I have always been interested in mathematics and teaching at the high school level. There is something about being presented with a problem and finding any possible way to reach a solution as you can, with whatever tools you're given, which I have always told my students was an important skill that math taught them, not just "formulas." I am introverted, but inquisitive by "nature." This, interestingly enough, brings me back to my earliest recollection of being taught that boys and girls were different. As I got older, I realized that being born female-bodied and producing female hormones prevented my exterior from reflecting how I felt on the inside and who I knew myself to be. So, I started doing research and looking into ways to change my body medically to reflect the person, that genuine self. That person was not the person that society kept telling me I was. It did not feel like me, thus the more I learned about medical advances, the more excited I became. Major obstacles always remained, though. I did not have the money initially for something as large of an undertaking as this gender confirmation surgery. I am a work in progress, as we all are. It has been over 10 years since I started my transitioning journey, but the more I think about it, it will never end. As language evolves, as our minds evolve, so do we, and so does our understanding of the way we model our world mathematically. That is why I continue to teach and learn mathematics, because I know that it can help us come closer to reflecting the amazing diversity that lies in our very own backyards, and because I know that someday, I may be able to contribute to the knowledge-base of what we choose to teach, why we choose to teach it, and how we choose to teach. These are all crucial questions to ask, not just of ourselves but for our society. If we continue to teach and learn binaries, then what are we saying to our gender- and sexually diverse student population?

CONCLUSION

Meyer (2007) writes, "By developing a more critical understanding of gender, sex, sexual orientation and how these identities and experiences are shaped and taught in schools, educators can have a profound impact on the way students lean, relate to others and behave in schools" (p. 17). This learning theory model I grew up with is known as scientific inquiry, which is a model that helps students identify solutions for problems that are presented (Joyce, Weil, & Calhoun, 2015). Like scientific inquiry, my main goal in approaching teaching was to provide my students with a set of tools from which to choose, as no scenario in life really ever needs the same set of tools, for every single person. By doing this in a way that helped scaffold my students' learning and (dis)advantages that they had in life, being that it was an economically disadvantaged school, I did not realize at the time that I was incorporating the positive self-concept model (Joyce, Weil, & Calhoun, 2015). I wanted all of them to succeed, and use mathematics as a tool to help get them and their families out of poverty.

As a man of transgender experience who happened to be an educator, I am proud of my journey, because it showed my students that we do not always have to fit in a box and that it is okay to live outside of the norm. As a matter of fact, that to me is the point of mathematics and scientific inquiry. Mathematics and science are not fixed disciplines. Like queer theory, they have evolved and changed to better reflect nature. Although imperfect, the more critical people are of mathematics, the more it can reflect our surroundings. Nothing changes when nothing is questioned. That is not to say that everything that mathematics does is wrong—it is just imperfect. Our own individual perspective and experiences influence how we see the world.

This chapter drew from philosophical perspectives in queer theory and queer history, my autobiographical reflection, in addition to learning theories in education, and reflected on how all of these have intersected at memorable points in my life as a teacher. By using my experience as an exercise in self-reflection and undergoing the stages of *currere* myself, my hope is that other educators might be exposed to *currere* and autoethnography in order to learn to be their "best-loved self" (Craig, 2013). Self-reflection is not an easy process, especially when interlinked with currere because of the deep memories and emotions. In my case, it only has brought about more questions than answers. However, it has helped me reflect on how I have educated and been educated throughout my life, and how I want to continue to educate about gender and sexual diversity. It has provided me with a greater self-awareness and cemented my perspectives on how I want to lead my life. In doing so, it has increased my awareness of issues that are relevant to my students. It is time that the lessons we learned as children about how gender works in society evolve into those that the new generation can have good memories about.

REFERENCES

Adams, N. 2017. Honoring known cases of deadly anti-trans violence in 2017. *GLAAD*, December 14, 2017. https://www.glaad.org/blog/honoring-known-cases-deadly-anti-trans-violence-2017

Anzaldúa, G. 1999. *Borderlands/La Frontera: The new Mestiza*, 2nd ed. San Francisco: Aunt Lute Books.

Brown, K. 1995. "Changed . . . into the fashion of a man": The politics of sexual difference in a seventeenth century Anglo-American settlement. *Journal of the History of Sexuality*, 6(2), 171–193.

Butler, J. 2006. *Gender trouble: Feminism and the subversion of identity*. New York: Routledge.

Bruner, J., Goodnow, J. J., & Austin, G. A. 1967. *A study of thinking*. New York: Science Editions.

Craig, C. J. 2013. Teacher education and the best-loved self. *Asia Pacific Journal of Education*, 33(3), 261–272.

Ellis, C., & Bochner, A. 2000. Autoethnograpphy, personal narrative, reflexivity: Researcher as subject. In Norman K. Denzin and Yvonna S. Lincoln (eds.), *Handbook of qualitative research*, 2nd ed., 733–768. Thousand Oaks: SAGE Publications.

Hatzenbuehler, M. L., Birkett, M., Van Wagenen, A., & Meyer, I. H. 2014. Protective school climates and reduced risk for suicide ideation in sexual minority youths. *American Journal of Public Health*, 104(2), 279–286.

Jennings, T., & Macgillivray, I. K. 2011. A content analysis of lesbian, gay, bisexual, and transgender topics in multicultural education textbooks. *Teaching Education*, 1(22), 39–62.

Joyce, B. R., Weil, M., & Calhoun, E. 2015. *Models of teaching*, 9th ed. Boston: Pearson Education, Inc.

Kosciw, J. G., Greytak, E. A., Giga, N. M., Villenas, C., & Danischewski, D. J. 2016. *The 2015 National School Climate Survey: The experiences of lesbian, gay, bisexual, transgender, and queer youth in our nation's schools*. New York: GLSEN.

Li, J., & Logan, K. D. 2017. Stories of an English language arts teacher in a high need secondary school: A narrative inquiry into her best-loved self. In Vicki Ross, Elaine Chan, Dixie K. Keyes (eds.), *Crossroads of the classroom: Narrative intersections of teacher knowledge and subject matter advances in research on teaching*, vol. 28 (pp. 137–156).

Macgillivray, I. K., & Jennings, T. 2008. A content analysis exploring lesbian, gay, bisexual, and transgender topics in foundations of education textbooks. *Journal of Teacher Education*, 59(2), 170–188.

McClive, C. 2009. Masculinity on trial: Penises, hermaphrodites and the uncertain male body in early modern France. *History Workshop Journal*, 68(1), 45–68.

Meyer, E. J. 2007. "But I'm not gay": What straight teachers need to know about queer theory. In Nelson M. Rodriguiez and William F. Pinar (eds.), *Queering straight teachers: Discourse and identity in education* (pp. 15–32). New York: Routledge.

Money, J., & Ehrhardt, A. A. 1972. *Man and woman, boy and girl: The differentiation and dimorphism of gender identity from conception to maturity*. Baltimore, MD: Johns Hopkins University Press.

Pinar, W. F. 1975a. The method of "Currere." *Counterpoints*, 2, 19–27.

———. 1975b. Currere: Toward reconceptualization. In William Pinar (ed.), *Curriculum theorizing: The reconceptualists* (pp. 396–414). Berkeley, CA: McCutchan.

———. 2012. *What is curriculum theory?* 2nd ed. New York: Routledge.

Slattery, P. 2015. *Annotated glossary for curriculum development in the postmodern era: Teaching and learning in an age of accountability*. New York: Routledge. http://cw.routledge.com/textbooks/9780415808569/data/glossary.pdf

Valenzuela, A. 1999. *Subtractive schooling: U.S.-Mexican youth and the politics of caring*. Albany: State University of New York Press.

Epilogue

Theodorea Regina Berry and Mariela A. Rodríguez

During the April 2018 meeting of the Texas State Board of Education, a motion was made that included naming a new course to be offered in Texas high schools—*Ethnic Studies: An Overview of Americans of Mexican Descent*. The vote on the motion failed "with 5 members voting Aye, 8 members voting No, and 1 member abstaining" (State Board of Education Minutes, April 2018, p. 4). Many constituents, including the lead contributing author of this text Dr. Angela Valenzuela, opposed the notion of such a name for a course. In a statement to the Board during the June 2018 meeting, Theodorea Berry noted that "the name matters" (Berry, 2018, p. 1). Berry continued, accordingly:

> The first part of the title, Ethnic Studies, speaks of a curriculum that focuses on ethnicity only and leaves absent social considerations of race, geographical considerations of nationality, and cultural considerations connected to language. The second part of the title of this course speaks to limitations of the knowledge to be offered (overview) and informs potential students about who determined what knowledge would be covered, who would be privileged, and who would be marginalized. In short, the title of this course speaks to a curriculum loaded with an imbalance of power.
>
> The title of this course should reflect the value placed on Mexican American's presence, knowledge, and contributions to American society with clarity and precision. There should be a centering of culture and identity, making the space and place secondary to the knowledge most worth knowing. The title of the course must make clear the multidisciplinary nature of the knowledge to be accessed: sociological, historical, cultural, economic, theological, aesthetic, political. Most importantly, the title of this course must reflect the individuals who should have the most to say about what students need to know about this particular demographic. Who should determine what knowledge is most worth knowing? The title of this course should be "Mexican American Studies". This title tells us what's most important to know. It tells us who is centered in this knowledge, in what context, and from various perspectives. Mexican American Studies, as the title for this course, provides clarity and precision.

In August 2018, Berry relocated to California to assume an academic administrative positon at San Jose State University and learned on her first day that the Department of Mexican American Studies was officially renamed the Department of Chicano/Chicano Studies (CCS). In a conversation with the department chair regarding the name change, he noted to Berry that the next step was a change to Chicanx/Latinx Studies. Who/what we call/name someone/something matters.

It matters for content because it speaks to our expectations of the information to be included. If the information fails to accurately and comprehensively address what it is called, then the name misrepresents the information. It matters for the goals, objectives, and purposes in schools because it speaks to the rationale and significance of the presence of the learners. If who is in our schools isn't reflected in the name, the name fails to appropriately represent the information. It matters for experiences as knowledge because it speaks to the cultural and historical roots of the knowledge. If the knowledge fails to honor all that is past and present, the name leaves absent all those who contributed to the knowledge.

We call this book *Latinx Curriculum Theorizing*, centering the knowledge and experiences within the Latinx diaspora in the context of content/subject matter, goals, objectives and purposes, as well as curriculum as autobiographical. This title centers the knowledge that is most worth knowing and who determines what knowledge is most worth knowing. The contributions to this book honor information, mission, and vision centered on the Latinx experience in U.S. education. This book honors the historical, cultural, social, political and linguistic knowledge, experiences and contributions of the Latinx diaspora in the context of education.

It is our hope that this book inspires all educators who are seeking innovative ways to support Latinx students. All of these students arrive at schools with their own strengths, experiences, language, and culture—and all should be valued.

REFERENCES

Berry, T. R. 2018, June. Comments on ethnic studies: An overview on Americans of Mexican descent: Curriculum perspectives. Lecture presented at the Texas State Board of Education Meeting, Austin, TX.

Texas State Board of Education General Meeting Minutes, April 2018. Austin, TX.

Index

Academia Cuauhtli, xxiii, 3, 4, 5, 6, 11; curriculum, 3
analytical moment, 143
autoethnography, 138, 139

belonging, 60, 102, 118, 121
black curriculum orientations, xi
Black Panther Party, 17, 27
Bobbitt, Franklin, xi, xiii, xix
borderlands, 35, 118, 119, 131
borderland identities, 33, 35, 37, 39, 43

Carmichael, Stokely, 15
Chicana feminist space, 7
Chicanx Latinx Studies (CLS), 104
Chicago, 13–15
Chicago Young Lords Organization (ChYLO), xxiv, 15, 16, 17; Aims of ChYLO, 16; history, 17; 12 point plan, 17, 18–19, 22
civil rights curriculum, 3
Committee of Ten, xi
Cooper, Anna Julia, xi
counter-storytelling, 82
Counts, George, xi
critical pedagogy, 84, 85, 107
Critical Race Theory (CRT), xxiv, 80, 81, 90, 102, 103, 107
cultural assault, 106
culturally relevant pedagogies, 107
culturally responsive pedagogy, 77
culturally sustaining pedagogies (CSP), 107, 112
currere, xxv, 137, 138, 139, 140, 144, 145, 148
curriculum, xi, xii, xiii, xxiv, 7, 23, 28, 54, 63, 66, 67, 70, 72, 77, 78, 80, 107, 131, 151; as experiences, xix, xxi; culturally relevant, 4; definition, xix, xx, 16, 33, 39, 40, 71, 137;
Eurocentric, 20; explicit, 105; hidden, 22, 105; null, 105
curriculum of oppression, 122, 132
curriculum studies, xi, xx, 22, 28, 77
curriculum theory, xii, xx

decolonial imaginary, xxiii, 3, 4, 5, 10, 11, 123
Deferred Action for Childhood Arrivals (DACA), 53
Dewey, John, xi
dialogue, 84, 85, 86, 90, 91, 122
Dual-Language immersion programs, 52
DuBois, William Edward Burghardt, xi

Encuentro, 90
engaged pedagogy, xxv, 118, 122, 131, 132
English Language Learner (ELL), 52
ethic of care, 118, 122, 132
Ethnic Studies curriculum, 4
experience, xix

feminist perspectives, 34
funds of knowledge, xxiv, 85

Goodlad, John, xi

identity, 34, 36, 53, 63, 69, 87
illegality, 65, 67, 70, 71, 72, 74
immigration, 87, 88; policy, 65
insurrection, 3, 7, 10
intersectionality, 80, 81, 82, 83, 86, 90, 103, 108, 110
invisible narratives, xxiv, 51, 53

Jefferson, Thomas, xi

King Jr., Dr. Martin Luther, 14, 15

language, 33, 35, 38, 41, 42, 62, 87, 88, 89, 103, 108
Latina/o Critical Race Theory (LatCrit), xxv, 68, 69, 70, 103
Latinx, 34, 35, 37; collective, xx, xxi; population, 51, 52, 104; students, xxi
Latinx revitalizing pedagogies, 107
LGBTIQ youth, 136
literacy, 79, 80, 91
Locke, Alain LeRoy, xi

mathematics, 33, 37, 38, 39, 41, 43, 44, 146, 147, 148; learning, xxiv, 33, 39; education, 33, 37, 38, 39, 40
mestiza, 33, 34, 35, 36, 37, 40
Montessori, Maria, xi

nepantla, 118, 122, 123, 131

oppression, 62, 103, 108
organic intellectualism, 19, 21, 22, 27
organic transformation, 19
outsider-within, 33, 34, 36, 37, 44

pedagogy, 7, 16, 67, 73, 107
portraiture, xxv, 118, 123, 124
practice, 19, 24, 25, 26, 27
praxis, 54, 81, 110
progressive moment, 142
public pedagogy, 51

queer theory, 136, 148

racial oppression, 100
regressive moment, 140
resilience, 101
resistance, 54, 55, 56, 101, 120

social justice, 3, 36, 44, 53, 54, 56, 62, 73
Southern Christian Leadership Conference (SCLC), 14
Spencer, Herbert, xiii
standpoint theory, 66
Stolen Education, xiii
synthetical moment, 144

Tenayuca, Emma, 8, 9, 10, 11
testimonios, xxv, 53, 55, 102, 104; collaborative, 51, 54
third space, xxiii, 4, 5, 6, 11
transgender visibility, 136
translanguaging, 109
TribalCrit, 101
Tyler, Ralph, xi

undocumented activists, xxiv, 65, 66, 67

voice, xxiv, 10, 81, 86, 90, 103, 122

Watkins, William H., xi
white-jacked, 58
white supremacist capitalist patriarchy, 101, 108
Woodson, Carter G., xi

About the Editors and Contributors

Theodorea Regina Berry, EdD, is professor and chair, Department of African American Studies at San Jose State University. Her research interests and scholarship focus on curriculum studies/theory, critical race theory/critical race feminism, and qualitative research methodology as she examines the lived experiences of black women as preservice teachers and teacher educators and explores the critical examinations of race, ethnicity, and gender for teaching and teacher education.

Crystal A. Kalinec-Craig, PhD, is assistant professor of mathematics education in the Department of Interdisciplinary Learning and Teaching at the University of Texas at San Antonio. She studies issues of mathematics teacher education that lie at the intersection of equity, culture, and language.

Mariela A. Rodríguez, PhD, is professor, Department of Educational Leadership and Policy Studies and Associate Dean/Director of Teaching, Learning, and Professional Development for the Graduate School at The University of Texas at San Antonio. Her research interests focus on school leadership that supports additive bilingual education programs, specifically dual language instruction.

***

Martha Allexsaht-Snider, PhD, is associate professor in the Department of Educational Theory and Practice at the University of Georgia, conducts research about family-school-community interactions in diverse settings, including U.S. Latinx communities and rural México. Her research also focuses on professional development and equity in mathematics and science education, with particular interest in educators supporting immigrant students in the United States and around the world.

Ann M. Avilés, PhD, is assistant professor in Human Development and Family Sciences in the College of Education and Human Development at the University of Delaware. Dr. Avilés's research interests include youth homelessness, educational policy, mental health, social justice youth development, critical race theory, and Latina/o critical race theory.

Richard D. Benson II, PhD, is associate professor in the education department at Spelman College in Atlanta, Georgia. Dr. Benson's research interests are history of education, protest movements in education, student/youth and community advocacy, the Black Freedom Movement, and transnational social movements.

Juan F. Carrillo, PhD, is associate professor at Arizona State University's Mary Lou Fulton Teachers College. Dr. Carrillo's research includes research on the schooling trajectories of Latino males in traditional and new gateway regions. Some of his current scholarship focuses on public pedagogy practices within Latinx communities in Arizona.

Erica R. Dávila, PhD, is associate professor in Educational Leadership in the College of Education at Lewis University. Dr. Dávila's research interests are educational policy, critical race theory, sustainability, and Puerto Rican studies.

Lynette Guzmán, PhD, is a postdoctoral research associate in the mathematics department at the University of Arizona. Her work supports prospective K–8 teachers to develop equity-oriented practices that value young people as knowers and creators with (and outside of) mathematics.

Alba Isabel Lamar is an educator, activist, artist, and PhD student of Curriculum, Instruction and Teacher Education at Michigan State University, which is situated on Anishinaabe land. Her work seeks to center Indigenous and Black knowledges in schools and focus on land-based, social and environmental justice pedagogies.

Cristina Valencia Mazzanti is a doctoral student in the Early Childhood program in the Department of Educational Theory and Practice at the University of Georgia. Cristina's identity and experiences as an immigrant, a Latina, and a multilingual person have inspired her to pursue research with other Latinx people focusing on the connections between mathematics and language to promote a more equitable education.

Lucia I. Mock Muñoz de Luna is a doctoral student at the University of North Carolina at Chapel Hill. Her research interests include community-led initiatives in education and human rights, education for Syrian and Palestinian youth, and interventions for ending white supremacy.

Ganiva Reyes, PhD, is an assistant professor in the Department of Teacher Education at Miami University, Oxford Ohio. Her research and teaching revolve around intersectionality, Chicana feminist theory, and pedagogies of care to provide a nuanced approach to topics of diversity and inclusion in teacher education. Her scholarship explores the intimate and interpersonal aspects of teaching, and how teachers need communal and institutional care and support in order to provide the same for their students.

Stacy Saathoff is a PhD candidate in the Department of Teaching, Learning and Sociocultural Studies at the University of Arizona in Tucson, Arizona. Her current research explores the social identities and lived experiences of Mexican and Mexican American adolescent young women in the southwestern United States.

Mario I. Suárez is a PhD candidate in the Department of Teaching, Learning and Culture in the College of Education and Human Development at Texas A&M University. Mr. Suárez's research interests involve queer studies in education, curriculum studies, STEM pathways for historically underrepresented students, and quantitative methods.

Jesus A. Tirado is a doctoral candidate in the Social Studies Education Program in the Education Theory and Research Department at the University of Georgia. His interests involve citizenship education, pedagogies of belonging, and the tensions within those concepts.

www.ingramcontent.com/pod-product-compliance
Lightning Source LLC
Chambersburg PA
CBHW020122010526
44115CB00008B/940